The International Library of Psychology

ABNORMAL PSYCHOLOGY

Founded by C. K. Ogden

The International Library of Psychology

ABNORMAL AND CLINICAL PSYCHOLOGY

In 19 Volumes

I	Psychotherapy with Children	*Allen*
II	Personality and Mental Illness	*Bowlby*
III	Inferiority Feelings	*Brachfeld*
IV	Abnormal Psychology	*Coriat*
V	Dimensions of Personality	*Eysenck*
VI	The Dynamics of Anxiety and Hysteria	*Eysenck*
VII	Psychology of the Normal and the Subnormal	*Goddard*
VIII	The Neurotic Personality	*Gordon*
IX	Mental Conflicts and Misconduct	*Healy*
X	The Concentric Method in the Diagnosis of Psychoneurotics	*Laignel-Lavastine*
XI	A Handbook of Psychiatry	*Lichtenstein*
XII	The Psychology of Emotion	*MacCurdy*
XIII	Psychosurgical Problems	*Mettler*
XIV	Personality and the Frontal Lobes	*Petrie*
XV	Psychotic Art	*Reitman*
XVI	Conditions of Nervous Anxiety and their Treatment	*Stekel*
XVII	Emotion and Insanity	*Thalbitzer*
XVIII	A Short History of Psychotherapy	*Walker*
XIX	Constitution-Types in Delinquency	*Willemse*

ABNORMAL PSYCHOLOGY

ISADOR H CORIAT

ROUTLEDGE
Taylor & Francis Group

First published in 1910 by
Routledge and Kegan Paul Ltd

Reprinted in 1999, 2001 by
Routledge
2 Park Square, Milton Park, Abingdon, Oxon, OX14 4RN

Transferred to Digital Printing 2006

Routledge is an imprint of the Taylor & Francis Group

British Library Cataloguing in Publication Data
A CIP catalogue record for this book
is available from the British Library

Abnormal Psychology
ISBN 0415-20922-6
Abnormal and Clinical Psychology: 19 Volumes
ISBN 0415-21123-9
The International Library of Psychology: 204 Volumes
ISBN 0415-19132-7
Printed and bound by CPI Antony Rowe, Eastbourne

PREFACE TO THE SECOND EDITION

It is extremely gratifying to the author that a second edition of this book should be called for within the space of three years. During this period abnormal psychology has made steady and important advances, particularly in the field of psycho-analysis with its various applications to the neuroses, wit, literature, mythology, and folk lore. For reasons of space, however, and because such material does not really lend itself to popular presentation, the important subject of psycho-analysis has been presented only in its general outlines. Several new chapters have been added, one on Freud's theory of dreams, one on the prevention of the neuroses, and one on colored hearing. This latter chapter has been reprinted, with a few modifications, from my contributions on colored hearing to the *Journal of Abnormal Psychology*. In addition, the chapter on the Subconscious has been rewritten, to conform with the most recent psycho-analytic conceptions. I have also added my researches on the nature and evolution of sleep and hypnosis. A large number of other important additions and changes have been made, to bring the book in line with the latest advances in abnormal psychology.

Isador H. Coriat.

Boston, November, 1913.
416 Marlborough St.

CONTENTS

PART I

THE EXPLORATION OF THE SUBCONSCIOUS

PART II

THE DISEASES OF THE SUBCONSCIOUS

INTRODUCTION

Abnormal psychology, or the study of abnormal mental phenomena, is one of the late developments of scientific medicine. It is not a mere fad, as some of its critics would attempt to make us believe, neither has it sprung up like a mushroom, within a single night. Abnormal psychology is the outcome of the work of small groups of investigators in France, Germany, and America, within the last twenty-five years. Beginning with a study of the phenomena of hypnosis, these researches gradually developed into a series of brilliant psychological discoveries. The most important of these is the principle of dissociation or of splitting of the mind. In a general way we speak of these matters as the theory of the subconscious. This theory has not only thrown an immense amount of light on the nature of human personality, but other peculiar phenomena, such as losses of memory or amnesia, automatic writing, crystal gazing, and such diseases as neurasthenia, hysteria, psychasthenia, have been stripped of the mystery which surrounded them for centuries. These phenomena, even more than the modern investigations on the ultimate nature of matter, form the " fairyland of science." Apart from any scientific knowledge, the general reader has a certain interest in these problems, either from curiosity or the light they shed upon human personality or perhaps from the mystery which seems to surround them.

Abnormal psychology has also its practical aspects. Its discoveries have made possible the psychic treatment of certain functional nervous disorders. Technically, this is known as psychotherapeutics. The interpretation of these functional states is based on the principle of the dissociation of consciousness. But psychotherapeutics would be in a very chaotic condition and barren of results, were it not for abnormal psychology, for a scientific psychotherapeutics must be based upon a sound psychopathology.

Most of the investigations on abnormal psychology are widely scattered in medical publications and in psychological journals of a highly specialized character, thereby making these researches almost inaccessible to the general reader. There has been no attempt, so far as known, to bring all this material together within the compass of a single book. It is with this object in view that the present volume was written. In it an attempt will be made, not only to summarize the principal work in this fascinating field, but also some personal observations and experiments will be added.

Most of the problems of abnormal psychology centre around the modern theory of the subconscious. While there is no consensus of opinion as to the exact interpretation of these subconscious phenomena, yet it is admitted by all psychologists that subconscious or dissociated mental states exist. Whether these states depend upon psychological or physiological activities, or whether they are normal or abnormal conditions, seems to be the chief ground of contention. It seems that subconscious manifestations present all grades of complexity, from the absent-mindedness of everyday life to the phenomena of hysteria and multiple personality. Before we can comprehend the more complicated aspects of subconscious mental states we must have a clear understanding of their simpler manifestations. The evidence seems to show that subconscious mental states are not always proofs of disease, but just where the physiological ends and where the pathological begins, is difficult to determine. No hard and fast line can be drawn, there is a decided overlapping, an almost imperceptible shading of one into the other. For in psychology as in pathology, the normal explains the diseased, and the diseased throws light on the normal. Absent-mindedness, the forgetting of familiar names, purposeless or thoughtless actions, all these may be designated as normal states of mental dissociation, because they occur in everyday life. On the other hand, such manifestations as hysteria or multiple personality or losses of memory are distinctly pathological conditions.

Therefore, in order that clearness may not be sacrificed, we must pass by slow gradations from the simplest to the most complex forms of subconscious mental states. We must understand the normal before we can hope to grasp the abnormal. Without adopting this method, we would become lost in a maze of psychological theories. After we have learned, so to speak, the grammar of abnormal psychology, by this meaning the psychopathology of everyday life, we are then in a position to understand the work on hysteria, neurasthenia, amnesia, multiple personality, etc. These subjects will be discussed from the standpoint of dissociated mental states, without entering into the field of psychical research. We shall see that these phenomena can be explained by purely psychological and physiological mechanisms based on well-recognized laws of body and mind, and that there is no need of supernormal interpretations.

This volume is, therefore, divided into two parts, which are indicated by the titles "The Exploration of the Subconscious" and the "Diseases of the Subconscious." In the first section, after a discussion of subconscious phenomena in general, we will pass to the methods of analyzing these phenomena and making them objective facts. The second section will be devoted to a study of certain functional disturbances which, either in whole or in part, are due to perversions of subconscious mental states.

In general what can psychotherapy, in its purely practicable aspects learn from these complex theories? What can psychotherapy do and how does it do it? That the principles are eminently practicable is shown by the results of psychotherapy. The modern concepts of the principles of mental dissociation and mental synthesis, of subconscious and unconscious mental states were the forces which were responsible for the birth of this new psychology in its practicable application to medicine. Popular ideas on suggestion are so loose and vague that a restatement of the scientific principles upon which suggestion is based may have a certain value. It seems to be the general idea that suggestion is a kind of magic wand in the hand of the physician, and that the waving of this wand can make diseases appear or disappear in the same manner that a rabbit appears to suddenly pop out of the magician's silk hat. So suggestion has come to have a certain occult or mystical meaning, in the same way that the term subconscious has been popularly interpreted as a supernatural state of mind. We hope to show that nothing of this sort is possible and that psychotherapy cannot change one iota of the laws of the mechanism of consciousness. Functional neuroses do not get well by a presto change method. Their treatment requires long study, numerous examinations, a knowledge of the theoretical and practical principles of abnormal psychology and of all the diagnostic methods of modern medicine.

BOSTON, *January*, 1910.

PART I

THE EXPLORATION OF THE SUBCONSCIOUS

ABNORMAL PSYCHOLOGY

CHAPTER I

THE SUBCONSCIOUS

1. *The Subconscious Defined*

THE term "subconscious," or as it is sometimes called "Unconscious," has been distorted by popular usage to mean almost anything beyond the pale of ordinary experience. It is applied in these pages only to certain well-attested psychological phenomena, phenomena which present themselves in different ways varying according to the standpoint or experience of the observer. The student of mental disorders interprets the subconscious in terms of derangement of certain functions of the nervous system; to one interested in the functions themselves, the subconscious means an inability to reproduce, at will and without the aid of a special technique, the images of past experiences; the psychologist regards the subconscious as an independent consciousness, coexistent with the healthy consciousness but detached from it.

Let it be stated at the beginning, however, that while this detached portion of consciousness is able to do any mental task, it cannot, however, perform so-called supernatural feats, at least so far as any reliable scientific evidence has shown. If the mind of an individual, suffering from hysteria, for example, is possessed by a system of independent, subconscious ideas, (or complexes as they are technically termed) of which the individual's personality is ignorant or unaware and yet that personality is under the control of these complexes, the term dissociation is applied to this group of independent, subconscious ideas. Dissociation therefore, is a pathological phenomenon, originating, as will be later demonstrated, from the resistance built up by mental repression or from conscious or unconscious mental conflicts.

Since these states of mental dissociation are clinical phenomena of the nervous system, we will first very briefly direct our attention to a few of these. The nervous system is the domain of consciousness, associative memory, and reflex action. The chief functional characteristics of the nervous system are—the storing up of impressions and their reproduction in the order in which they are stored up, reflex action, and conduction. The first of these functions, the storing up of impressions, is the most important, as it probably forms the physical basis of memory. However, the exact correlation of mental processes with physical changes in the brain is impossible. As Tyndall says, "The passage from physics to the phenomena of consciousness is unthinkable." Bergson has more recently attempted to correlate brain states with memory, but as with all attempts in this direction, only with indifferent success. He states, for instance,[1] "The cerebral mechanism does in some sort condition memories but it is in no way sufficient to ensure their survival." That a close relationship between brain and memory exists, however, is shown by certain clinical phenomena which follow a localized destruction of brain tissue through hemorrhage or tumors. As examples of this condition may be mentioned the loss of motor memories which cause motor apraxia and therefore disorders of voluntary acts and movements, or of auditory or visual memories, which produce the various types of speech-disorder known as aphasia. We may state in general, however, although this statement will not bear rigid critical analysis, that the brain probably stores up impressions in the manner that the phonograph cylinder stores up sound vibrations and reproduces these as sounds. Or the analogy might be carried

[1] "Matter and Memory," p. 84.

a little further, by referring to one of the phenomena of living nerve tissue. The retina of the eye stores up ether vibrations, and their persistence in the retinal nerve elements forms what is known in physiology as "after images." For instance, if one looks very intently at a bright light for a second or two and then closes the eyes, one will still see the image of that light for a brief period of time. The impression of light has outlasted the objective stimulus which caused it. Probably phenomena of a like nature take place in the brain, but of this we cannot be certain. No one has yet shown absolutely how physical changes in the nerve cells can cause mental phenomena, or *vice versa,* how mental phenomena can cause physical changes excepting perhaps in the domain of the physiological accompaniments of the emotions. Our knowledge is limited to the statement that the brain is the organ of consciousness, but exactly how brain activity produces consciousness is a riddle which probably will never be solved.

Consciousness is a feature of all brain activity, but whether it is a result of this activity, or whether it runs parallel to it, opens up the enormous field of the interaction of mind on body and body on mind, and has given rise to many philosophical speculations. If we assume that it is probably the action of the molecules within the nerve cell which produces consciousness, we must also assume that what comes to me as consciousness would be visible to an outsider merely as molecular activity. Even in the deepest hypnotic and somnambulistic states, consciousness is very active, but it is probably absent or reduced to a very low level in sleep and certainly completely absent in deep chloroform or ether anesthesia, although even in the latter state, as recent investigations have shown, afferent impulses, such as pain, may be transmitted by the sensory nerves from the periphery to the brain. Strong says,[1] "The doctrine thus reached is variously expressed by saying that brain action 'causes,' 'generates,' 'manufactures,' or 'calls into existence' states of consciousness; that consciousness is dependent on the brain." This doctrine of the causal relation between mind and brain activity is called the theory of automatism. It is directly opposed to what is known as parallelism, which states that brain activity and mind run side by side—in other words, are simultaneous events.

The storing up of objective experiences is principally through the complex organs of sensation,—the eye, the ear, and the skin. These experiences are stored up in the nerve cells of

[1] C. A. Strong: "Why the Mind Has a Body."

the brain, their traces forming what are known as physiological dispositions or complexes. The revival of these stored-up experiences is called memory; but only those experiences are capable of revival which have produced sufficient traces. Memory may preserve not only what is worth having, but also what is not worth having, for instance, in the various psycho-neurotic disturbances. Usually these experiences are stored up in the order in which they are received, and the revival of one portion of the experience tends to revive the others which are connected with it. This forms the physiological basis of association. Of conscious experiences or rather of experiences which remain in consciousness we are usually aware, and we can revive and suppress them at will. In other words, they lack automatism and independent activity. When an experience is stored up, but cannot be voluntarily reproduced, we speak of it as dissociated or subconscious. A synthesis cannot be formed except through special devices. A mental dissociation is, therefore, directly opposite to a mental synthesis. By the former, we mean that experiences are detached or split off—by the latter, that these split off experiences are made whole again.

In normal mental life, except under special and very transitory conditions, stored-up experiences do not tend to become split off from consciousness. When an experience or complex has become dissociated, it tends to act automatically, and cannot be controlled by the will. This is well seen in those abnormal mental states which are termed obsessions and in some forms of automatic writing. In certain hysterical states, in functional losses of memory, or in multiple personality, the subject is not aware of the dissociated experiences. The chief factors in dissociation, whether simple or complex, seem to be automatism, independent activity, lack of awareness, and the inability to reproduce conserved experiences. By what is known as "tapping" the subconscious, as in hypnosis and in states of abstraction, in crystal gazing or automatic writing or through various other devices, we can bring these dissociated activities into full consciousness, or in psychological terms, produce a synthesis.

2. The Modern Theories of the Subconscious

We are now prepared, after this brief introduction, to discuss the principal dominant theories of the subconscious. The recognition of the subconscious (or unconscious) mental life, constitutes the basis of modern psychopathology and psycho-analysis. However, for some psychologists, particularly those who have not had experience in investigating abnormal mental phenomena, everything psychic is a priori conscious and hence for them an unconscious mental process is an absurdity and a contradiction of terms. Consciousness, however, is not the indispensable characteristic of mental life, for psycho-analysis has shown, particularly in the analysis of dreams and the study of hysterical patients, that subconscious mental process, even of a most complex nature and of which the individual is not aware, may lead an active existence and so influence thought and behavior. All psychopathologists, however, agree on one fundamental principle, however conflicting their interpretation of the various phenomena may be, namely, that our minds are made up of certain states, for some of which we are conscious and for some not conscious or unaware. Whether in normal minds these extra or subconscious states are merely isolated phenomena, such as ideas or feelings, without being grouped into systems, or whether they are composed of more complex states capable of independent activity, is the crux of the whole question. By some this splitting of consciousness is always considered an indication or sign of disease, but it can be shown that normal everyday activities exist in which there is a transitory dissociation, although this may consist of merely isolated ideas without organization. Of course, it is in the realm of mental pathology that we find the best known examples of subconscious phenomena.

The theories of the subconscious are several and can be divided into various groups.[1] The first theory states that the subconscious is that portion of the field of consciousness which at a given moment is outside the focus of attention. It is a marginal state in which the sense of awareness is more or less prominent. If we are aware of a certain matter it is conscious; if we are only partially aware of it, it is suppressed or dormant; if we are not aware of it, then it is subconscious, or dissociated.

The second theory is that subconscious activities consist of dissociated or split-off ideas. These are split off from the main stream of consciousness and may become isolated, like the losses of sensation in hysterical anesthesia, or changes in the personality, as in amnesic states and multiple personality.

The third theory is Frederick Myers' poetical though most unpractical theory of the subliminal self.[2] Myers' doctrine is purely metaphysical and states that consciousness or what

[1] For a more detailed statement of these theories the reader is referred to Dr. Prince's article in the symposium on "The Subconscious."—*Journal Abnormal Psychology,* Vol. II, Nos. 1-2, 1907.

[2] "Human Personality and Its Survival of Bodily Death."

he calls the superliminal self, is only a small portion of that underlying great reservoir of consciousness which he terms the subliminal self, this latter making up the greater portion of our personality. We are only conscious of a small portion of our consciousness; the greatest part of it is submerged in the same way that the greatest portion of an iceberg is submerged and only a fragment shows above the surface of the water. He bases his ideas upon the psychological theory of thresholds of a mental level, above which sensation must rise before it can be manifest. Below this threshold of sensation lies what he calls the subliminal self. Or to draw an analogy from physics, consciousness is only the visible portion of the spectrum—the invisible, ultra portions are our subconscious selves.

The fourth theory states that the subconscious consists of dissociated experiences, things forgotten and that cannot be recalled, in other words, out of mind. To use a physical term, this is consciousness at rest, or consciousness which is not active. These inactive states of consciousness, while they may be recalled as memories either spontaneously or through certain technical devices, for the moment are out of mind, because our thoughts are occupied with something else.

The fifth theory is the physiological idea of the subconscious, the theory known as unconscious brain-thinking or unconscious cerebration, which states that all subconscious manifestations, such as hysteria, automatic writing, the subconscious solution of mathematical problems, are merely pure nerve processes unaccompanied by any thought whatsoever. According to Münsterberg, the subconscious is not psychical at all; he would interpret it merely as a physiological process.

A more practical theory, and one better supported by the evidence, is that active thinking processes may exist although we may not be aware of them. These subconscious mental states of which we are unaware may have intense emotions, may fabricate, or may even work out complex intellectual problems.

Thus the phenomena called automatic writing, which will be described at length in a subsequent chapter is, briefly stated, obtained by placing a suitable subject in a state of abstraction, putting a pencil in his hand, whereupon without any act of willing or conscious control, words, sentences, and even mathematical sequences are written.

One automatic writer, Mlle. Hélène Smith, reported by Flournoy,[1] described thus in detail,

[1] Th. Flournoy: "From India to the Planet Mars."

the conditions on the planet Mars. For some time these descriptions were held to signify that the subconscious subject was capable of supernatural communications, but careful analysis established two facts, both of which this chapter is concerned with emphasizing, *first,* that subconscious processes were not mechanical reproductions, but might be very complicated new combinations of ideas; and, *second,* that Mlle. Smith, in her automatic writings, told nothing that might not have been gathered from her previous reading and experiences, in other words, it is unnecessary to call upon spiritual realms for an explanation. Concerning this latter, Flournoy states, that several years before the automatic writing developed to such a degree in his subject that she claimed to be able to communicate with the planet Mars, she had more than once directed her conversation to the habitability of this planet and to the discovery of the famous canals.

In addition as the result of certain experiments with hypnosis, and the galvanic reactions in cases of multiple personality, it has been shown that under these circumstances complex calculations and translations could be done, and it would be inconceivable to think that these were pure physiological processes without thought.

At the sixth International Congress of Psychology, held at Geneva during August, 1909, a discussion of the subconscious formed one of the important subjects. This discussion was led by Max Dessoir, Pierre Janet, and Morton Prince. Max Dessoir drew a close analogy between the field of consciousness and the field of vision. From the psychological standpoint, in the visual field we have the centre of the field which corresponds, according to Dessoir, to the focus of consciousness, and the periphery or edge, of the field, which corresponds to the subconscious. In the periphery or edge, the contents of consciousness are either very dimly perceived or not at all, and these peripheral contents can become dissociated, split off, from the main or focal consciousness and lead an independent existence. Morton Prince suggested that the term subconscious be discarded and the word co-conscious be substituted in its place. The expression "co-conscious," relates to dissociated mental processes of which the subject is not aware, such processes (in passing from the simple to the complex) as automatic writing, hypnosis, and hysterical states. These processes are not mere blind automatisms, but possess intelligent psychological qualities, such as reasoning, calculation, memory, and volition. Furthermore, in cases of multiple personality, these disintegrated mental processes may lead an independent existence, in every way analogous to a normal mind. He would limit the term "unconscious" to certain physiological brain dispositions, such as conserved memories, which do not become psychic processes until stimulated.[1] Janet in this discussion limited the term subconscious to certain phenomena observed only in hysterical conditions, or in other abnormal mental states resulting from a weakened power of mental synthesis.

We will now pass to a brief statement of Freud's theories of the unconscious, a theory which is both unique and far-reaching in its possibilities. Freud's idea of the unconscious has aroused considerable discussion, not only for its rather revolutionary conception but because of the influence of his theory upon the psycho-neuroses, literature, wit, folk-lore, in fact

[1] Dr. Prince has also suggested the following classification. He would use the term "subconscious" in a generic sense, as implying all detached states of consciousness. This term he further subdivides into "co-conscious," meaning an active thinking process, and "unconscious," which is equivalent to unconscious brain thinking, a process which is unaccompanied by consciousness of any sort. The following scheme will make this clear:

Subconscious

Co-Conscious | Unconscious

the whole field of human mental activity.[1] The practical application of the theory has made possible all recent psycho-analytic conceptions and interpretations.

According to Freud, a psychic element may not only be unconscious but likewise exceedingly active and dynamic. For instance, in the hysterical patient, an hysterical convulsion may be incomprehensible to both subject and observer, yet this convulsive attack may be representative of and produced by a dramatic incident in the subject's life, but which lies unconsciously active in the memory, in other words, the patient is unaware of the cause of the convulsion. An unconscious idea, therefore, may be weak and fail to penetrate consciousness or it may be strong and over active (overdetermined). The unconscious is not always pathological, because it may produce certain phenomena in everyday life, such as slips of the tongue, errors of speech or memory, and, above all, in dreams of normal individuals, which latter, as demonstrated by psycho-analysis, may arise from the most complex unconscious ideas. The mental mechanisms entering into dream formation, as

[1] Freud's theory of the unconscious can be found scattered through his various publications on dreams, hysteria, wit, the psychopathology of everyday life, the sexual theory, and in his more recent contributions in which he analyzes the mind and superstitions of the savage and primitive man.

will be shown in a subsequent chapter, have furnished us with the best data for an insight into the nature of the unconscious.

The term "unconscious" as used by Freud, is not synonymous with "unconscious" in everyday speech. The latter connotes lack of consciousness or an unintentional or involuntary action. According to Freud, the unconscious means something in consciousness of which one is not aware, but which can be made known and brought into consciousness through the technique of psycho-analysis. Unconscious thoughts are therefore, existent and active in the normal individual as well as in the neurotic. Unconscious thoughts or ideas frequently remain so, because a force termed resistance prevents them from becoming conscious. On the activity of this resistance with the consequent repression of unconscious thoughts, is based the Freudian conception of hysteria. The act of repression usually meets with ill success, because the repressed impulses (wishes) and complexes continue to exist in the unconscious and thus send disguised substitutes into consciousness in the form of psycho-neurotic symptoms. Thus when unconscious thoughts break through into waking consciousness, we have disease, because the unconscious wish thus comes into conflict with reality: when unconscious thoughts break through a partially sleeping consciousness, dreams are produced. The repression is, therefore, the process which forces these unconscious thoughts out of consciousness and leads to a mental dissociation. Thus a mental dissociation is the result of this mental conflict and not according to one conception, as due to a weakened mental synthesis.

Unconscious thoughts may not only be of recent date (adult), but may also reach into the deepest strata of the unconscious to the earliest years of childhood (the infantile unconscious), which latter is usually a repressed sexual or erotic instinct associated with a wish to forget. The word "sexual" is used by Freud in its broadest sense, like the word "love" in English. If an unconscious thought of which the subject is unaware can be brought to memory with slight effort, even momentarily, it is termed "fore-conscious." The unconscious is rich in expression, as in the neurotic; in symbolisms, as in dreams; in oddities, as in wit; and in symptomatic actions, best seen in the absent-minded behavior of everyday life. It has also been shown through psycho-analysis, that unconscious individual phantasies which produce dreams, may, if they are active in the childhood of the race, give rise to myths and legends. Thus there is a psychological analogy between dreams and folklore; both use the same material for their fantasies.[1] In artistic literary creations likewise, the unconscious wish may often be disclosed by psycho-analysis.[2]

The unconscious exerts a persistent and dynamic influence on everyday life, so much so, that no element of thought or behavior is accidental, arbitrary or due to chance, but every conscious mental occurrence bears a direct, causal relation to its unconscious source. On this deterministic view-point is based all psycho-analytic investigation and the psycho-analytic therapy of the functional neuroses. For instance, if a subject is requested to make free associations to a given word or theme, the associations are really not free, but are conditioned by the unconscious or fore-conscious complexes. In dreams too, an identical mechanism can be

[1] K. Abraham, "Dreams and Myths," 1913.

[2] For interesting examples of the application of the psycho-analytic method to the study of literary creations, see a paper by Ernest Jones: "The Œdipus-Complex as an Explanation of Hamlet's Mystery."—*American Journal of Psychology,* January, 1910,—also my book, "The Hysteria of Lady Macbeth," New York, 1912. Thus psycho-analysis has shown that Hamlet's inhibition lay in a repressed love for his mother which was more powerful than his hostilities and that Lady Macbeth's hysteria and somnambulism arose from a repressed wish for a child. The action of both characters is thus explained on psycho-sexual mechanisms.—See also A. R. Chandler's interesting paper, "Tragic Effect in Sophocles Analyzed according to the Freudian method." *The Monist,* January, 1913.

found, the symbolism or the distortion of the dream bears a direct relationship to the latent (or unconscious) thoughts producing the dream. As stated by Freud,[1] "The unconscious must be accepted as the general basis of the psychic life. The unconscious is the larger circle which includes within itself the smaller circle of the conscious; everything conscious has its preliminary step in the unconscious, whereas the unconscious may stop with this step and still claim full value as a psychic activity. Properly speaking the unconscious is the real psychic; its inner nature is just as unknown to us as the reality of the external world and it is just as imperfectly reported to us through the data of consciousness as is the external world through the indications of our sensory organs."

Because of this persistent action of the unconscious, we are all victims of our unconscious thoughts or complexes. Thus our moral or religious or political views of life are tinged by our latent, unconscious ideas, and yet, by a process of self-deception, we conceal the origin of our views and motives. This concealment, called rationalization, is responsible for the frequently erroneous idea that logic plays a part in our thoughts and motives.

[1] "The Interpretation of Dreams" (translated by A. A. Brill) —New York, 1913.

3. *The Subconscious Mechanism in Everyday Life*

In everyday life a number of these dissociations may take place; for instance the forgetting of a name, absent-mindedness, slips of the tongue and pen, purposeless actions, the feeling of having experienced an entirely new sensation before or having previously been in a place which we are visiting for the first time (paramnesia or illusions of memory). The forgetting of a name is a very prominent instance of a normal dissociation of consciousness. How many times has it occurred that when one tries to recall the name of a person or a place it lingers in a most aggravating manner on the tip of the tongue but later, perhaps hours later, probably while engaged in something else, when we have put the thing out of our mind, the name will suddenly flash into consciousness. Here is an example of a normal amnesia, and the principle of the sudden return of the forgotten name while in a later state of abstraction, when the effort to remember the name has been put out of mind, is of great value in abnormal psychology, particularly in the psychological device of the synthesis of certain amnesic states, as will be pointed out later in the chapter on memory. This temporary dissociation leading to the forgetting of a name may be caused by repression. The name is forgotten because it is associated with a painful or disagreeable experience which has been repressed in the unconscious and the forgetting is a purposeful act, whose function is to protect the mind from the recalling of the experience. Thus an unconscious but purposeful motive can be detected on analysis, namely, that the forgetting is determined by a painful mental process. An individual, for instance, attempted in vain to recall the name of the Swiss neurologist Veraguth, and only some hours later, the name suddenly flashed into his mind. In order to attempt to find out the reason for the forgetting of a name that was very familiar to the individual, free association procedures gave the following:—"Veraguth—Verabad-Bad (the German for bath)—Bath—water—mineral water." Thus with the free association method the disturbing complex became clear—in other words —while in Switzerland the previous summer the subject was suddenly taken ill with a disorder which required the use of a certain mineral water and thus was unable to travel as had been planned. The association of the disagreeable experience in Switzerland was the inhibiting force which prevented the recall of the name. Sometimes also, following severe intellectual work, a temporary forgetfulness for recent things may take place. When subjects are in a state of abstraction or absent-mindedness, a question may be asked to which they apparently pay no attention. Ten or fifteen minutes later they will suddenly look up and answer. The question was there, but at the moment it was asked, the person was in this state of abstraction and there was an immediate dissociation of the question, it became split off from the main stream of consciousness. When the state of abstraction was terminated a synthesis took place, the question became conscious where before it was subconscious. Here we have an example of the conservation of an absent-minded experience, although the conserved experience was dissociated. As will be shown later, suggestibility is increased in normal abstraction or absent-mindedness, a feature which makes it closely related to the artificial hypnotic states. Although absent-mindedness may be looked upon as a special condition, yet it is nothing more or less than a severe form of inattention or concentrated attention, as shown by the negative hallucinations which sometimes occur in this condition, namely, a failure to perceive what is immediately in front of the eyes. Normal forgetfulness is thus in some way allied to the pathological amnesias, being both a dissociation and repression of memories;

absent-minded acts and apparently purposeless actions are simpler forms resembling the automatism of automatic writing or some hysterical symptoms, but having the same mental mechanism.

What takes place in normal absent-mindedness to show that we have a state of temporary mental dissociation? In absent-mindedness the attention is focussed on one thing, either internal or external. This focussing of attention narrows the field of personal consciousness and the portion of consciousness which lies outside this narrowed field is subconscious or dissociated. In this dissociated state, many acts may be done automatically, such as buttoning of a coat, tearing up papers, etc. But all these automatic acts are preserved and can be revived later by appropriate methods. All absent-minded states are not dissociations, it is only severe grades where attention is intensely focussed on some stimulus from without or some idea from within, that can be termed dissociated.

"This duality of the mind in normal absent-mindedness has been pointed out by various observers. Its phenomena simulate those of artificial abstraction as they occur in automatic writing and hysterical states. There is nothing surprising in this, as the term 'absent-mindedness' means dissociation of consciousness, a failure to perceive that which before was perceived and a failure to be conscious of acts intelligently performed. On the other hand, normal absent-mindedness is a distinctly special condition. We don't go about in an absent-minded state. Absent-minded phenomena are manifestations of the temporary disintegration of the personal self. But here the significant fact, the most significant of all, should not be lost sight of, that in the normal process of abstraction we find evidence of the existence of a normal prearranged mechanism for dissociating consciousness and producing subconscious states." [1]

Dissociation is plainly a function of the mind or brain as was shown above. These normal dissociations are not limited to absent-mindedness and forgetting of names, but may comprise other phenomena of our everyday life, such as the solution of problems by the secondary consciousness during sleep, slips of the tongue and pen, certain apparently accidental and purposeless actions, and those tricks of mind called illusions of memory. In a most interesting little volume Freud has discussed in detail some of the phenomena of the unconscious, which we have briefly mentioned here, under the title of the psychopathology of everyday life. In it he shows that these apparently aimless acts and phenomena are motivated by mental mechanisms unknown to consciousness, mechanisms hidden

[1] Morton Prince: "Problems of Abnormal Psychology."—*Psychological Review,* March-May, 1905.

in the unconscious and which can be revealed only through psycho-analysis. Here again we see the fruitful results of the concept of determinism. Thus mechanisms occurring in the abnormal are found also in the normal.

Both this observer and others have thus explained the acts of everyday life, many of which seem purposeless, accidental, and without reason unless carefully studied. The mechanism which produces disturbances in the thoughts and actions of normal people is identical with the mechanism which causes the disturbances in the insane and in abnormal mental dissociation. Automatic acts may be caused by an unconscious, suppressed complex. Dreams are frequently the manifestation of hidden wishes or memories; the haunting of the mind by a popular melody resembles a pathological obsession. It is popularly supposed that most mental life is forgotten beyond recovery, but it has been shown that a great deal may be recovered through proper devices, provided sufficient traces had been left in the nervous system.

Examples of the forgetting of a name resulting from the linking of the name with a disagreeable experience, have already been given. A slip of the tongue may arise as a manifestation of a suppressed thought or from an unconscious wish. This mechanism is not only seen in everyday life, but also in some cases of stammering. The same remarks can be applied to slips of the pen,—for instance, the case of writing the date of the previous year throughout January. This is not always due to habit, but in a number of cases it can be traced to a disinclination to admit to one's self that the new year has brought them a year nearer to old age, in other words, such slips of the pen betray in all of us, the wish (conscious or unconscious) to remain young. In writing the preface to the second edition of this book, such a slip of the pen occurred in writing "November 1914" instead of "November 1913," thus betraying my wish to bring the book as near up to date as possible.

The phenomena of hypnosis and a great many of the phenomena of hysteria seem to be merely more intense and protracted states of absent-mindedness or abstraction, which, we have shown, is a dissociation of consciousness. So we see that there is nothing supernormal or supernatural in these subconscious or dissociated manifestations, startling as some of these phenomena may appear. The gradations from the normal to the abnormal are slow; there is no distinct line; there is an overlapping of types, and one cannot say where the normal ends and where the abnormal begins.

A few other examples will show in further detail the presence of temporary subconscious phenomena in everyday life. In the first instance to be given it can be demonstrated that normal abstraction is a mental condition of increased suggestibility and thus resembles the artificially produced state of hypnosis. In the second case it can be shown that normal forgetfulness is a dissociation of memory, allied to the pathological amnesias. In common with these amnesias, it is possible to restore or synthetize the lost experience because the experience is really not lost, but is present in the subconscious. In the third example, that of a dream analysis furnished an interesting instance that unconscious manipulations of numbers appearing in a dream were not accidental, but represented important unconscious mental conflicts of the subject.

In the first case, three men were members of a party of seven seated at dinner. Dessert was being served and some of the party were already supplied. One of the members of the dinner party, Professor H., was talking to another member, Mr. G., in a low tone, and the latter was listening very intently. The dessert consisted of chocolate pie and squash pie, and as some had already been brought in Mr. G. had time to decide which he preferred. Mrs.

R., who was sitting beside Mr. G., inquired which he would have. The latter was so abstracted in the conversation, that apparently he did not hear, and even on a repetition of the question, he gave no reply. Meanwhile another member of the party, in a spirit of jest, spoke softly to Mrs. R., but in such a manner that Mr. G. could hear, and said, "Mr. G. always takes chocolate pie." Immediately Mr. G. quickly replied, "Chocolate pie, please." This was done because it was well known to the other members of the party that Mr. G. had a profound distaste for chocolate pie. Meanwhile the waiter had brought the dessert (chocolate pie) to Mr. G., who by that time had finished his conversation with Professor H. Then, as if just coming to himself, Mr. G. turned to his companion and said, "Who said chocolate pie? I wanted the other kind."

In the second case, a woman had given a check for a certain amount. For certain reasons, some two years later, it became necessary for her to recall the signature on the check, the exact date and place and the bank on which the check was drawn. She remembered that she had read the check carefully over at the time it was given to her, but two years later she could not recall by any amount of conscious effort, the date on the check. When she was placed in a state of abstraction by listening to a monotonous sound stimulus, in a few minutes all the data on the check were recalled. She was now able to recollect the exact date, the name of the bank, the name of the person to whom the check was payable, the number of the check, and finally the signature. By means of crystal gazing it was also possible to produce a vivid visual hallucination of the check.

In the third case, a young man whose betrothal was not approved by his mother who wished him to honorably terminate it, had the two following dreams.

Dream I. He seemed to be in a lawyer's office. The assistant was making notes and writing figures on sheets of paper, which figures when added made the sum 3990.

Dream II. He seemed to be standing near a large building, in front of which was a moving-van with the figures 317 painted thereon.

An analysis of the figures occurring in these two dreams demonstrated how complicated may be the various manipulations of figures taking place in the unconscious and furnished an exact demonstration of the subject's mental conflict. This number symbolism was as follows:—

$$317 = 3 + 1 + 7 = 11$$
$$3990 = 39 + 9 + 0 = 48$$

$48 + 11 = 59$ (the age of the subject's mother)
$3 + 9 + 9 + 0 = 21$
$3 + 1 + 7 = 11$
$21 + 11 = 32$ (the age of the subject's fiancée)

Thus the numbers occurring in the dreams were not accidental, but revealed the struggle taking place in the unconscious. This struggle was symbolized by the numbers, which represented both the age of the subject's mother and that of the subject's fiancée.

4. *How the Subconscious Becomes Diseased*

Passing from the consideration of the subconscious as a mere psychological mechanism to a condition of specific disease, we also pass from a comparatively simple set of problems to a complex and much discussed field. Here we shall find the theory that subconscious activity is not mechanical but reasoning and is dynamically active or what is called the psychological theory, more helpful and more easily applicable than in the simple forms.

When the subconscious assumes extraordinary and painful attributes it may be said to be diseased, and then exhibits in a marked manner the independent or split-off existence which has been noted above, so much so that the entire range of such diseases are often included within the term dissociation. In these cases, it is not only the dissociation, but also the continued activity of the dissociated or unconscious portion of consciousness, due to a process of repression which causes the mischief.

What is the cause of this dissociation and why does it at one time simply produce an absent-mindedness and at another time an hysteria? It seems that when absent-mindedness becomes protracted we have hysteria, and when normal failure to recall a name takes in the events of a period, we have amnesia. Dissociation remains normal, therefore, so long as it is transitory. When the dissociation is prolonged and assumes a continued activity, due to repression and to the inability of the repressed thoughts to enter consciousness, then it becomes abnormal. It is probably this fact above all others which determines whether a subconscious process be normal or pathological. Concerning the exact cause of this repression and dissociation, we are in the dark. We know that exhaustion, certain emotions, unconscious mental conflicts, and certain experimental devices are able to produce a mental dissociation, but exactly how this dissociation is brought about, abnormal psychology cannot at present offer a final solution.

Janet interprets the abnormal phenomena, applying them more particularly to hysteria and hysterical dissociations, as being merely a chronic form of absent-mindedness, and concludes that clear-cut phenomena, analogous to the subconsciousness of hysteria, are infinitely rare in a normal mind. His conception, that a mental dissociation, particularly as seen in hysteria, is caused by an inborn weakness of mental synthesis, is somewhat unsatisfactory as shown by recent psycho-analytic investigations. It explains only a portion of the problem; it makes no attempt to solve the more fundamental aspects of the unconscious mechanism, particularly repression, mental conflicts, and the persistence of childhood complexes. In general he states, that when these normal dissociations "are really noted by competent observers, they cannot but be regarded as unhealthy accidents of a more or less transient character, and of a somewhat sinister omen." Breuer and Freud, on the contrary, state that severe dissociations are secondary to the development of what they term the "hypnoidal state" which is a condition of abstraction in the normal sense. According to this view, the pathological process is a dynamic one. In the conscious mental life, an active conflict is persistently taking place, in order to force certain ideas into the unconscious. The mechanism is therefore based upon a process of repression and when this repression fails, certain pathological symptoms tend to arise. This conflict and repression is mainly concerned with the sexual instincts of early childhood (pertinently termed the pre-historic period of our lives), and may cause either hysteria or an obsessional neurosis. When an unhealthy mental accident takes place in this hypnoidal state, there arises an inability to form a synthesis with the normal consciousness. Hence the abnormal state tends to be indefinitely prolonged, producing a pathological mental condition, sometimes hysteria, at other times recurrent automatic ideas called obsessions. "Abnormal psychology, then, points strongly to the conclusion that there is a normal physiological dissociating mechanism which is the function of the nervous organization. It is this mechanism which brings about such spontaneous normal states as absent-mindedness, sleep, normal induced states like hypnosis; and through its perversions the dissociations underlying abnormal phenomena."[1]

A feeling on the part of the subject, that the personality has disappeared or has changed from the normal to the abnormal, is often an evidence of mental dissociation. This Dr. Jekyll and Mr. Hyde existence may occur in

[1] Morton Prince: "Problems of Abnormal Psychology."—*The Psychological Review*, 1905.

many functional conditions, such as neurasthenia, psychasthenia, and in certain cases of delirium or mental depression. In hysteria or multiple personality, the new personality may lead an independent existence.

Probably the most marked forms of functional neuroses are caused by the action of abnormal ideas or emotions. These ideas and emotions are usually present in groups (complexes) and are linked together as abnormal associations. All complexes are not abnormal, however, for the formation of normal complexes forms the basis of all our educational processes. Habits and highly skilled movements are complexes which are the result of frequent repetition. They are really unconscious memories, having an automatic action.

Now these stored-up complexes, whether conscious or dissociated, may influence the entire psycho-physical life. They may appear in dreams but in a fantastic and distorted manner; they may produce hysterical phenomena, or the dormant complex, if stimulated, may cause recurrent attacks of fear or obsessions, or it may produce certain inhibitions of thought as in the association tests. Sometimes, too, the complex or even an isolated idea related to the complex, may produce changes in the electrical resistance of the body or certain physiological effects, such as an acceleration of the pulse rate. The stored-up emotional complex is distinctly the most important factor in abnormal psychology. Complexes may be formed in various ways, in everyday life, in dreams, or in states of abstraction.

All stored-up complexes may either produce themselves spontaneously or can be artificially reproduced by means of special methods. This artificial reproduction of the unconscious complex is at the basis of all psycho-analysis. So we see that this reproduction may have a beneficial effect because once the complex is discovered it can usually be rendered harmless. If complexes were always present in memory it would be unnecessary to dig for them through psychological methods. But they are not always present in memory; in fact, a complex may be unconscious and lead to a mental dissociation. Dissociated complexes are removed from the censorship of the conscious mind and, therefore, act in an abnormal manner. Under conditions which are not at present clearly understood, this complex may suddenly begin to act. So we see that this dissociated state may tend to become automatic, and it is this automatism which gives rise to many pathological states of consciousness.

All psychotherapy is based upon one or more

of these fundamental principles. If there is a state of dissociation the obvious remedy is synthesis, as can be shown in many hysterical manifestations. If certain experiences are stored up, but cannot be spontaneously reproduced, then we must have recourse to some form of artificial reproduction. In this way we can fill up the blanks in the mind which are caused by certain types of functional amnesia. If a complex had an automatic or independent activity, then an effort should be made to bring about a control and finally an inhibition of this automatic state.

From the evidence that can be gathered, from both normal and abnormal mental life, it seems that before a mental state can be termed dissociated or subconscious, it must possess several qualities. First this mental state must have an automatic activity. Second, it must act independently from the rest of consciousness. Third, there must be an absence of awareness for this mental state. Fourth, there must be an impossibility of voluntarily reproducing the mental state in consciousness. Fifth, it ought to be possible to reproduce the detached mental state by an artificial method. A dissociation may be normal, as in absent-mindedness; it may be artificially produced, as in hypnosis; or it may be abnormal, as in hysteria.

CHAPTER II

AUTOMATIC WRITING AND CRYSTAL GAZING

AUTOMATIC writing can be best understood by giving a brief account of a series of elaborate experiments carried out by Mrs. Verrall.[1] The phenomena of automatic writing were Mrs. Verrall's personal products. She carried out a long series of experiments, some 322 in number, upon herself, and obtained as many " consciously " written pieces of script. That she was already accustomed to having her subconscious mental life " tapped," so to speak, is expressly stated. In 1889-1892 she had recorded and later published a series of observations on herself in crystal gazing. She allowed this faculty to remain dormant, however, until after repeated attempts, she found herself able to produce automatic writing in 1901. The method employed to develop the faculty is instructive. She says, " On January 17, 1901, I spent a quarter of an hour or more in sitting perfectly still in a dim light with a pencil in my

[1] Mrs. A. W. Verrall: " On a Series of Automatic Writings."—*Proc. Soc. for Psychical Research,* Vol. XX, October, 1906.

hand, with a view to giving myself the opportunity of recognizing any impression that I might have. I continued this daily. Unless my attention was actively engaged in some other direction, the pencil did not move; if I tried to occupy my attention with reading, the pencil merely produced some of the words of the book or occasionally traced characters resembling those on a brass table on which the pencil and paper lay." These attempts were continued daily for about two weeks and only three attempts were made during the following month. Then, on resuming the experiments, the first successful result was obtained. A strong impulse to change the position of the pencil was felt, and, "in obedience to the impulse I took the pencil between my thumb and first finger and after a few nonsense words, it wrote rapidly in Latin. On the first occasion, March 5, 1901, my hand wrote about eighty words almost entirely in Latin, but though the words are consecutive and seem to make phrases, and though phrases seem intelligible, there is no general sense in the passage."

These early attempts resulted in mere rubbish, but by continued "practice," the writing became the logical expression of ideas. "Whole phrases were intelligible," until they finally developed into elaborate compositions, written indifferently in English, Latin, and Greek, the experimenter having an excellent command of the two latter languages. Rude drawings were also included in these phenomena. Curiously enough, although Mrs. Verrall was perfectly familiar with French, and constantly dreamed in this language and was apt to use it absolutely in imaginary conversation with herself, there was no trace of this language in the script. The subject was entirely unaware of what her hand was writing, although she was apt to perceive a word or two, but never understood whether it made sense with what went before. "Under these circumstances," the report states, "it will be seen that though I am aware at the moment of writing what language my hand is using, when the script is finished I often cannot say till I read it what language has been used, as the recollection of the words passes away with extreme rapidity." In each experiment, as a rule, the writing ceased after a sheet of paper was covered, that is from 70 to 90 words, but as many as 265 have been produced. The content of the writing embraced all sorts of topics; for instance, allusions, descriptions of persons or places, exhortations, messages, reminiscences, anecdotes, philosophical and quasimathematical disquisitions, enigmatic or oracular sayings, etc. On occasions, Latin and Greek verse was produced, although the subject disclaimed normally any ability to write English verse.

One interesting point mentioned is the influence of the content of writing upon the writer, notwithstanding her ignorance of that content. "Thus, once I found the tears running down my face when the writing was over; the contents apparently alluded to two friends of mine who had died under tragic circumstances." On another occasion her left hand, which was not writing, was very cold and she had a recollection of feeling a breeze on her left side. These observations are in accord with similar phenomena frequently described in abnormal mental conditions when subconscious ideas produce emotional feelings in the subject, whether of exaltation, depression, or fear. In the great majority of occasions while writing, Mrs. Verrall was in a "perfectly normal condition," although often she felt sleepy and a few times lost consciousness of her surroundings. Telepathic experiments, with the avowed object of determining whether information unknown to the writer could be conveyed by automatic writing, were practically unsuccessful. The failure of these telepathic experiments is of particular value in freeing automatic writing from any supernormal interpretation and placing it beyond doubt on the basis of the reproduction of past experiences or fabrications founded on these experiences.

Sometimes there were concomitant phenomena, such as a "sudden impulse" to write (21 out of 306 occasions) and a feeling of fatigue and discomfort in the right arm. There was, however, no anesthesia of the writing hand and none of that intense abstraction, with its systematized anesthesia of all the sensory and motor functions, which has been observed in hysterical automatism. In these hysterical cases, however, the state of abstraction may be so deep that little or nothing is left of the waking consciousness. Under these circumstances a kind of a new alternating personality has been formed and it is this new personality which does the writing. The real self thus becomes a mere narrow automatism, perhaps almost completely asleep, while the secondary self is active, wide awake, and intelligent. This production of automatic writing while the subject was plunged into a state of deep abstraction, was found in the Beauchamp case and in Janet's case of Mme. B. To a certain extent it was also present in the Lowell case of amnesia, although here the writing consisted of mere scraps of dissociated experiences.

Automatic writing is a phenomenon of great experimental value. It is one of the simplest forms of mental dissociation, and thus through it can be easily studied such questions as whether we are dealing with mere mechanical repetitions of previous experiences or with unconscious activities accompanied by thought, and also whether these simple states are abortive, alternating personalities. Automatic writing also shows how automatism and independent activity enter into states of mental dissociation. Thus we have in automatic writing not only a device for tapping the subconscious, but also a simple form of experimental evidence for the analysis of many disputed points.

To interpret automatic writing as a mere physiological nervous process without ideation is incompatible with the observed facts, because not only are records of previous experiences reproduced, but also elaborate fabrications, mathematical reasoning, arithmetical problems, moods, feelings, and emotions. Sometimes a kind of an abortive secondary or alternating personality will make its appearance, on other occasions an alleged new language may be fabricated, such as in Hyslop's case of Mrs. Smead and Flournoy's case of Mlle. Hélène Smith. In both of these latter, there were alleged communications with the planet Mars, with the formation of an elaborate Martian language.

In automatic writing the subject may or may not be aware of what the writing hand is producing, but all cases show automatism and independent activity. The test of automatic writing is not the sense of awareness, but rather the independent activity of the consciousness that is doing the writing. Automatic writing may occur in a number of conditions in which there is a splitting of consciousness or in which the mind of the subject lends itself to an easy dissociation. Automatic writers may show other signs of mental disintegration (such as crystal gazing), and it has also been found to occur in multiple personality and in certain forms of functional amnesia. In both these latter the writing reproduces experiences which the subject cannot voluntarily recall to consciousness as memory. Yet the ability to do automatic writing is not always an evidence of disease, as the phenomenon may occur and be increased through practice in perfectly normal and well-balanced individuals.

Now in Mrs. Verrall's experiments, the content of the writing did not represent mechanical repetition of previous experiences, such as might be done by physiological automatisms of nervous processes without accompanying thought, but there were often elaborate compositions of an original character. The data offered by the author in these observations are of extreme value for the study of subconscious phenomena, in that they show the possibilities of the splitting of consciousness and the formation of large organized systems of subconscious thought in healthy individuals. They are examples of subconscious activities in everyday life, occurring in subjects who are free from the manifestations of any disease.

Mrs. Verrall's data, therefore, contradict the view maintained by some academic psychologists that subconscious phenomena, like tics and choreiform movements, are produced simply by physiological nerve processes without thought. They also contribute to an understanding of abnormal conditions, for with these normal phenomena in mind we can readily understand that when the subconscious ideas have an undesirable character, like fearful or horrifying or repugnant ideas or experiences, they may influence the personal consciousness and the whole organism unfavorably and produce abnormal phenomena such as occur in hysteria. This was well seen in the hysterical condition of Miss F., who forms the subject of Chapter VIII. Here a horrifying experience became detached from the personal consciousness and caused a series of hysterical attacks. It was only when a synthesis of these detached experiences was formed with the waking consciousness that the attacks ceased.

Now, in all Mrs. Verrall's experiments, there was nothing to show that the content of the automatic writing did not represent the previous knowledge and experiences of the subject. The most pertinent example of pure fabrications of a highly imaginative character occurring in automatic writing is seen in the " Martian Cycle " of Flournoy's celebrated case of Mlle. Hélène Smith.[1] Here the alleged supernormal knowledge of the trance personality was as much fabrication as the communications themselves. For instance, in Mrs. Verrall's account, the fact that allusions to Neoplatonic phraseology appeared in the script before these writers were read, can well be explained on the basis of a hasty but forgotten glance at their works, or even at some forgotten essay.

Much that has been stated concerning the mechanism of automatic writing can be applied to crystal gazing. In spite of the part played by crystal gazing in necromancy and Eastern mysticism, nothing can be reproduced as a crystal vision which has not already been a part of personal experience, although this experience may have been dissociated. In the production of these visions the subject gazes into a crystal globe

[1] See Flournoy: " From India to the Planet Mars," pp. 139-274.

and at the same time attempts to keep the mind a blank and free from external stimuli. The state of abstraction thus produced in crystal gazing "taps" the subconscious experiences in the same manner that they are tapped through automatic writing. After a short time isolated or complex pictures appear in the crystal. These are usually very vague at first, but later become more distinct. Like automatic writing, crystal visions may take place in normal individuals, although they are produced with greater ease in those persons who have an abnormal instability or who are victims of a pathological disintegration of the personality. In the Beauchamp case, the crystal visions threw considerable light on the experiences of the various personalities. In one of our cases (Mrs. Y.[1]), it served as a device for reproducing some of the incidents of the split personality.

Mrs. Y. showed four multiple hypnotic states for which she was amnesic in her waking condition. The crystal visions in this patient were revivals of past experiences. Some of these experiences the patient remembered; others could only be recalled in hypnosis. For instance, in one of the hypnotic states for which there was no memory on awakening, the emotional reaction was one of hatred and disgust. When a

[1] See chapter on "The Splitting of a Personality."

crystal vision of the same experience was produced, the emotional reaction was the same. It seems that whatever device was used for synthesis, either hypnosis or crystal gazing, the reproduced memories were associated with certain emotions. These emotions had attached themselves to the dissociated experiences, and when these experiences were revived by either of the methods, the associated emotions likewise appear. The following is a partial record of the crystal visions belonging to dissociated experiences in the life of the subject, the details of which were given in hypnosis and not remembered on awakening.

"I see my husband choking me, that terrible man choking me, with his hand around my throat."

"I see Dr. J. chatting with me. I am in his office. It is so strange I am sitting there and seem to be in a hurry."

"I see my brother, a surgeon in the British army. He is just home from Burmah. He is in a gray suit and standing beside me and my sister. It is trimmed with red and he has all his decorations. The scene is on a beach."

The ease with which crystal visions were produced in Miss Beauchamp, was one of the evidences of the facility with which disintegration took place in this subject. One of the incidents offers a good example of the manner in which subconscious experiences may be reproduced as crystal visions.[1] The report follows, Chris and Miss Beauchamp being different personalities of the same subject. Chris or Sally was mischievous, fond of fun, and playing practical jokes; while Miss Beauchamp was quiet, sedate, and demure.

In the course of the interview of May 1, reported in the last chapter, Chris remarked that she smelled the odor of a cigarette which I had been smoking. I offered her one. Delighted at the idea, she accepted, but smoked the cigarette very clumsily. The fact that smoking is something absolutely repugnant to Miss Beauchamp's taste added to Chris's enjoyment. Her manner was that of a child in mischief.

"Won't she be cross?" she laughed.

"Why?"

"She is not in the habit of smoking cigarettes. I shall smoke though." Miss Beauchamp when awakened, entirely ignorant of what she had been doing, complained of a bitter taste in her mouth, but could not identify it, and I did not enlighten her. At the next interview I remarked to Chris, "Wasn't it funny to see Miss Beauchamp when she tasted the tobacco in her mouth, and did not know what it was?"

Chris laughed and thought it was a good joke. "Yes, she thought you had been putting quinine in her mouth, but did not dare ask her." This remark, later verified

[1] "The Dissociation of a Personality," pp. 54-56.

by Miss Beauchamp, was one of many which showed Chris had knowledge of Miss Beauchamp's thoughts.

The sequel to this episode was amusing. At a later period I was engaged in making an experimental study of visions, and for the purpose had Miss Beauchamp (BI) look into a glass wherein she saw various visions of one kind and another. That is to say, the phenomena of so-called crystal visions were easily produced, and she proved an excellent subject. These visions were, for the most part, reproductions of past experiences. In one experiment she was horrified and astonished on looking into the globe to see the scene of the cigarette rehearsed in all its details. She saw herself sitting on a sofa—the identical sofa on which she was at the moment seated—smoking cigarettes. Her eyes, in the vision, were closed. (Chris's eyes were always closed at this time.) It was amusing to watch the expression of astonishment and chagrin with which she beheld herself in this Bohemian act. She indignantly repudiated the fact, declared it was not true, and that she had never smoked a cigarette in her life. The childlike expression on her face in the vision—Chris's face—which she characterized as "foolish" also annoyed her.

In another case of the automatic writing, which came under personal observation, the first efforts of the subject produced only scattered and disconnected words. By practice, however, the ability to do the writing increased, and the productions became more complex, until she was able to carry on communications with an alleged control. In this subject, there was neither abstraction nor a trance state and the sense of awareness during the period of writing, was almost complete. The thoughts seemed to precede the writing by the fraction of a second, but they were automatic and independent of the subject. She had no control over these thoughts or over the movements of the hand which was doing the writing. It was very curious to watch this subject during this process. The eyes were widely opened as she watched the pencil in the moving hand. Sometimes the writing was faint, but on other occasions the hand wrote rapidly and with such great force that the pencil point became frequently broken or the sheet of paper torn. Under some conditions mere marks and scrawls would be produced; at other times, words and sentences. As a rule, however, even the sentences were rather vague in their meaning, while any elaborate fabrications were entirely absent. The subject was very easily hypnotized and on several occasions, while in a normal condition, she spontaneously experienced a sense of unreality. These phenomena in connection with the automatic writing were evidences of the ease with which mental dissociation took place in this subject. Thus automatic writing and crystal gazing are merely technical devices utilized in psychopathology, by means of which experiences long forgotten and impossible of recall by voluntary effort, may be revived.

Sometimes also, automatic writing may merely fulfill or realize the wish of the subject, the same as in dreams and thus give rise to symptomatic actions. An interesting example of a fulfilling of a wish once came under personal observation. It related to a young woman who had made several ineffectual attempts to consult me while I was on a vacation. She had in the past experimented some with a planchette (a mechanical device for automatic writing) and one day she decided to "ask" the instrument the date of my return. The pencil thereupon persistently wrote the figure five and then added "September 5," which the subject took to mean that I would return on that day. Although I actually returned several days earlier, she did not call until September fifth, which date I found on questioning, to be most convenient for her. Thus, through her actions she realized her wish for convenience, a wish which was revealed some time earlier through automatic writing.

CHAPTER III

TESTING THE EMOTIONS

WHEN we approach the study of the emotions, physiology and psychology become inseparable. Before the mental accompaniments of the various emotions can be understood, we must have a clear comprehension of the physiological or physical aspects of these mental states. While this chapter will be devoted principally to the abnormal aspects of the emotions, yet it will be necessary to give a summary of the various theories of normal emotional processes, to which will be added the more recent experimental researches on the question, such as the electrical phenomena (the psycho-galvanic reflex) and a modification of these phenomena, namely, the pulse reaction tests. Like sleep, the emotions are instinctive and are inseparable from our everyday psychic existence. As a preliminary, there can be applied to the emotions the same important question as can be applied to sleep, namely, at what step in evolution did the emotions first appear? This question is more easily propounded than answered, for the emotions are very complex phenomena and enter into all the phases of our every-day existence. In animals, possessing a well-organized nervous system, well-marked emotional expressions occur, yet these seem to be absent from the lower organisms, in which the nervous system is either entirely absent or is limited to a mere collection of ganglion cells. If this be true, then the manifestations of the emotions must have arisen at some phase of natural selection and possibly the physical expressions of certain emotions were a strong factor in the early struggles for existence. Since emotional expressions require a certain active state of consciousness, it may be said in general, although, of course, this statement is open to certain modifications and corrections, that the emotions can only take place in organisms whose nervous system has reached such a state of development that this active consciousness possesses a certain intensity. Emotions, therefore, would be completely absent from all organisms whose nervous system was in a very rudimentary condition, incompletely developed in those animals possessing a moderately complex brain, and reaching their highest expression in the higher animals and man, where the nervous system has assumed a great complexity of structure.

Emotional reactions are highly complex functions of the nervous system and their intensity and complexity are parallel with the development of the brain. While there seem to be no special brain centres for the emotions, yet if the brain is removed or profoundly diseased, as in certain states of dementia and in some physiological experiments, the emotions either pass into simple reflex acts or are entirely absent. This is well seen in the emotional apathy of the terminal stages of such mental diseases as general paralysis and dementia præcox.

The higher animals, such as the cat, dog, certain birds, monkeys, and anthropoid apes, not only have a wide range of emotions, but the physiological expression of these emotions is almost as graphic as in man. Of course, none of these animals can express the finer emotions, such as meditation, laughter, blushing, modesty, etc., but the more primitive and elementary emotional expressions, such as anger, fear, and surprise are as well developed in some of the higher vertebrates as in man. Whether or not the accompanying mental states are as intense, we have no means of judging, but certainly if the physical expression of these states can be taken as an indication, they must be so in every particular, although in animals we are hopelessly cut off from any introspective evidence.

Taking the emotions in their widest sense, as comprising both the physiological symptoms and their mental accompaniments, we arrive at the important question,—what is the cause and interpretation of these various manifestations? It is a fact of common experience that certain reactions of the bodily organs are characteristic of certain emotions, bodily manifestations which have been known from time immemorial and have pervaded the literature and art of all nations. These physiological accompaniments of the emotions take place in all the organs,—respiration becomes affected, the heart beat becomes either fast or slow, there is either an inhibition or an excitation of the secretory and mechanical factors of the stomach and intestines, the muscular system changes in its tension, and even the skin reacts in various ways. The sight or even the idea of a tempting morsel of food will "make the mouth water," while fear inhibits the salivary secretion, so that an excessive dryness of the mouth takes place. In states of bravery the limbs are held tense by the muscular contractions;—in fear, the limbs tremble, the heart-beat becomes accelerated, the "hair of the flesh stands up." Mental states of anxiety or apprehension frequently accompany pathological states of rapid heart reaction, known in medicine as paroxysmal tachycardia.

We see, then, that the emotions possess two distinct phenomena,—the physical or physiological, relating to the viscera, and the psychical or state of cerebral action. Some authorities state that emotion begins as a mental state, and it is this mental state which influences the various organs and the vascular apparatus. For them, the emotions are primary cerebral reactions, the visceral expressions being purely secondary. This theory is supported by certain important facts. If the hemispheres of the brain are removed in an animal (Goltz's experiments) it will not show the slightest vestige of emotional reaction. Even the coarser emotions, such as anger and pleasure, will be absent. In states of dementia or mental enfeeblement and in certain other mental diseases, the finer emotions are likewise absent. In other words, there is a condition of what has been called emotional apathy or emotional atrophy. The opposite view, which may be termed the peripheral theory of the emotions, as held by James, Lange, and Sergi, states that the mental state of emotion is secondary to the actions of the viscera, particularly the circulatory organs. These organs are thrown into a state of activity and excitation through certain peculiar stimuli.

Professor James says, "Our natural way of thinking about these coarser emotions is that the mental perception of some fact excites the mental affection called the emotion and that this latter state of mind gives rise to the bodily expression. My theory, on the contrary, is that the bodily changes follow directly the perception of the exciting fact, and that our feeling of the same changes as they occur is the emotion. Common sense says, we lose our fortune, are sorry and weep; we meet a bear, are frightened and run; we are insulted by a rival, are angry and strike. . . The more rational statement is that we feel sorry because we cry, angry because we strike, afraid because we tremble, and not that we cry, strike, or tremble, because we are sorry, angry, or fearful, as the case may be. . . If we fancy some strong emotion and then try to abstract from our consciousness of it all the feelings of its bodily symptoms, we find we have nothing left behind, no 'mind stuff' out of which the emotion can be constituted, and that a cold and mental state of intellectual perception is all that remains."[1] In order to disprove this hypothesis, Sherrington has shown,[2]

[1] William James: "The Principles of Psychology," Vol. II, pp. 442 *et seq.*

[2] C. S. Sherrington: "The Integrative Action of the Nervous System."

that if an experiment be performed on an animal in such a manner so as to remove all sensation of the bodily organs, the skin and muscles, upon which Professor James lays so much stress in his peripheral theory of the emotions, that the animal thus experimented upon shows all grades of emotional expression. Here the brain was left intact but the peripheral sensations were obliterated, yet no alteration occurred in the emotional character of the animal. Furthermore, the changes in the electrical resistance of the body under the influence of certain emotions as measured by a delicate galvanometer and also the emotional fluctuations in the pulse rate, force us back to the fact that the emotions are central and not peripheral in origin. To the ordinary individual, this central theory of the emotions is the most logical one; he trembles because he is afraid, he strikes because he is angry, etc.

It has also been shown, by the investigations of the Russian physiologist Pawlow,[1] how the secretions of the stomach and intestines are largely influenced by the mental state of the animals on which he experimented. The results obtained have also been confirmed in experiments on man. Gastric and salivary secretion took place in dogs when the animals were

[1] See the interesting book by J. P. Pawlow: "The Work of the Digestive Glands," 1910.

tempted with food, but not with indifferent substances, such as stones or pieces of rubber, whereas threatening a dog with a whip entirely arrested gastric secretion. These experiments showed that the stimulus of a pleasant emotion, associated with food, called into activity the secretion of the gastric and salivary glands, while the depressing emotion of fear had an exactly opposite, inhibitory influence. It is a matter of common observation how the sight or even the abstract idea of an appetizing, tempting morsel of food will make the mouth water, while the states of fear, and also in the pathological fear neuroses, an opposite condition takes place, the secretion of saliva is inhibited and a dryness of the mouth results.

Furthermore, Cannon has shown, in some investigations on the movements of the stomach and intestines in animals, the intimate relationship existing between emotional states and the mechanical factors of digestion, and also that the secretion of the adrenal gland may be influenced by emotional stimulation. He states, for instance—

"Any signs of emotional disturbance, even the restlessness and emotional mewing, which may be taken to indicate uneasiness and discomfort, were accompanied in the cat by total cessation of the segmenting movements of the small intestines, as well as complete quiescence of the gastric mechanism. During more than an hour of continuous watching such signs of anxiety have been attended by entire inactivity of every part of the alimentary canal."

Studies along these lines are of value in the interpretation of pathological effects of certain emotions upon the gastro-intestinal functions of man, and they throw considerable light upon the visceral expressions of some of the fear neuroses. Such investigations help to explain the mysterious effect of certain psychical processes upon the body. The various publications of Pawlow had already pointed out the influences of mental states in animals upon the secretions and motor power of both the stomach and intestines. Observations in man have shown the same phenomena to occur as the result of certain emotional conditions. Cannon does not restrict the word emotions to violent affective states, but uses the term in a wider, popular sense, as including all affective experiences. The emotions precede the bodily change, the nervous connections of the viscera acting merely as conduction paths. It was demonstrated by Cannon, that if these nervous connections were severed, mental excitement caused no inhibitory effect upon the movements of the stomach or intestines. Pawlow also showed that if the nervous connections of the stomach were severed, there was no flow of gastric juice in his so-called sham feeding experiments. If we take these physiological investigations (Sherrington, Pawlow, Cannon), as the basis of a theory, it would seem to follow that the visceral expressions of the emotions were secondary to the psychical state.

Both the motor power and secretory activity of the alimentary canal are largely dependent upon the nature of the excitation in the nervous system. Normal secretion is favored by pleasurable sensations; unpleasant feelings, such as fright and rage, are accompanied not only by a failure of secretion, but also by total cessation of the movements of the stomach and intestine. The sight of food to a hungry subject causes a flow of gastric juice. The inhibitory result of emotional states can persist long after the cessation of the exciting condition. Many of the abnormal motor and secretory digestive disturbances of man are caused by the emotional state of the subject. These physiological experiments show how profoundly the mental state may affect favorably or unfavorably, not only the secretions but also the movements of the stomach and intestines.

We are now prepared to briefly discuss the more exact methods of detecting the emotions, methods which not only have the qualitative value of giving us a finer insight into the mental side of the feelings, but which also have a certain quantitative value. In other words, we are able to measure the emotions the same way as by other methods we can measure the depth of sleep or the intensity of a sensation of sound, light, or pain. These newer methods no longer make us dependent on the coarser bodily expressions of feelings, such as blushing when we are ashamed, crying when we are in grief, or trembling when we are afraid. Yet in many cases the shame, grief, or fear may be suppressed by the subject and show no outward manifestations. Further, these feelings may be connected with a special episode or experience which the subject is anxious to hide for fear of detection, or purposely conceals, because even the thinking of the experience may be mentally painful. We shall see later how large a part these "strangulated emotions" play in the genesis of certain hysterical manifestations. How then are we to detect these hidden suppressed emotions, when we have no gross bodily symptoms to guide us and give us a clue? How are we to know that certain words which we speak, or certain incidents to which we may refer, arouse in the mind of the subject an emotional meaning? What is the effect of this aroused emotion upon the finer physiological processes of the body or upon the actions of the mind? It is just here that experimental psychology comes to our rescue.

Recent investigations on the emotions have furnished us with exact methods of psycho-physical research in this direction.[1] In states of abstraction, produced by having a reclining subject listen to a monotonous sound stimulus, such as the beating of a metronome, there results after a time a lowering of the pulse rate. This lowered or rest pulse rate remains permanent, so long as the subject continues in this quiescent mental state. If, while he is in this condition, the subject be given certain abstract problems to solve, or certain startling and painful stimuli be used, or if he be made to think of indifferent words, the pulse rate remains unchanged. The condition of mental serenity in the abstract state is unaltered. [See Fig. I.] On the contrary, if the subject be asked to recall individual emotional experiences or to think of isolated test words having a direct association or relation to these experiences, there results an almost immediate increase in the pulse rate. This increase lasts only for a limited time, however. That is to say, only words or mental processes suggesting emotions can cause an increase in the

[1] Coriat: "Certain Pulse Reactions as a Measure of the Emotions."—*Journal Abnormal Psychology,* Vol. IV, No. 4, 1909. Peterson and Jung: "Psycho-Physical Investigations with the Galvanometer."—*Brain,* Vol. XXX, 1907.

rate of the pulse. All other words or mental processes remain ineffective. This is not a blind automatic phenomenon, however, for there seems

Fig. I.—A pulse curve in a normal subject in a state of abstraction. In this experiment the subject was requested to do some problems requiring mental effort, such as ordinary mental calculation, or to think of ordinary words that had no personal emotional meaning. Notice that no change took place in the pulse curve. It remained a straight line. The numbers above the curve refer to the pulse beats per minute.

to be a selective action of the nervous mechanism controlling the heart beat, to the influence of certain emotions.

A few examples taken from personal observations will make the matter clearer. For instance, in a patient who was afraid to remain alone because of an abnormal state of fear, if asked to think of the word *alone,* the pulse rate rose from 88 to 104 per minute. An indifferent word, such as *snow,* caused no increase in the pulse rate. Here the word *alone,* through association, recalled to the patient's mind all the emotions of the pathological fears, whereas the word *snow* stimulated no emotion whatsoever. In another subject, who had a fear of dogs, indifferent words were ineffective, whereas if the subject were asked to think of the word *dog* or of words relating to this particular animal, the pulse rate would increase over the usual rate from 12 to 20 per minute. [See Fig. II.] In still another patient, during a series of experiments, the test words *book* and *glass* were given as indifferent stimuli. To my surprise each word caused a marked acceleration of the pulse. Later questioning revealed the interesting fact, that some time previously she had *dreamed of broken glass,* and on consulting a popular *dream book,* found that this dream signified *trouble.* The idea of trouble thus evolved as an emotion was woven into the patient's delusions, although previously she had failed to mention, in fact purposely concealed, these particular episodes. They were revealed, however, by the pulse reactions. [See Fig. III.] Thus we seem to have, not only a method for measuring and detecting known emotions, but also a method for discovering suppressed or concealed emotions, and furthermore, another experimental proof that the psychical state is the cause of the physiological

FIG. II.—A portion of a pulse curve from a subject who had an unreasonable and abnormal fear of dogs. Note the sudden rise at 1, the pulse rate increasing from 96 to 116 beats a minute, when the word *dog* was mentioned.

reaction. The pulse rate thus becomes a delicate index for the emotions and for the stimulation of complexes. For these pulse reaction

Fig. III.—A portion of the pulse curve, from the experiments on the subject mentioned in the text. Note the two sudden rises in the curve at 1 and 2, when the words *glass* and *book* were used as test words. Both these words had a strong emotional meaning for the subject. The figures at the top of the curve refer to the number of pulse beats a minute.

phenomena, the name of the psycho-cardiac reflex is proposed. This reflex, which has been of value in the analysis of certain abnormal mental states, is due to the action of the nervous system upon the rate of the heart beat.

Other experiments show these phenomena in a still more remarkable manner. The apparatus used is more complicated however, and the cause of the reactions not so clear. It has been demonstrated that if a weak electrical current be passed through the body from a galvanic cell, the subject being connected with the battery by means of the palms of the hands placed flat on a metal plate, and this current be measured by a delicate instrument called a galvanometer, that the emotions will cause variations in this electrical current. These variations occur particularly when words having an emotional meaning are called out to the subject, indifferent test words or ordinary intellectual processes causing no reaction whatever. [See Fig. IV.] The activity of the sweat glands in

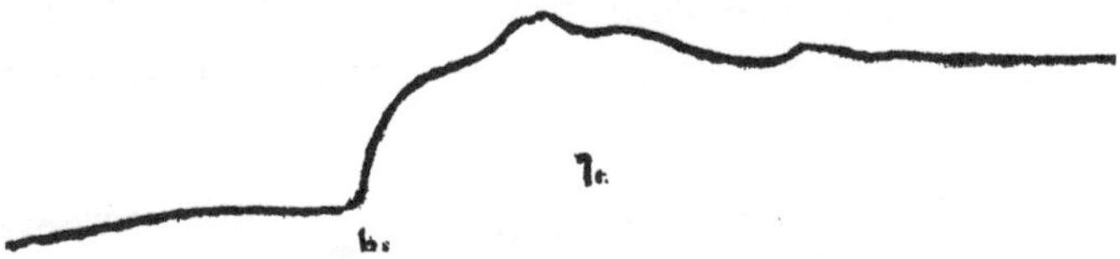

FIG. IV.—A galvanometric curve in one of Jung's cases. The subject was a total abstainer. Ordinary test words up to 6 produced no effect. When the word *restaurant* was mentioned at 7, there was an immediate rise in the curve. Later the subject confessed that in the past he had once been arrested for drunkenness, and because of this occurrence he had since been a total abstainer. In this particular case, the word *restaurant* stimulated strong emotional memories, hence the electrical reaction.

the skin is under nervous influence; changes in this activity through emotional disturbances alter the resistance of these glands, and this perhaps is the cause of the electrical variations. A more recent investigation has shown that the galvanic phenomenon may be of muscular origin. It is of interest to note that in those mental conditions in which the emotions are absent, such as in the states of dementia, the electrical reactions are also absent. Where the emotions are intense and active, as in hysteria, the electrical reactions are very marked and prolonged. In some pathological conditions, as in cases of multiple personality, it is not necessary that the test words relate to emotional states present in consciousness. Subconscious mental experiences can cause electrical variations in the same manner as conscious processes, a fact which is also true of the pulse variations. [See Fig. V.] It has also been demon-

FIG. V.—A portion of a galvanometric curve from a case of multiple personality reported by Dr. Prince. The subject had an intense fear of cats, probably originating in an experience of childhood, which was revealed through automatic writing. Here a subconscious mental experience caused the electrical reaction. When the test word *cat* was mentioned at 1 there followed an immediate rise in the galvanometric curve.

strated, that deflections of the delicate galvanometer can take place even when the battery is not used. Here the electrical variations under the influence of the emotions seem to be caused by a current generated in the body itself. These electrical phenomena associated with the emotions have been called the psycho-physical galvanic reflex, or more simply, the psychogalvanic reaction.

In these pulse reaction tests and in the psychogalvanic reaction, we seem to have methods of precision in investigating and measuring the effects of the emotions. Whether these emotions are present in consciousness, but suppressed, or only present as subconscious emotional complexes, the electrical and pulse effects are the same. Both methods are merely more exact modifications of the association tests for the detection of emotional complexes. In these latter, however, the reactions are inhibitions or lengthenings of thought, whereas in the former the phenomena are either physiological or electrical. All of these test methods, however, are reactions to emotional conditions and have no relation to purely intellectual processes.

The pathological effects of certain emotions are of great interest. It is well known that harrowing experiences may lead to sudden death and that emotional effects enter largely into certain individual religious conversions or by a kind of mental contagion are the prime factors in religious revivals. The rhythmic character of the emotions and their motor accompaniments are of great interest in all revivals. Frequently hysterical phenomena make their appearance,—trance, stupor, mutism, blindness, hallucinations, visions. A series of emotional shocks may bring about grave nervous disorders such as neurasthenia, hysteria, association, and fear neuroses, certain hysterical dissociations, or they may lead to profound changes in the personality, as in cases of extensive general amnesia or in multiple personality.

According to Féré, an emotion may be considered as morbid or pathological when its physiological accompaniments take place with extraordinary intensity, when the emotion is produced without a sufficient determining cause, and when the emotional effects are unduly prolonged. Emotions are most likely to lead to pathological phenomena when at the time of the emotion a state of exhaustion or fatigue was present. In fact, an emotional experience is most liable to recur again under states of fatigue.

This is well illustrated in the evolution of certain fear neuroses, in which exhaustion, pain, or certain suppressed feelings precede the first attack of fear, which then becomes automatically repeated as a kind of an unconscious or subconscious automatism. Sometimes, instead of the psychical accompaniment, the physiological symptoms of the original emotion persist and are repeated, as in certain cases of functional intestinal disturbance or in the persistence of a rapid heart beat without any organic basis. Under other conditions an attack of a previous organic nervous disease may be induced by a severe emotional shock, as in the case of the epileptic attack of Othello. After the harrowing experiences of a railroad accident, the sudden shock of the accident, even with little or no physical injury, may lead to distressing types of hysteria and neurasthenia, from which the person may not recover for months or years, even without litigation or even after the claim for damages has been satisfactorily arranged. These form the large class of cases known as the traumatic neuroses. Here it is the psychical and not the physical shock which caused the disintegration.

Suppression of certain memories or experiences having a strong emotional meaning can lead to hysterical symptoms, such as paralysis, contractures, convulsions, or even changes in the mental state or the personality of the individual. It is not necessary that the suppressed or "strangulated emotions" remain in consciousness, for under certain conditions they can exercise their pernicious effect even if they are subconscious by a process termed "conversion" by Freud. Sometimes a complete confession on the part of the subject of the emotional experiences which he is voluntarily suppressing will have a profound influence in relieving, or even curing, the abnormal symptoms which seem to be dependent on this suppression. The mechanism of this therapeutic procedure, as will be later pointed out in more detail, is due to the breaking down of the resistances which prevented the unconscious thoughts or emotions from reaching consciousness. This disintegratory effect of the emotions in leading to certain pathological phenomena of dissociation, has been shown in a number of published cases. In Janet's case of Mme. D. the sudden mental shock of the false news of her husband's death caused almost immediately an hysterical attack with delirium and convulsions, which lasted several days. At the end of this time it was found that not only had the patient forgotten everything that occurred for six weeks previous to the attack (retrograde amnesia), but continued to forget everything as fast as it happened (continuous amnesia). In the chapter on memory, however, it will be pointed out that, in this case, the memories were not entirely obliterated, but were simply dissociated from her conscious perception. These dissociated experiences could not only be recalled when the patient was hypnotized but also appeared in dreams. In the case of Miss Beauchamp, the genesis of the changes in the personality could be traced to an emotional shock. Furthermore, in the case of Mrs. Y., who developed a form of hysterical paralysis with four distinct hypnotic personalities, it was possible to trace the origin of the hysterical condition back to a series of harrowing emotional experiences.[1] In a case of nocturnal paralysis, the origin of the condition was the emotional shock incident to the sudden death of the patient's child. Peculiar functional attacks simulating epilepsy may also recur by association with the emotional experience which caused the first attack of convulsions. In other words, the emotions can so act as to lead to a splitting of consciousness and thus cause changes in the personality, losses of memory, psycho-epileptic attacks, and certain recurrent states of fear (recurrent psycho-motor states). Any emotional complex or experience which has become dormant or quiescent can be thrown into activity again through association, either from within or without, and thus lead to certain pathological phenomena (hysterical, psycho-epileptic, phobias, obsessions). These various phenomena, to a limited degree, have also their prototype in everyday life. The fear of thunder-storms, the sense of nausea that occurs in some persons at the sight or odor of certain foods, as for instance, strawberries or peppermint, the sense of awe that overwhelms others at the sight of the sea, the feeling of disgust for snakes, worms, or crawling things, are instances in question. Here certain dormant experiences

[1] This case forms the subject of Part II, Chapter IV.

with an emotional coloring (fear, nausea, awe, disgust) are awakened through association, some of which can be traced back to a forgotten episode in childhood.

In contrast with this disintegrating effect of painful emotions, the integrating or curative or rather the synthetic effect of pleasurable emotions and confidence is a well-known fact in psychology. As Bain says, " States of pleasure are concomitant with an increase and states of pain with an abatement of some or all of the vital functions." This psychological mechanism is of great value in certain psychotherapeutic procedures, such as the successful treatment of certain states of depression, exhaustion, and fear. This has been experimentally proven by some studies of the physiological accompaniments of feeling. Claparède states as follows concerning this condition, " Each one of us can testify that, under diverse conditions, confidence gives strength, it is dynamogenic. A neuropath is most often a being who mistrusts himself, who shrinks and inhibits himself; in a word, one who strains his reflexes of defence. Confidence, which is the antagonist of this mental defence, acts in relaxing these reflexes of defence; at the same time it sets free the energy which had been stored up, potentialized by the activity of defence. This available energy, this energy in a nascent state, can then be usefully employed in the physical or psychic re-education of the patient." Here we have a biological interpretation of the doctrine of reserve energy.

The practical application of this theory was well exemplified in the synthesis of the various personalities of Miss Beauchamp and also in the following personal observations. A highly intelligent woman, under the stress of a series of harrowing experiences, which she was compelled to voluntarily suppress during a number of years, developed a gradual change in her personality. Whereas previously she had been cheerful, fond of company and travel, and interested in general affairs, she became moody, depressed, and seclusive, easily exhausted, lost her interest in things in general, and became self-centred and abnormally self-conscious. The treatment of this condition consisted in the stimulation of pleasurable emotions and of a sense of elation and well-being, which after a time changed, or rather synthetized her, back to her normal self. In another case, one of psychasthenia with a marked feeling of depersonalization, the same procedure was eminently successful. This patient characterized her normal self as a " solid substance, living, growing," and her abnormal self as a " bloodless nothing—if I shut my eyes I do not think or feel, as though my thoughts went through me without resistance." Here again the integrating, synthetizing effect of the emotion of well-being and joy was successful in effecting a cure.

Thus we see that the emotions can act either for good or evil. They may be reactions of defence or have painful effect in certain pathological mental states. On the other hand, the suppression of painful emotional experiences or emotional shocks, either singly or in series, may lead to certain abnormal phenomena in the mental life of the individual, such as changes in the personality, losses of memory, or hysterical manifestations. On the body mechanism itself the emotions have a profound influence, producing changes in electrical resistance, in the pulse rate, stimulation or inhibition of glandular secretion or of the motor power of the gastro-intestinal tract, variations in the respiration and in the tension of the muscles. Recent investigations would lead us to believe that these multitudinous psycho-physical and psycho-physiological phenomena are of central and not peripheral origin. The phenomena of the relation of certain test words to associations of an emotional character (the association tests) and the mechanism of the inhibition of thought in these experiments, are of such importance that their discussion will be left for another chapter, although here again it is emotional states, and not intellectual conditions, which determine the type of reaction.

Wit and laughter may also be interpreted as emotional reactions and both have been extensively investigated by Bergson[1] and Freud.[2] According to the former anything which breaks away from the elasticity of living beings and becomes stiff, mechanical and stereotyped, or in other words becomes a caricature of life, tends to provoke laughter. Freud bases his theory of wit upon his well-known conceptions of the unconscious and finds in it many of the same mental mechanisms as occur in dreams. He divides wit, according to the reactions which it produces, into purposeful, or that which shows a definite aim, and harmless, or that in which no definite aim can be discovered. Concerning the mechanism of wit, it seems, according to Freud, that a foreconscious thought is left for a moment unguarded and thus becomes the object of an unconscious elaboration. Thus wit, like the dream, is an involuntary mental occurrence and brevity is common to both wit and dreams. In fact, "brevity is the soul of wit." This brevity is due to a process of condensation and from this condensation mechan-

[1] Henri Bergson, "Le Rire," 1911.

[2] S. Freud, "Der Witz und sein Beziehung zum Unbewussten."

ism, arise many plays on words. Wit is a social product, whose aim is to acquire pleasure, and in wit there may often be detected an infantile type of thinking. An interesting confirmation of Freud's theory occurred in a case of automatic laughter which I had occasion to analyze. Here it could be shown that an unconscious emotional complex expanded and became an impulsive motor reaction (laughter) which for the time being dominated the field of consciousness. Thus the laughter was the result of an unconscious repression.

CHAPTER IV

ANALYZING THE EMOTIONS

THE association of ideas or the linking of ideas in consciousness has engaged the attention of psychologists from the days of the Greek philosophers up to the present time. The fact that a word or idea should immediately suggest a related word or idea is one of the peculiarities of the mechanism of thought, and on this peculiarity was based some of the older systems of the so-called associationist psychology. For years, however, the study of association remained barren of practical results, but with the advent of precise instruments to measure the reaction time, with the investigations of the physiology of the reflexes, and the propagation of nerve impulses, the association of ideas became filled with a new interest. It is a matter of common observation that it is easier to remember rhymed poetry than blank verse or prose, and this is due not to the rhythm but in a great part to the association of rhyme. Many of the schemes used by schoolboys for remembering historical dates or the sequence of rulers or presidents, is based upon the law of association.

In normal individuals, the association time is usually very short, but measurements of this time by modern electrical instruments have shown that it is not instantaneous, as was formerly supposed. It takes time for an impulse to travel along a nerve path or for a sensory impulse from the eye or ear to reach the brain and call forth a related impulse. In a way, the association mechanism resembles certain physiological reflexes. It is only when instruments of accuracy are used, that the time for one idea to call forth a related idea can be measured. Therefore, before the advent of experimental psychology and physiology, the association of ideas was looked upon as a more or less mysterious process, a function of a kind of a metaphysical consciousness. Investigations in normal individuals and in certain abnormal mental states have shown, however, that the association mechanism is based upon well-defined laws of body and mind, upon brain physiology and not upon metaphysical conceptions. Association, therefore, like the emotions, can be best explained through physiological psychology. We will discuss the subject from this standpoint alone, giving only as much of the work on normal associations as will enable the reader to understand the various abnormal associative processes.

There is an intimate relationship between the psychology and physiology of the brain. There can be no mental process without a previous brain process. Precise measurements have shown that it takes a definite and appreciable length of time for nerve energy to be propagated, and even in the quickest of our associations there is an interval of a large fraction of a second between one idea and another. Habit lessens this time interval; fatigue, alcohol, and other drugs, and the presence of an emotional meaning connected with a certain word greatly increase this interval. This last factor, the inhibition or slowing of thought through emotional factors, is of great value in some of the analyses of abnormal psychology. To this factor, however, we will return later.

Certain bundles of nerve fibres, or tracts in the brain, seem to be especially concerned with the processes of association, in the same way that certain parts of the brain are the centres for sight, smell, language, etc. Now in man these so-called association areas occupy a large portion of the cerebral hemispheres, and when we realize how all intellect seems based on association and associative memory, we have here a beautiful example of the relation of function to structure. The exact localization of these association areas in the brain has recently attracted a great deal of attention. For some of these centres, the evidence is certain; for others, it is still problematical. After we eliminate the sensory or motor paths of the brain, and the centres for language and special senses, there still remains a large portion of what were formerly termed the "silent areas." Now these "silent areas," in the light of recent investigations, possess a function of great importance and interest, namely, association.

In the development of the nervous system, the nerve tracts of the brain receive their covering or myelin sheaths (called medullation) in different order and sequence. Those nerve tracts which will be used first by the new-born child, first become medullated, that is the sensory fibres, because the child makes use of its sensory organs before it uses its motor organs. When the child begins to walk, then the motor paths of the brain become medullated. Last of all, the association areas receive their myelin sheaths, because these subserve the highest functions of intelligence,—language and memory. In mental diseases associated with any degree of dementia or mental weakness, the association areas are nearly always found in a condition of degeneration.

The materials of thought and association are largely the results of habit and training. Association is due to the manner in which one elementary brain process may excite another elementary brain process, which has taken place at a previous time. So we see that the processes of association are brain processes and its physiological law may be expressed as follows: When two elementary brain processes have been active together or in immediate succession, one of those, on recurring, tends to propagate its excitement into the other. Normal associations are due largely to the habits in which the nervous system has become "set," as it were. Associations will not only show a subject's mental make-up or his interests, but will also betray his hidden motives and desires and concealed facts in his experiences. Hence the value of the association method to test the intellectual capability of the subject or to lay bare his innermost feelings and secrets. For instance, let us take the word "man." To this word the scientist would probably associate the word "vertebrate," the physician, the word "disease," the minister, the word "morality."

I had previously pointed out that the reproduction of stimuli, experiences, or reactions is usually in the same order in which they are received. This psychological mechanism finds its physiological parallel in the phenomena of chain or sequence reflexes. According to Loeb and Sherrington, the crawling of an earthworm, in which the threshold of each succeeding reflex is lowered by the excitation just preceding its own, is a chain or sequence reflex of this kind. Association may be interpreted in part as a *psychical* chain reflex, for as soon as one elementary brain process becomes started, it stimulates the next succeeding group, so that each process is reproduced in the order in which it originally occurred. Memory forms the highest type of association. In fact, all memory, with the probable exception of certain scrappy automatisms which occur in some cases of functional amnesia, is associative memory. It is this associative memory which is responsible for the higher intellectual processes of man, for even in monkeys and the higher apes the associations are of a very elementary, simple type.

What, then, is the value of associations in abnormal psychology; how are we to interpret the findings, and how are the tests carried out? It would lead us too far into technicalities to give the enormous mass of literature which has recently been called forth by the association tests and therefore only the most important and practical points will be briefly discussed. These technical methods have shown that the associations cannot only reveal the normal mental make-up of an individual, but may also betray his abnormal mental make-up as well. In other words, the interpretation and study of a series of words used for the association tests in normal individuals apply with equal force when we come to study certain diseases. When we give a subject a word and ask him to reply with the first idea which this test word suggests, it will be found that a definite time elapses between the test word and the reaction. This time, if measured with the chronoscope or the stop-watch, will be found to vary from the fraction of a second to several seconds. This could not be otherwise, if we remember the complicated circuit which the reaction takes. The spoken word is first heard by the ear, then carried to the brain; there it awakens or stimulates previously stored-up brain processes which are related to this word; then it reaches the language centre and awakens the image of the related word, and finally it is spoken by the subject. In reality the circuit and the brain process are far more complex than I have indicated. In any case it takes time for the impulses to travel along the nerves and tracts in the brain. As will be shown later, certain things may influence either the time, or the reaction, or both; the time may be normal, or shortened or lengthened, the reaction to the test word may be normal, peculiar, or entirely lacking. The facts which determine any abnormality in association are many.

Let us make the experiment somewhat more complicated, as it is usually carried out in laboratories and in clinical investigations. A series of fifty to one hundred words is read off to the subject, care being taken that the words are ordinary and indifferent. In most cases, the suggested word will be found normal and the time reaction short. But supposing in the midst of this list we insert a few words that touch a "sore spot," as it were; that is, words relating to certain emotional experiences in the subject's life. A peculiar thing will be found to occur. Whereas the reaction time for normal words was short, in the words having an emotional meaning the time will be found to have been considerably lengthened. A retardation or inhibition of thought has taken place, if we wish to speak in psychological terms; or, if we wish to take a nomenclature from physiology, we say that the normal path of association has become blocked. What causes this retardation, this blocking, this interference with a normal reaction, and this alteration of the processes of thought? Evidently the test word has stimulated a dormant group of ideas or complexes which had an emotional meaning, and it is this emotional tone which has delayed the process of thought. A painful idea has been awakened by the test word and the subject's efforts to suppress the painful idea, to keep it in the background of the mind, take a certain length of time. Hence the delayed time between the test word and the reaction word. While the intellectual status may determine the kind or type of association, yet the reaction time is influenced by emotional and not by intellectual factors.

Thus a response to a test word may show certain peculiarities called " complex signs " and the word which causes this disturbance is termed a " complex indicator." These complex signs are as follows—

1. Unusually long reaction time.
2. Strange reactions, errors or no reactions at all.
3. Stereotyped repetition of the test word.
4. Forgetfulness.
5. Persistence of disturbance for the next or following association.
6. Surprise at the stimulus word.

7. Laughing at a reaction. (When a complex is struck the subject will often automatically laugh.)

8. Superficial associations.

The method is often valuable in the preliminaries of a psycho-analysis, in giving one hints concerning the patient's emotional complex.

Other abnormal phenomena may also take place in the association mechanism, such as flight of ideas, absence of reaction, automatic repetition of test words, indifferent reactions, etc. It would lead us too far into technicalities to enter into all these finer details, and, therefore, we will limit our discussion, as far as possible, to the delayed reaction time. The associations are influenced by the type of complexes, that is whether or not they have an emotional coloring. These complexes may cause an inhibition of thought and so delay the reaction; they may completely arrest, temporarily at least, the normal mental activity and so cause an absence of reaction to the test word; they may cause indifferent reactions or finally only sound associations, such as rhyming and flight of ideas. As will be shown later, this latter is largely dependent upon a disorder of attention. In order for a complex to produce the retardation of thought it must not only have an emotional coloring, but must be preserved in the unconscious, although it may be dormant and suppressed. Subconscious complexes are incapable of causing any retardation in the association tests, although if identical words be used, these same words will be found capable of causing electrical reactions and modifications in the pulse rate.

The use of the association method has thrown considerable light upon the delusions and hallucinations in dementia præcox and also upon the dream life in both this disease and hysteria. When a test word strikes a particular experience that has been stored up, but remains dormant, immediately an abnormal reaction takes place, either retardation or refusal to co-operate or an indifferent reaction word.

By means of this method we are able to prove that many insane ideas, delusions, hallucinations, and dreams take their origin in previous experiences, which were preserved in the unconscious as dormant complexes or memories. Investigations along these lines by certain German investigators (Jung, Freud, Bleuler, and the Zurich school), have thrown an immense amount of light upon hysteria and upon the psychogenesis of dementia præcox.

The results and the value of the association method in hysteria are given in a psycho-analysis of a case of hysteria.[1] We will, therefore, limit ourselves to a brief discussion of a case of dementia præcox. Dementia præcox is a mental disease which usually occurs in adolescence and early youth, its chief characteristic being that, no matter what may be the character of the insane ideas or the abnormal activity, there is a termination in a peculiar and characteristic mental weakness. This mental weakness is primarily of the nature of an emotional deterioration or indifference, rather than any intellectual change. It is only within recent years that the disease has been fully recognized and only still more recently has the psychology of the disease found a fairly satisfactory explanation. The psychological interpretation of dementia præcox is certainly a healthy reaction from the vague theories of auto-intoxication and the barren results of pathological anatomy. Examinations of the brain in subjects who have died from this disease, have yielded nothing of importance. In no other disease, outside of hysteria, have purely psychological investigations yielded data of so much importance. In the recent work of Jung,[2] an attempt is made to give a logical explanation of the behavior and utterances in this disease, which were for-

[1] See Chapter IX: "The Analysis of the Mental Life."

[2] C. G. Jung: "The Psychology of Dementia Præcox," 1909. (Translated by Peterson and Brill.)

merly looked upon as strange and at random.

In dementia præcox, there is often a peculiar blocking of thought and a dissociation of the inner mechanism of will and action. For instance, in one case of dementia præcox the subject replied to all the association test words by an indifferent "I don't know," or by merely echoing the test word. He later explained these reactions by stating that he could not think of anything. It has also been shown in this disease that it is the experiences of the subject preserved in the mind as unconscious or dormant memories which cause the various hallucinations, delusions, insane ideas, and abnormal activities. These unconscious residuals have a distinct emotional coloring, and hence, when the association tests are used for analysis, words related to these complexes cause a disorder of the mechanism of association. This disorder may be either retardation, or mere repetition of the test word, or complete refusal to co-operate, all of which are manifest "blockings" of the mechanism of association. Of interest in dementia præcox is the instinctive tendency to conceal these unconscious complexes, leading to stupor, contrary actions and behavior and apparent emotional indifference and apathy. Thus the unconscious complexes, in dementia præcox, the same as in dreams or in hysteria, are often symbolically expressed. As Jung expresses it—"Let the dreamer walk about and act like one awakened and we have the clinical picture of dementia præcox."

The evidence seems to show that in dementia præcox we are dealing with some form of mental dissociation. But why one form of mental dissociation should cause a curable hysteria and the other an incurable dementia præcox, cannot be definitely answered at present. Without entering into details, it might be briefly stated, that in hysteria the emotions are merely suppressed or detached, while in dementia præcox the emotions are destroyed. Hence, on the one hand, we get the increased emotionalism in hysteria, and on the other hand, the decreased or even absent emotions in the subject of dementia præcox. Further analysis by the pulse, electrical, and association tests, seems to show, however, that in dementia præcox the emotional indifference is only superficial and that the emotions may be subconsciously active. The subjects, however, pay little or no attention to their submerged emotions, while in hysteria, the opposite takes place.

We are now prepared to study a series of associations in a case of dementia præcox, and to show how the various phenomena of this particular case took their origin in the subject's previous experiences. These experiences remained conserved as dormant unconscious complexes or memories. It was these memories that caused the vivid hallucinations and the fantastic dream states. Words relating to these unconscious complexes or taken directly from them, greatly influenced the time and type of the associations. The retardation in many of the tests was due to the words relating to unconscious complexes, which had a strong emotional coloring, hence the blocking of thought with the consequent slowness of reaction. The unconscious complexes not only influenced the type and formation of the hallucinations and dreams, but they also were the factors in causing the inhibition of thought as shown by the association tests. Hence the complex had a twofold disturbing action; on the formation of the insane ideas and on the retardation of thought as shown by the special tests.

The patient was an intelligent young woman, thirty years of age. At the age of twenty-eight she went on a pleasure trip, and during her travels, she consulted three palmists who informed her that while on this trip she would meet the person who would eventually become her husband, although there would be considerable trouble and delay. To a certain extent this occupied her mind and worried her, and while on her way home she became acquainted with a young professional man. Shortly afterward she began to have series of dreams, such as the hearing of pistol shots, of a certain person wearing a black necktie, at another time of a police officer about to arrest her, that her father and mother were in prison for some terrible crime. Later other dreams followed, such as being on a sinking ship, or in a rowboat alone at night, or of travelling interminable distances on a railroad train. These dreams symbolized certain things to the patient; the dream of the black necktie meaning that the professional man had committed suicide, the sinking ship meant trouble, the rowboat signified her destiny. Finally peculiar words that she had been unaccustomed to using would suddenly flash into her mind, such as "tripod," "harlequin," "suicide," "Jezebel," "ineffable woe," "ineffable joy," etc. To these words a symbolic meaning was also attached. Finally these words became hallucinatory in character and took the form of voices, and the patient became literally bombarded by auditory hallucinations. In the series of associations which follow it will be noticed that long reaction times coincide with the words or ideas which formed either the complexes, the hallucinatory phenomena, the dreams, or the previous experiences.

Stimulus Word	*Reaction Word*	*Reaction Time (Seconds)*	*Stimulus Word*	*Reaction Word*	*Reaction Time (Seconds)*
Chair	Frame	4.8	*Affinity*	Like	4.2
Tripod	Three	2.2	Ring	Round	2.8
Glass	Square	2.8	*Book*	Vellum	2.6
Black	Darkness	4.	Police	Uniform	3.4
House	Home	1.8	*Jezebel*	Wickedness	4.8
Harlequin	Fool	6.4	Dress	Gown	3.8
Ship	Ship	4.	*Prison*	Bars	8.
Heart	Red	6.2	Joy	Happiness	2.8

The slowness of reaction showed that the emotions aroused by certain test words were blocked, could not find a normal path of discharge. This was due to the fact that the test words aroused painful memories in the experiences of the subject, such as certain incidents in her life, her dreams, and her hallucinations and delusions. For instance such words as "prison," "black," or "ship" referred to the dreams and their symbolic interpretation; "harlequin" and "Jezebel" referred to the hallucinations. In this case also, the same test words caused an increase of the pulse rate.

In certain other mental diseases the association of ideas may be disturbed along different lines. In dementia, the associations are very narrow and may be applied to mere mechanical repetitions of the test word. In experimental fatigue and hunger and after the ingestion of even moderate doses of alcohol the associative process is slowed. The most marked disturbance of association of ideas is found in mania.[1] The chief characteristics of this mental disease are extreme restlessness and increased activity, loquacity, exaltation, and a marked disorder of attention, leading to rapid comments upon the surroundings and upon any new sense impressions. The disturbance of association in mania is expressed by the term flight of ideas. Its chief characteristics are jumping from one idea to another, usually by means of rhyming or sound associations, or in extreme cases, there may be an actual incoherence of ideas. It is not the apparent increased rapidity of association that leads to flight of ideas, because no matter how rapid may be the association time, it still may be rational. The flight of ideas is really due to a disorder of attention. When a normal person passes from one group of ideas to another, the tendency is to remain attentive to the first group, to keep the ideas in the foreground of the mind, and not allow the attention to be distracted by external occurrences. In mania, however, just the opposite takes place. Here attention is lacking or much diminished, it dwells for a short time only on one idea, the subject is extremely fickle, dis-

[1] The term mania is used as expressing the exalted phase of the periodic mental disease known as manic-depressive insanity.

tracted by outward sense impressions, and turns to anything new with great avidity. Hence the jumping from one idea to another.

For instance, a maniacal patient was given the word "hot" as an association test word. Now, in a normal individual, the reaction word would probably be "cold" or "weather," but here it would stop. But observe this patient's string of associations. To the word "hot" he responded as follows—"Weather, not cold, hot beans, hot times in war, heat ironing, that's what women do, if more wood is wanted, fill the wood-box." Another maniacal patient was given the word "spider." Here rhyming associations took place, "Ida, rider, spider, spy I, who do you spy, through my little eye."

Recently the application of the association tests for the determination of concealed facts in crime has attracted a great deal of attention. For this purpose the list of ordinary test words is loaded with special words pointing to the trend of suspicion. In reaction to these special words, there results either a refusal to co-operate, or a lengthening of the reaction time. The method is very promising of practical results, but only by the accumulation of further data in the future can we determine if we have here an infallible device to probe into hidden memories. If so, the psychological inquisition of the future will not consist of threats, tortures, and the rack, nor of the equally painful so-called "third degree," but the criminal will be brought face to face with the scientific psychologist. It has already been pointed out how words having an emotional meaning may slow the reaction time. Now this retardation may take place either because the words had something to do with the crime, or because the subject was afraid that the associated word which first came to his mind would betray him and, therefore, he makes an attempt to substitute a less dangerous word. But either of these mental processes, either substitution or the emotional reaction of a bad conscience, would cause a slowness in answering, and this retardation can easily be measured, either with a chronoscope or, what is just as accurate for all practical purposes, a stop-watch. Innocent, indifferent words would be given very quickly, as the subject would feel that he need not be on his guard, having nothing to conceal. Sometimes, on a suspicious word, the reaction may be an indifferent association, if the subject is clever, but the suppressed memory would linger in consciousness and betray itself in the following association. Also when suspicious words are used, the association suggested by this word will occasionally unmask the subject.

The following is an example in a case of juvenile delinquency which came under personal observation.[1] Only the most striking reactions will be given. The patient, a girl of seventeen years of age, for several years had been cross and stubborn, and would frequently remain away from home. There was also some suspicion of certain irregularities, of disorderly conduct, and of frequenting cheap vaudeville entertainments. All this was absolutely denied by the patient. Owing to the manifest untruth and lack of sincerity in the patient's attitude, an attempt was made to get at the concealed facts in the case by means of the association tests.

Test Word	*Reaction Word*	*Reaction Time (in seconds)*
Dark	Night	1.
Square	Four corners	2.
Hard	Not bent	3.
Drink	Water	1.
Bad	Unconscious	4.
Lie	Hasty	9.4
Street	Walking	6.4
Sea	Water	0.4
Untruth	Spoken in haste	9.4
Bed	Sleep	2.4
Deceit	To speak against	14.6
Vaudeville	Gayety	13.6
Conduct	Don't know	16.4
Sweet	Candy	1.4

[1] "The Mental Condition of Juvenile Delinquents," *Psychological Clinic,* Vol. I, No. 5, October 15, 1907.

The lengthened reaction time to such test words as "lie," "street," "untruth," "deceit," "vaudeville," the refusal to co-operate when the word "conduct" was used, and the peculiar reaction of the word "walking" to the test word "street," or of the word "gayety" to "vaudeville," pointed strongly to purposely concealed facts. When the patient was directly accused of these matters, she broke down and confessed that she had been telling an untruth.

CHAPTER V

SLEEP

Sleep has been called a mystery, and it is a mystery well-nigh inscrutable. The very multiplicity of the theories on sleep shows how inadequate they are to explain the phenomenon, which from the earliest dawn of history has puzzled savage and scientist alike. To primitive man or to the uneducated savage, there was something uncanny in this " darkness and light that divided the course of time." The outward resemblance of sleep to death only served to increase the mystery.

The modern scientist has approached but little nearer to the final solution of the problem. Many theories have been proposed to explain sleep, from the earlier ideas that sleep is due to a lack of blood in the brain to the more recent biological and physiological conceptions. Each theory has its enthusiastic advocates and each can cite apparently unanswerable facts as a positive proof. In sleep, we seem to be dealing with definite alterations of the personality, but just how the waking personality falls into the state we call sleep and *how* this latter again changes to the waking personality, is the great enigma. Yet this cycle occurs in one form or another throughout almost the entire organized world.

As a preliminary, it will be of interest to briefly pass in review the various theories that have been propounded to explain sleep. These theories fall naturally into five groups, namely physiological, histological, chemical, psychological, and biological. The pathological theories of sleep belong to a separate category and comprise only the abnormal sleep states as manifestations of certain diseases of the nervous system, such as hysteria, epilepsy, somnambulism, narcolepsy, and the African sleeping-sickness. However, it is the more recent biological and physiological conceptions which have, in a measure, cleared the way for a fairly satisfactory, if not a final solution. Any theory of sleep must be based upon sound physiological data, because sleep is a physiological phenomenon occurring in everyday life and not the manifestation of a disease process. Sleep is a function of living matter, and is necessary for all living beings, at least for those organisms which possess a central nervous system. The periods of immobility and rest which are observed in the lower organisms are probably conditions strongly allied to sleep and out of which sleep phylogenetically arose. It is to the nervous system, however, particularly the brain, that attention must be directed in any attempt to solve the problem of sleep.

Physiological Theories of Sleep

Sleep is due to changes in the cerebral cirılation. A lack of blood in the brain causes what is known as cerebral anæmia. This cerebral anæmia may be due to a dilatation of the blood-vessels of the skin, which causes a fall of blood pressure in the brain. Sleep naturally results, in the same way that a lack of blood in the brain causes that transitory loss of consciousness known as fainting.

According to these circulatory theories of sleep, cerebral congestion, or an increased amount of blood in the brain, produces insomnia. Observations on exposed brains after the skull has been trephined for injuries, seem to bear out these circulatory theories on sleep. Mosso's famous observations in cases of this type, showed a cerebral anæmia during sleep. Yet strong pressure on the carotid arteries in the neck, for a short time, thus interfering with the passage of blood to the brain, causes a state of consciousness analogous to fainting, rather than genuine sleep. Tarchanoff showed that in puppies the brain becomes pale when the animals are asleep and that at the same time, it reacts less readily to electrical stimulation. Salmon has recently formulated an ingenious though unsatisfactory theory of sleep, based upon the functions of the pituitary body, a secretory gland which lies at the base of the brain. He points out the very marked relation between somnolence and pituitary tumors and therefore claims that sleep is due to a hypersecretion of the pituitary body and insomnia to a diminished secretion. There exists an analogy between the winter sleep of animals and our daily sleep, as this winter sleep is also due to the diminished secretory activity of the tissues.

Histological Theories of Sleep

These are the theories which explain sleep as being produced by certain movements which the nerve cell prolongations are supposed to possess. These prolongations are technically known as the dendrites. All nerve cells possess dendrites which touch each other and by means of which nerve currents are supposed to be transmitted from one cell to another. According to this theory these nerve currents are necessary for consciousness and when there is any break in these currents, that is, when the dendrites spontaneously grow shorter, so that they no longer come into contact with one another, sleep results. The theory is a fascinating one and it has also been utilized to explain the mechanism of certain dissociations of consciousness, such as dreams, hysteria, and hypnosis.

Chemical Theories of Sleep

Even modern physiological chemistry has tried its hand in the interpretation of such a purely psychological mechanism as sleep. It supposes that poisons are elaborated during the day, as the result of muscular and nerve activity, that these poisons are narcotic (sleep producing) in action and when they reach a certain amount, drowsiness, and then sleep, results. These poisons have a direct action upon the central nervous system, particularly the brain. In sleep, the poisons are no longer formed because in this condition there is a minimum of nerve and muscle activity. These toxic substances are eliminated during the night and when elimination is nearly complete, awakening results. This cycle of self-poisoning of the nervous system is repeated day after day. It is really a kind of auto-intoxication. A modification of this theory states that sleep is produced by a lack of oxygen in the brain. An excess of carbonic gas is, therefore, formed and the somnolent effect of this gas is a fact well attested by experience, such as occurs in improperly ventilated and crowded rooms.

Psychological Theories of Sleep

Sleep is an inhibition, a resting state of consciousness. Mental activity or consciousness is dependent upon peripheral incoming stimuli, and when these are absent, a lowering of mental activity follows and sleep results. According to this theory, if all peripheral stimuli are cut out, sleep will naturally follow. When we attempt to sleep, we voluntarily cut off all distracting external stimuli; we darken the room, lie quietly, stop all muscular activity, close the eyes, etc. In favor of this hypothesis are the observations on human subjects who have a general cutaneous anæsthesia and who fall asleep when sounds are excluded and the eyes are closed. Strümpell, for instance, reports the case of a sixteen-year-old subject with total anæsthesia of the skin to all stimuli, an absence of the muscular sense and of fatigue, no sense of taste or smell, blindness of the left eye and deafness of the right ear. If in this subject the right eye was bound and the left ear stopped, the brain was deprived of all stimuli from the external world and after a few minutes, the subject fell tightly asleep. Heubel showed, in experiments which were performed on animals, principally frogs and birds, that mental activity was dependent in great part on incoming peripheral sensory stimuli; when these were absent, the intensity of consciousness tended to diminish and sleep resulted. He states for instance:—"If the external causes of excitation are completely and permanently withdrawn, there appear, especially in birds, unmistakable signs of sleep. Their eyes become tightly and continuously closed, the respiration becomes regular, often surprisingly slow and the muscles relax."

Biological Theories of Sleep

The interpretation of sleep as one of the essential life phenomena is the basis of the biological conceptions as elaborated by Claparède, Sidis, and Coriat. In fact, Claparède interprets many abnormal psychic conditions from a purely biological standpoint. His biological theory of sleep has attracted considerable attention.[1] According to him, sleep is not due to fatigue because fatigue frequently produces insomnia. Sleep is a negative state, a cessation of all activity. It is a reaction of defence to

[1] E. Claparède: "Enquisse d'une Théorie Biologique du Sommeil."—*Archives de Psychologie*, Vol. IV.

protect the organism against fatigue, rather than a psychological process, the result of fatigue. It is an instinct; we sleep not because our nervous system is poisoned or exhausted, but because there is an inhibition of attention for the present situation, really the active development of disinterest. In fact, we tend to become drowsy and fall asleep when we become disinterested. He asks the very pertinent question—At what step in evolution did sleep first appear? and in reply he states, " Sleep did not necessarily exist at all times; it is, in fact, a contingent phenomenon, and is not implied in the conception of life; the lower forms of animal life, microbes and infusoria, do not manifest any sleep. If sleep has developed, it is probably due to the fact that those animals whose activity was broken by periods of repose or of immobility have been favored in the struggle for existence, for they have been enabled, thanks to the accumulation of energy, during these periods of immobility, to manifest in consequence a more intense activity. As to these periods of immobility, they are themselves derived from the function of inhibition of defence, which plays such a great rôle in the animal kingdom (simulation of death)."

According to Trömner, sleep is not dependent upon fatigue and he asserts that sleep and hypnosis have much in common. Sleep is an active process of instinctive inhibition and he assumes on various theoretical grounds that the optic thalamus is the seat of this instinctive action. That there is no relation between fatigue and sleep is shown, in that infants, who are least liable to fatigue, sleep the greater part of the time. Boris Sidis [1] interprets sleep from the standpoint of the threshold of cell energy. These investigations showed that sleep is due in the main to the cutting out of all peripheral stimuli. Relaxation and not fixation of attention is necessary for sleep, for this latter frequently produces insomnia. Suggestibility is absent in the sleep state. Three essentials are necessary for the production of sleep, namely monotony of sensory impressions, limitation of voluntary movements, and inhibition. Of these three, the monotony of sensory impressions is the most important factor. In going to sleep, there is always an intermediary subwaking or hypnoidal state. This subwaking state is present, not only in man, but in the lower animals, such as dogs and kittens. Like Claparède, Sidis also considers sleep from the evolutionary standpoint. Sleep, therefore, biologically considered, is a reaction of protoplasm. It is as much an

[1] Boris Sidis: "An Experimental Study of Sleep."—*Journal Abnormal Psychology,* Vol. III, No. 1-3, 1908.

instinct as sex or hunger. Sleep is normal, psychological, not an evidence of the pathological, the diseased. Sleeping and waking are merely different manifestations of normal life-processes. When the organism becomes fatigued as the result of continued stimulation, those stimuli which have exhausted themselves or ceased to act on the organism by reason of their monotony, drop out and are replaced by new ones, until the whole round of stimuli has been gone through. Then the organism ceases to respond to the stimuli and falls asleep. Organisms, therefore, fall asleep when the threshold for stimulation rises, and waken when the threshold falls.

Neither monotony of sensory impressions nor limitation of voluntary movements is necessary for sleep. Sleep likewise does not result from a fatigue of the organism by continued stimulation, but only if the actual stimulus be decreased, either to zero or to the threshold of conscious perception. The motionless states produced in animals by sudden peripheral excitations are not sleep, but a form of hypnosis. If a stimulus is present, but just falls short of producing a sensation, then for the organism it is just as if no stimulus existed at all. It has been shown beyond a doubt, however, that sleep takes place when the peripheral sensations are cut off or greatly diminished. Now it is well known, that the activity of consciousness is maintained by these sensations, which pour in from the eyes, ears, muscles, and the afferent nerves of the skin. When these are cut off or reduced to a minimum, sleep results. The nervous system receives the active energies supplied to it by stimuli of all kinds and is merely a conduction path connecting peripheral organs with the center,—a receptive surface with an afferent organ in combination. The greatest mass of stimuli pouring into the brain comes from the muscles and it is for this reason that a diminution of muscle tonus (or tension) either accompanies or precedes the onset of sleep. Thus the problem of sleep becomes essentially a psycho-biological problem and seemed so promising that I investigated the function of sleep from this standpoint.[1]

My experiments were performed on animals and also on a series of human subjects, in whom I could check my procedures and thus have the advantage of introspective evidence, a thing manifestly impossible in animals. The animal experiments on crayfish, frogs, and guinea pigs were undertaken merely to establish the nature

[1] Isador H. Coriat, "The Nature of Sleep."—*Journal Abnormal Psychology,* Vol. 5, 1912.

"The Evolution of Sleep and Hypnosis."—*Ibid,* VII, 2. 1912.

of motionless states in animals, in order to determine whether these were genuine sleep, hypnosis, or states of cerebral inhibition. Thus I was able to trace the mechanism of sleep from animals with a primitive nervous system, up to man.

When a crayfish, frog, or guinea pig was thrown suddenly on its back and held in a firm position for a few minutes, it would remain motionless even in a strained and uncomfortable attitude for a prolonged period of time after the experimenter's hold had been released. The entire body would be immobile, the limbs rigid, eyes widely opened, and the reflexes exaggerated. The animal would not move on external stimulation, such as jarring of the table or the flashing of an electric light in the widely opened eyes. In other words the animals were cataleptic, resembling deeply hypnotized human beings. There were no signs of genuine sleep; that is, relaxation of the limbs, closure of the eyes, and slow, regular respiration were absent. Thus, the interpretation of these motionless states in animals, as sleep, as had been done by other observers, was shown to be without sufficient foundation.

Experiments on human subjects demonstrated that they fell asleep after listening for prolonged periods to monotonous auditory stimuli, but only if there was a concomitant state of muscular relaxation. That this sleep was genuine and not allied to hypnosis, was demonstrated by the fact, that some of these subjects were able to relate short dreams on awakening. Subjects also fell asleep without listening to monotonous stimuli if muscular relaxation could be induced. Muscular tension, however, even of one limb, under like conditions of listening to monotonous stimuli, entirely inhibited sleep.

It was possible to measure the degree of muscular relaxation by a modification of an instrument called the capillary electrometer, both on subjects in whom sleep was experimentally produced and in already sleeping subjects after they had retired for the night. It was definitely shown by means of this instrument, that sleep and muscular relaxation were parallel phenomena, viz., in subjects gradually falling asleep, the muscular relaxation gradually diminished, while in subjects deeply asleep, the state of muscular relaxation was reduced to zero. With hypnotized subjects, however, the instrument showed no variation in muscular tension, the same as in the artificially produced motionless states in animals.

Analyzing my series of experiments, it was found that listening to a monotonous sound stimulus tended to produce a drowsy state and finally sleep. Sleep also took place when the element of monotony was not used, thus demonstrating that this factor was unnecessary for the production of sleep. A limitation of voluntary movements may thus produce sleep, but this limitation must be of the nature of a muscular relaxation and not a muscular tension. Further experiments with electrical currents demonstrated that sleep failed to result so long as the stimulus was felt. Only when the current was reduced to zero or when the lowest threshold of perception was reached, which for the subject was the same as zero, did sleep take place. Thus sleep was a reaction to stimuli and when, in conditions of muscular relaxation, stimuli ceased to pour into the brain and keep it active, sleep resulted.

The dependence of sleep on muscular tonus is shown by the fact that when we "fight" against drowsiness we do so by voluntarily placing our muscles in a state of tension. When we allow ourselves to relax, sleep results. Sometimes great fatigue tends to keep one awake, because the fatigue symptoms are localized in the muscles. Sleep is an instinct, an inhibition of muscular tension. Monotonous stimuli keep us awake by pouring themselves into the brain and keeping it active, and sleep can only take place if these stimuli are reduced to zero or to the threshold. Yawning before sleep is an effort to bring about muscular relaxation. Thus muscular relaxation is a necessary condition for sleep in all the higher animals. In the lower organisms sleep was probably limited to motionless states of relaxation, which had all the characteristics of a simple, elementary instinct or tropism. Those organisms survived which possessed these relaxed reactions to their greatest extent, and from these sleep arose. All motionless states in animals are not sleep, however, neither do they resemble sleep, but are probably a variety of hypnosis, as demonstrated by my experiments.

These experiments on the nature of sleep and hypnosis suggested several other directions to which inquiry might be directed—namely,

1. How did sleep evolve?
2. What is the biological necessity for sleep?

Although it has been noted that primitive, moving unicellular organisms, when observed for hours at a time, were unceasingly active and showed no motionless states, yet sleep must have arisen at some stage of evolution from these primitive organisms. Presumably those organisms survived which possessed these motionless states to their greatest extent, and from these motionless states could probably be traced the phylogenetic origin of sleep. In the higher animals, however, that is, in those possessing a complex nervous system, these motionless states, as demonstrated by my experiments, were not sleep but a form of cerebral inhibition, a genuine hypnosis. Furthermore, the animals experimented upon possessed genuine spontaneous sleep states, whereas the motionless states induced in them were artificial and experimental.

In the lower organisms these motionless states are not intelligent reactions, but probably blind mechanisms, and we must therefore not allow the interpretation of such phenomena to lead us into anthropomorphism. Neither can they be said to arise from fatigue, because such states may be observed in organisms which have not been subjected to stimuli that would lead to fatigue. Lower organisms, however, are very sensitive to light, but whether this influence to light is a chemical or a mechanical phenomenon cannot be discussed at present. For instance, many motile forms collect in regions of a given light intensity, some orient themselves towards the source of light and others away from it into shadows or where the light is diminished. We are dealing here with a process variously termed heliotropism or phototaxis.[1] These light re-

[1] On the various tropisms and the reactions of organisms to light, and the interpretation of these phenomena from the standpoint of comparative psychology, see the publications of Loeb, Pieron, Bohn, Jennings, Verworn, Claparède, and Mast.

actions may be decidedly rhythmic in character and because they usually result from sudden changes in the intensity of light, they seem compulsory and mechanical. It has been found, for instance, that a sudden increase in the intensity of light will cause restlessness in earth worms and fresh water planarians. Diminution of the intensity of light inhibits these restless reactions and causes the creature to come to rest, or if such a creature goes from a light area to a dark one its activity becomes reduced to a minimum, it becomes motionless and seems to fall asleep.

It seems probable that out of these periods of immobility and rest sleep arose. Light is a distance receptor and the activity of these organisms ceased when these particular receptors failed to throw its nerve elements into activity. The same mechanism probably takes place in the sleep of man and the higher animals from the inhibition of distance receptors. If sleep is an instinct, it was not so in the primitive organisms, but in these creatures it was a tropism, a mechanical or chemical necessity for repose under conditions where light was absent. From this tropism-like reaction, sleep arose, a veritable impulse of living matter to higher and higher rhythmic activities, motility on the one hand, with its freedom of action and the consequent development of the nervous system, periodic immobility on the other, in the effort to protect this nervous system from the pernicious effects of over-activity. Thus those organisms which showed these rhythmic reactions of immobility and repair were those which survived in the biological struggle for existence.

Let us investigate these complex reactions to light more closely. Sometimes instead of attaining a definite axial position or orientation to the source of stimulation, the organism as a whole will move from light to shadow or vice versa. Whether or not these reactions are adaptive or mere mechanical automatisms is one of the most important questions of comparative psychology. Probably the phenomenon, at least in the more primitive organisms, is not psychic, the light in these cases acting as a mere directive stimulus. The fact that in brainless planarians can be demonstrated the same sensitiveness to light, but that the reaction time to arrive at immobility is longer, speaks in favor of the mechanistic hypothesis.

Histological investigations on planaria and earth worms seem to indicate that the photosensitive elements are distributed over the body surface. That the reaction to light is a mechanical or a chemical response without the involvement of consciousness or perception, a mere mechanism, is demonstrated by the fact that brainless organisms become motionless when the light intensity is suddenly reduced, or what amounts to the same thing, when shadows are suddenly thrown over the bodies of the creatures. These reactions to shadows seem to be defence reactions, because a shadow would naturally herald the approach of an enemy. Then the organism becomes motionless, a condition under which it would be less likely to be perceived. Analogous conditions are sometimes found in the higher animals, namely, simulation of death, but here the defence reaction is intellectual and not mechanistic. Thus these latter reactions are in a general way adaptive and serve a purpose in not only protecting the creature from external influences, but likewise have a reparative action.

Sleep, therefore, in these lower organisms seems a mere rest state, a negative heliotropic reaction, because of the poverty of the creature in receptor organs. As the animal evolved, as the spinal cord became a complicated reflex mechanism and the brain the dominant organ of consciousness, the various receptors became more numerous and complicated, and parallel with this there arose rhythmic states of activity alternating with rest or sleep.

It is well known that we cannot get along without sleep and so the important question arises—why is sleep biologically necessary? Genuine sleep only exists in organisms with a developed nervous system, and it has been shown that the motionless states in lowly organisms, when in shadows or in darkness, are not sleep. Sleep also seems to be due to a cessation of activity of the receptor organs and this in turn causes a diminished activity of the central nervous system. In sleep, the brain and spinal cord alone seem to be the seats of diminished activity, for the body metabolism during sleep does not differ much from that of the waking state. Sleep is an organic need, in the same way that hunger is an organic need. The effect of complete sleeplessness, as shown by experimental evidence, is to cause severe changes in the nerve cells. Therefore, the activity of the nerve cells furnishes the key to sleep. The Nissl bodies (or granules) of the nerve cells accumulate during repose and disappear in activity, particularly under conditions of fatigue. In the brains of chickens and dogs which have been suddenly killed during sleep there has been found an increase of the Nissl bodies. This substance, therefore, accumulates in the nerve cells during their functional inactivity, when the sensory stimuli pouring into these cells from without are greatly diminished. Normal nerve cells, or nerve cells in a state of rest, show these Nissl bodies with great clearness. It is only in the fatigued cell or the cell which has been poisoned by toxic substances or through the influence of increased temperature in fever, that these bodies are disintegrated and in many cases completely disappear, giving the cell a washed-out appearance (chromatolysis). Therefore, sleep is a mechanism for the repair of nerve elements which have become disintegrated from the bombardment of stimuli received by the various surface receptors and receptor organs of the special senses. Those organisms which by reason of rest and immobility when they went into darkness or shadows, showed the greatest repair, were the very organisms which survived in the evolutionary struggle and sleep evolved out of these motionless states. This reparative power is absolute, for no matter how great the fatigue or long the insomnia, only a few hours of complete sleep are necessary as demonstrated by some exact experiments on the loss of sleep in man.

In ordinary sleep, the eyelids are lowered, and a position is assumed by the sleeper which tends to a relaxation of all the voluntary muscles. Certain changes take place in the pulse and respiration, the blood-pressure falls, the muscles become relaxed, the threshold of consciousness becomes very low. The reflexes are diminished or may entirely disappear. The restorative and refreshing effect of natural sleep upon the tired nervous system is a fact well attested by everyday experience. A profound sleep is refreshing; a broken sleep, even in snatches that are profound, or lying in a half-sleeping state, such as frequently occurs in insomnia, fails to restore the fatigued organism. But even the pernicious effects of a complete insomnia are completely balanced by a few hours of profound sleep, as has been shown by certain experiments on the loss of sleep. Sleep rests and refreshes one because of the muscular immobility and relaxation during sleep, the internal organs become less active, the nervous system rests, there is a decided lowering of mental tension. In other words, during normal sleep, there is a distinct reparative action.

What happens if the body is deprived of sleep? We will consider this question under two heads:—the complete loss of sleep from an experimental standpoint and the involuntary partial sleeplessness known as insomnia. It is well known that absolute loss of sleep has a very pernicious, sometimes even a fatal effect upon the organism. In man, however, even the severest types of insomnia complained of by patients who are sufferers from some form of nervous or mental disease, are never absolute sleeplessness. In China and during the Inquisition in Europe, forced deprivation of sleep was not only a form of torture, but also was used as a form of capital punishment.

Manaceine's experiments on young puppies showed that the animals suffered more from loss of sleep than from deprivation of food. When the animals were absolutely deprived of sleep from periods varying from 96 to 120 hours, the result was invariably fatal, even if sufficient food were given during this interval. She concludes from her experiments, that sleep is even more necessary to animals endowed with consciousness, than food. In animals which have been starved to death, but few changes can be found in the brain, while in animals which died of enforced insomnia, the most profound and irreparable changes occurred, such as capillary hemorrhage and fatty alterations in the nerve cells. The experimental loss of sleep, as applied to man, was carried out in a very systematic manner by Professor Patrick and Dr. J. A. Gilbert, of the University of Iowa.[1] This was the first time that such

[1] G. T. W. Patrick and J. A. Gilbert: "The Effect of the Loss of Sleep."—*Psychological Review,* September, 1896.

experiments were carried out on man, previous investigations having been limited to dogs. The subjects were kept awake for about ninety hours and a series of psychological tests comprising reaction time, motor ability, memory, attention, etc., were made at six hour intervals. In one of the subjects, during the second night, hallucinations of sight developed; the air seemed full of colored particles which appeared like gnats and were in constant dancing motion. In all the subjects, memory became very defective and the power of attention was greatly lowered. After the experiments were finished, sleep brought about a complete restoration, in about one-sixth to one-third of the time of the enforced insomnia.

The development of hallucinations in the above experiments is of interest. One of my cases of hysterical insomnia was constantly troubled by grimacing faces; another case of protracted sleeplessness would see a panorama of animals just as he dozed off, at other times he would hear a voice constantly repeating "Let down the jib." All these sense deceptions occurred in the half-sleeping condition, never when the subject was fully awake or fully asleep.

Ordinary insomnia is a very common complaint. One of the most common causes is physical pain. It also occurs in many forms of nervous diseases, particularly neurasthenia. In this insomnia of neurasthenia, the subject is frequently in a half-waking and half-sleeping condition, with a hazy state of consciousness and limitation of muscular activity. Or sleep may be secured in snatches, but the slightest noise awakens the sleeper. Therefore, in spite of their statements, these individuals never suffer from complete insomnia; they sleep more than they realize. Extreme physical exhaustion alone may produce insomnia, a proof that sleep is not absolutely dependent on exhaustion of the nerve centres. Sleeplessness may also be due to an emotional shock, as in certain cases of hysterical insomnia. For instance, a patient became greatly frightened by an insane woman entering her store and throwing an entire box of lighted matches among some paper. The patient immediately became greatly agitated, began to dream of the episode at night, and one week later, an insomnia developed, which continued for five years, up to the time she came under observation.

Sometimes insomnia may be due to the development of a fixed idea that sleep is impossible. One patient said, "I cannot get it out of my skull that I am not going to sleep." Janet had studied in great detail a case in which the sleeplessness was due to a fixed idea.[1] In this case, the patient developed a severe attack of typhoid fever four months after the death of her child. During convalescence from this illness, she suffered from an almost continual visual hallucination of her dead child, particularly at night. After this sleeplessness developed, and when she first came under Janet's observation, the patient claimed that she had not slept a wink for two years. This almost complete loss of sleep was verified by careful observation. During the day she complained of fatigue, and the facial expression was that of one half asleep. Drugs failed to induce sleep; hypnosis produced only light states of short duration, in which the patient would awaken suddenly, with an expression of terror. At night also, she would go into a half-drowsy condition and awaken suddenly, much terrified, saying that she had had a bad dream, but which was only vaguely remembered on awakening. When questioned during her somnolent state, it developed that the so-called dream consisted of an hallucination of her dead child. The insomnia was due to the fact that the hallucination developed immediately after the somnolent condition took place; the patient would then become

[1] Pierre Janet: "Nevrose et Idées Fixes," Vol. I, pp. 354-374. (Chapter on "Insomnie par Idée Fixe Subconsciente.")

terrified and waken. Here was clearly a case of insomnia due to a subconscious fixed idea.

The depth of sleep is variable. We have the lighter subwaking states in which consciousness is almost perfectly preserved, the deeper somnolent conditions in which dreams occur, and finally the deepest grades of sleep, in which consciousness is reduced to such a low threshold that it may be considered as being almost entirely obliterated. In these somnolent states the sense of the lapse of time is only partially obliterated, in deep sleep completely so; we may have slept for hours but on awakening we have the illusion that it has been only a few minutes. Sleep is most profound in the early part of the night or within the first half-hour after falling asleep, and it becomes more shallow during the early morning hours. In some experiments with the capillary electrometer on sleeping subjects, it was found that the greatest depth of sleep was reached in about an hour and that this period corresponded with the greatest degree of muscular relaxation. It is of interest to note that it is just during these early morning hours when sleep is lightest, that dreams are most apt to occur. The depth of sleep is measured either by the height from which a metallic ball must be dropped to awaken the sleeper or by the intensity of an electric current from an induction coil. However, if there is an element of expectation, a very slight noise will awaken the sleeper, as in the case of a sleeping mother being awakened by a slight movement of her child.

This subwaking state to which we have several times alluded, where the individual hovers between sleep and waking, is of great practical and scientific interest. When it occurs spontaneously, it is technically known as the hypnagogic state; when it is experimentally produced by listening to a monotonous sound stimulus, while the individual is in a state of muscular relaxation with limitation of voluntary movements, it is called the hypnoidal condition (Sidis), or the state of induced or experimental distraction (Coriat). The spontaneous hypnagogic state may be only momentary in duration or it may last for fifteen minutes or more. It occurs just as one is falling asleep or as one is awakening from slumber. It appears that we never go to sleep or waken suddenly. There always intervenes this hypnagogic state between sleep on one side and awakening on the other, a state bordering on hypnosis, really a natural hypnotic state, particularly when it occurs just before the individual falls asleep. When sleep takes place, however, the relation of sleep to hypnosis ceases.

This hypnagogic state occurs in all individuals and is markedly protracted in insomnia, particularly in those subjects who complain of absolute loss of sleep. In this hypnagogic state, many peculiar psychic and motor phenomena may appear, and there is also obtained, as in real hypnosis, a condition of increased suggestibility, so that it possesses a certain therapeutic value.

We will first consider a condition of muscular activity which is peculiar to the hypnagogic state. It is well known that even on being suddenly awakened from a deep sleep, full consciousness is not immediately regained. Complete consciousness is reached only after passing through this intermediary hypnagogic state. In this state, there is sometimes an extreme difficulty in opening the eyelids, at other times a complete inability to move the limbs. After a time, however, and by continued effort of the will, the eyes can be opened or the limbs moved. When this point has been attained, consciousness has become completely restored and the hypnagogic state has entirely disappeared. Now this transitory paralysis of the limbs and eyes occurs frequently in normal individuals, but is only momentary. Sometimes, however, the phenomenon either occurs frequently or is greatly prolonged. Under both these conditions we are dealing with what I have called nocturnal paralysis.[1] When this paralysis is frequent or unduly prolonged, it becomes a genuine functional nervous disorder. In one of my cases, this inability to move the limbs lasted for fifteen minutes. A brief report of a case which came under personal observation will illustrate the matter more clearly than any description. It refers to a patient in whom these distressing attacks of nocturnal paralysis had persisted for a number of years. After a sound sleep he would awaken suddenly, know where he was and who he was, but could not recall his name. Therefore, consciousness was not completely clear, a prominent characteristic of the hypnagogic state. In the attack the eyes were closed and the limbs rigid. He was unable to open the eyes, to move the limbs, or to cry out. The duration of the individual attacks averaged about three minutes and they occurred about once a week. In another subject the condition of nocturnal paralysis was vividly described as " I feel like a doll whose eyes can be opened but who cannot move the limbs."

The condition in all these cases is only a dis-

[1] " Nocturnal Paralysis."—*Boston Medical and Surgical Journal*, Vol. CLVII, No. 2, July 11, 1907. (" Some Further Studies on Nocturnal Paralysis," *Ibid.*, Vol. CLVII, No. 23, December 5, 1907.)

sociation of consciousness reacting most strongly on the motor mechanism. It bears no relation to epilepsy, as one writer would lead us to believe. Neither does sudden awakening from sound sleep bear any relation to the disorder, for in some personal experiments on sleeping animals which were suddenly awakened by a loud noise, not even a temporary muscular rigidity took place.

Other peculiar phenomena occur in this hypnagogic state. Hallucinations of hearing may take place, as in the case of the patient cited above, who heard a voice repeating, "Lower the jib." Sometimes there are heard loud sounds like a gong or a piece of falling metal, and the half-sleeping subject is suddenly awakened by these sense deceptions. Occasionally there are shock-like startings of the body or a sensation as if falling. A condition called catalepsy may also arise, in which the limbs can be molded like a piece of lead pipe and kept in a strained position for some time, without any apparent sense of fatigue. Horrible dreams may take place with a sense of great fear, as in the night terrors of children. Occasionally, the hallucinations are those of touch, either a light touch or a sensation as if we were gripped in a vise. When this latter occurs, there is usually associated a terrifying dream with great fear and a sense of impending suffocation or death. This is the so-called nightmare. In the case of a woman, there arose a sense of an awful calamity about to overtake the patient; a deformed man would seem to spring on her, and she would think, " It has overtaken me, this is the end of all." Then she would cry out and the scream would awaken her. In another case the patient felt as if she were grasping something, a pencil or a person's wrist; sometimes the sensation would be as if the fingers and toes were swelling to the bursting point. These nightmares have also been interpreted as nocturnal states of anxiety, based upon certain repressed sexual conflicts. The phenomena of nightmare, as shown by Ernest Jones, explain the mediæval theory of a fiend who sits upon one's bosom and hinders respiration.

These hypnagogic hallucinations have been utilized with great imaginative effectiveness by Guy de Maupassant in his description of a nightmare. In his novelette " Le Horla " he describes the development of an incipient mental disease. The sufferer in question was a victim of insomnia and believed that he was pursued and haunted by an imaginary being. Then in terribly laconic sentences, the author gives us a most vivid description of the following condition, which is really a hypnagogic hallucination, a kind of a night terror. "Then I lay down and waited for sleep as one waits an execution. . . . My heart beat and my legs trembled; my entire body started in the warmth of the sheets, up to the moment when I suddenly fell asleep, as one falls into an abyss of stagnant water when dreaming. . . . I slept—a long time—two or three hours—then a dream—no, a nightmare took hold of me. I felt that I was lying down and that I was asleep—I felt it and saw it—and I also had the feeling that some one approached me, looked at me, touched me, mounted on my bed, knelt on my chest, took my neck between his hands and squeezed—with all his force to strangle me. I struggled, bound by this atrocious power. . . . I tried to cry out—but was unable to;—I tried to move—I was unable to; I tried with fearful efforts, panting for breath, to turn, to throw off this Being who crushed and stifled me—I was unable to. And suddenly I awoke, covered with perspiration. I lit a candle. I was alone."

There are a number of conditions which outwardly resemble sleep, yet are distinct from it. The so-called African sleeping-sickness, which occurs with the greatest frequency in the region around the Congo River, is a condition of gradually increasing stupor, which terminates in death. It is caused by a micro-organism belonging to the Protozoön group, which is found in the blood and central nervous system, and is transmitted by a certain African fly. A morbid disposition to sleep, coming on in sudden attacks, and characterized either by mere drowsiness or complete unconsciousness, is sometimes seen in hysteria and particularly in epilepsy. This condition is called narcolepsy and the attacks are designated as narcoleptic attacks. A form of stupor, outwardly resembling sleep, is seen in some forms of mental disease, particularly adolescent insanity. The sleep of anesthetics, such as ether or chloroform, is due to the direct chemical action of volatile drugs upon the brain. Here the analogy with sleep ends, because the depth of unconsciousness produced by these anesthetics is much greater than in normal sleep, as shown by the complete insensibility to pain. It must be admitted, however, that before ether or chloroform anesthesia becomes complete, there is always a preceding semi-drowsy state, the same as occurs just before normal sleep.

Hypnosis only outwardly resembles normal sleep. The relation of sleep to hypnosis will be discussed in the chapter relating to this latter condition. Sleep-walking or somnambulism, in which many complicated and seemingly natural acts are executed with a loss of memory for these acts, occurs not only in the disease hysteria, but also in normal individuals. Somnambulism, however, is not sleep, but a special mental state arising out of sleep through a definite mechanism. It may assume various types, either the ordinary form of sleep-walking or may develop to the high degree of actual changes in the personality. In both instances, it is probably a form of mental dissociation. The amnesia is only an apparent one, as the memory may be recovered by appropriate methods. In one case of somnambulism, it was possible to restore the memory for all the complex acts of the period, although this period was of an hour's duration.[1]

[1] For a complete discussion of somnambulism and its psychoanalytic application, see my book, "The Hysteria of Lady Macbeth," New York—1912. (Particularly Chapter II.)

CHAPTER VI

DREAMS

Dreaming, like sleeping, is one of the mysteries of our psychic life. For centuries, dreams have had a peculiar fascination for man. The world of dreams, because it was so distorted and so fantastic, has been interpreted as having an entirely different significance from the waking world. The occult significance of dreams has given another coloring to literature, folklore, and even religion. But while the ancients were particularly concerned with the prophetic nature of dreams, the modern investigator has busied himself in an attempt to fathom out the psychological mechanism of "the stuff that dreams are made of."

In this chapter we will discuss the subject of dreams from the purely psychological standpoint, as manifestations of certain forms of dissociations of consciousness and of unconscious wishes. We will leave untouched, as foreign to our subject, the statistics of dreams or of their interpretation from the standpoint of symbolism, prophecy, telepathy, atavism, or premonitions of the future. These latter aspects belong more strictly to the field of psychical research, than to that of abnormal psychology, and though many remarkable dream experiences have been collected, the effort to establish a supernormal basis has not been successful. The attempts to interpret the underlying mechanism of dreams are recent. Modern science has stripped much of the cloak of mystery from dreams and laid bare to critical view the cold, dry facts. These facts in themselves are just as interesting as any supernormal interpretations, and what is more to the point, are more valuable.

The modern investigations of dreams have assumed several distinct aspects. In order that the reader may have a clear view of the entire field, the following summary of these investigations may be made:

1. Investigations of dreams from the supernormal standpoint, what is generally known as the field of psychical research just referred to.

2. The study of dreams from the purely statistical standpoint, as in the investigations of Sante de Sanctis and Miss Calkins and her pupils.

In both of these publications the method used was that of introspection, the dreamer being asked to record his dream immediately on awakening. Miss Calkins investigated the dreams of normal persons. She found that dreams occurred usually during the light morning sleep and that there was a very close connection between dreaming and the experiences of waking life. Illusions of memory and distortions of facts, and of the time element were quite frequent. She divided dreams into two types—the presentation type, or those occasioned or accompanied by peripheral excitation, and the representation type, those of purely central or cerebral origin. The largest number of dreams were visual in nature, then followed in order, auditory, touch, taste, and olfactory dreams. As our visual apparatus is most active during the waking state, so visual dreams are the most frequent, while pure auditory dreams occur frequently in musicians.

Sante de Sanctis not only studied the normal dreams in children, adults, and the aged, but also the dreams of criminals and animals, the insane and in certain nervous diseases, such as hysteria, epilepsy, neurasthenia. He concludes that even animals and very young children dream, and that the dreams of old people are less vivid than in adults. These dreams of the aged tend to disappear quickly on awakening, in harmony with the weakness of memory for recent events in old age. In hysteria the dreams are very intense and have a strong emotional coloring. In epilepsy the dreams are less complex than in hysteria; neurasthenics dream frequently, the dreams resembling those of hysteria, but are less intense and not so well recalled on awakening. The insane frequently dream of their hallucinations and delusions.

3. The purely psychological researches of the mechanism of dreams, such as the publications of Freud [1] and Tissie [2] and Mourly Vold [3] and the investigations of the content of dream consciousness, as in the dreams of the blind.[4] Vold's investigations have led him to believe that cutaneous or motor stimuli are the most frequent causes of dreams and that frequently childhood memories are interwoven in the dream life.

4. The interpretations of dreams from the standpoint of dissociated mental states, as in multiple personality, functional amnesia, and the dream-like hallucinations resulting from the action of certain toxic drugs, such as alcohol, opium, and hashish. Part of these belong to purely scientific literature, as in the modern studies of dissociations of consciousness, and part to the dream-hallucinations of certain

[1] Sigm. Freud: "Die Traumdeutung," 1909.

[2] Ph. Tissie: "Les Rêves," 1890.

[3] J. Mourly Vold: "Ueber den Traum," 1910.

[4] J. Jastrow: "The Dreams of the Blind." (In "Fact and Fable in Psychology," 1900.)

imaginative writers, for instance De Quincey and Baudelaire, yet possessing a certain scientific value. Finally we have introspective accounts of intelligent patients who have recovered from alcoholic delirium. These two latter groups, the mechanism of dreams and their occurrence and interpretation in states of mental dissociation, will form the chief subject-matter of this chapter.

Freud has been foremost in the investigation of the mechanism of dreams. So important are Freud's investigations on dreams, as revealing the mechanism of the unconscious and the psycho-analytic treatment of certain functional neuroses, that they will be discussed in the following chapter.

Dreams are not phenomena of accidental origin, but have a hidden meaning and are related to either dissociated, suppressed, or dormant past experiences, and originate chiefly in the subconscious mental life. In dreaming, the experiences may be distorted in their character (called paramnesia), or the time element may be disturbed (anachronism), either by the imagination or by external stimuli. The central nucleus remains, however—the element of recognition is not absent. For instance, we may dream of something that we knew took place long ago, not to ourselves, but to others, and yet it may seem to happen at present and we may be the chief actor in that particular dream. Dreams are not insignificant and without value. They lay bare the innermost secrets of the heart, past experiences, wishes, desires. Our subconscious mental life is filled with experiences struggling to enter consciousness, and in sleep, when there is no longer any dissociation, these experiences enter consciousness and are interpreted as dreams. In sleep, the censorship of the normal waking consciousness is removed, the suppressed or dissociated experiences gain the upper hand and, colored by the imagination, they form new combinations resulting in a weird phantasmagoria. The mechanism of dreams is, therefore, similar to the dissociations of an everyday waking life, into which these subconscious elements so largely enter.

Dreams have two principal sources:—(1) Those arising from external stimuli during sleep and becoming distorted in consciousness, and (2) those having purely an internal origin, as manifestations of conscious, suppressed, or dissociated experiences. In those dreams caused by external stimuli, the intensity of the dream-state is much greater than the stimulus which gave rise to the dream. A number of external conditions may thus be factors in the development of a dream, such as the position of the body, a loud noise, or a sudden light that strikes the face of the sleeper, uncovering of the bedclothes so as to expose a portion of the body, hunger, thirst, impeded respiration, pain, etc. For instance, in Maury's experiments on dreams, when the sleeping subject was tickled on the lips and nostrils with a feather, there arose a dream of terrible torture, the subject dreaming that a mask of pitch had been placed on his face and then pulled away so that the skin of the face came with it. When water was dropped on the forehead, he dreamed that he was in Italy perspiring freely and drinking white wine.

A dream may sometimes follow a glance at a book or newspaper account. One subject dreamed of a man on a lonely island in the middle of the ocean, and traced this to the reading of newspaper accounts of Dreyfus on Devil's Island. In another person, after a glance at a book treating of Egyptian life and manners, the following dream took place the same night. He dreamed that he was in an ancient Egyptian city, and about him were massive buildings and monuments, adorned with hieroglyphics. Crowds of people were present; it seemed to be the occasion of some great festival or holiday. He was taken to the roof of a high building by a number of men in military dress, there he was bound hand and foot and lowered a short distance below the roof by means of a rope. One of the soldiers took an axe and cut the rope, and he fell an immeasurable distance to the ground. At this point, just before touching the ground, he awoke.

These are all examples of simple dreams. Sometimes external stimuli give rise to very complex dream experiences, as in the elaborate taste dream related by Hammond.[1]

"A young lady sought to cure herself of the habit of thumb sucking acquired in babyhood by covering the offending thumb with extract of aloes. During the night she dreamed that she was crossing the ocean in a steamer made of wormwood and that the vessel was furnished throughout with the same material, and the emanation so pervaded all parts of the ship that it was impossible to breathe without tasting the bitterness; everything that she ate or drank was likewise impregnated from the flavor. When she arrived at Havre she asked for a glass of water to wash the taste from her mouth, but they brought her an infusion of wormwood, which she gulped down because she was thirsty. She sent to Paris and consulted a famous physician, begging him to do something which would extract the wormwood from her body. He told her there was but one remedy, and that was ox-gall. This he gave her by the pound, and in a few weeks the wormwood was all

[1] This account is taken from Manaceine: "Sleep," pp. 260-261.

gone, but the ox-gall had taken its place and was fully as bitter and disagreeable. To get rid of the ox-gall she was advised to take counsel of the Pope. She accordingly went to Rome and obtained an audience of the Holy Father. He told her that she must make a pilgrimage to the plain where the pillar of salt stood, into which Lot's wife was transformed, and must eat a piece of the salt as big as her thumb. She did so and awoke to find that she had sucked all the aloes off the thumb."

Dreams are manifestations of a persistent consciousness during sleep. We dream only when this consciousness persists, or is active to a certain degree. Therefore, two things are necessary for dreaming—the persistence of a certain amount of consciousness during sleep and a certain activity of this persistent consciousness. It has been said that a sound sleep is dreamless, but if dreams do occur in sound sleep, we have no proof of the fact, because we have no memory of them on awakening. It is extremely doubtful, however, if there is enough of this persistent consciousness in a really sound sleep, to form any dreams. Of course lack of memory after a deep sleep is no proof that there was no conscious activity during this time and dreaming did not take place, because in deep hypnotic states mental activity goes on, but there is no memory of this activity on regaining the normal waking condition. The same might be true of deep sleep. If dreams only occur in light sleep or in the intermediate sleep states, we remember them, but this does not prove that dreams are absent in deep sleep, because we do not remember them. Under ordinary circumstances, we are able to recollect only a small portion of our mental activity during sleep. However, the weight of evidence seems to show that dreams occur only in light sleep or in the intermediate (hypnagogic) sleep states. The latter, as was previously pointed out, is a kind of a natural hypnotic condition. In light hypnosis, isolated dream-like hallucinations may take place, as in one of my subjects who insisted that I pulled his coat sleeve while he was hypnotized, when in reality I sat at some distance from him. In Patrick's and Gilbert's experiments on the loss of sleep, one of the subjects reported a dream while he was standing up gazing at a piece of apparatus. At this time he was evidently partially asleep, although he considered himself fully awake. In some of my experiments on the artificial production of sleep, fragmentary dreams occurred. One of the best proofs that dreams occur only in the intermediate sleeping states is—that we scarcely ever finish a dream. We always awaken at a particular part, at a critical moment, namely, the part at which the emotional element, usually fear, is the most vivid. The dream is unfinished, probably because we are on the road to awakening while we dream. As we become more and more awake, the dream ceases. This awakening at a particular vivid moment of a dream was seen in Janet's case of insomnia due to a subconscious fixed idea, and also in our case of Mrs. Y., who displayed four hypnotic personalities. As this latter case will be studied in full in another chapter, we will give only the essentials of a peculiar recurrent dream. At the moment of falling asleep, the patient would experience with great intensity the following dream. She would see a surgeon robed in white and with his sleeves rolled up, working at the back of the head of the patient herself and taking stitches in the scalp. This dream was only momentary, and every time she experienced it she would awaken immediately.

The most interesting dreams are those which occur in certain dissociations of consciousness, such as hysteria, multiple personality, amnesia, and in recurrent dream states. Studies of the dream life in these conditions have furnished us with valuable information concerning the exact nature of these dissociations and have proven that dreams are merely waking experiences which appear during sleep, but of which the waking subject has no memory except as a dream. In states of psychopathic dissociation, dreams have their origin in the waking experiences of the individual. They are experiences of the original primary personality of which there is no memory in the waking state. These dreams appear without apparent reason, are strange and peculiar, and not synthetized with the waking or sleeping personality.

In the case of Susan N.,[1] a study of the dreams proved valuable and interesting and illustrated these points in an admirable manner. In this case, after an attack of prolonged stupor, the patient awoke to find that the memory of her whole previous life, from the time of her birth, was completely obliterated. In sleep, however, the patient dreamed of episodes for which she had no memory in her waking state and the dreams were, therefore, interpreted as purely imaginative creations. Strangely enough, identical dreams were frequently repeated. The dream records were taken verbatim from the patient and one of these is as follows:

"One dream stands out very clear. This was several weeks ago. It seems as if a man and woman came to see me, and they told

[1] Isador H. Coriat, "The Lowell Case of Amnesia."—*Journal Abnormal Psychology,* Vol. II, No. 3, August-September, 1907.

me they were relatives of mine and were willing to take care of me. So they sent me off with them, and we travelled quite a distance. On part of the road there seemed to be trees growing on both sides, not very close together, and after a time they came to a house, and after they took me inside the man commenced to beat me and the woman to pull my hair out. The man had coarse whiskers, and I think I'd know the woman if I should see her." This dream was repeated several times in an identical manner. As an interesting and valuable sequel to the above, one afternoon later in the year the patient was taken for a drive to her old home, in an effort to ascertain if she could recognize any of the scenes of her childhood and early youth. But everything was strange and unfamiliar to her; the old cemetery, a former schoolmate who was encountered in the village road, and even the building in which she had formerly taught school. She was taken up the road to the house where her brother and sister lived, and on reaching it, she immediately said, "This is the house of my dreams. I can see very plainly the man dragging me off the wagon and the woman pulling my hair up those two steps and through the piazza into the kitchen in the back." On being confronted by her sister, the patient exclaimed, "That is the woman of my dream," and although immediately recognized by her sister, Susan N. disclaimed all knowledge of her and was very frigid in her manner. In sleep, the patient had merely reproduced an episode which had occurred during her past life previous to the stupor. While sleeping, there was no dissociation, consciousness was completely synthetized. As she had no memory of this episode in her waking state, it was interpreted as merely a dream.

In Sidis's case of the Rev. Mr. Hanna, many of the lost memories appeared during dreams.[1] In this case, as in that of Susan N., the patient had lost all memory of his life experiences. This extensive amnesia followed an accident. But that the loss of memory was only apparent, that all the events were retained in the subconscious mental life, as in the Lowell Case of Amnesia, was proved by an extensive investigation. All the dreams of Mr. Hanna, the places spoken of, as well as the persons mentioned, were fully identified by the patient's father. Sometimes the dream pictures were very simple. On one occasion, he dreamed of "a horse with long ears and with a tail like a cow. Never saw anything like it. The horse produced such queer sounds." The animal seen in this dream

[1] "Multiple Personality," 1905.

was evidently a donkey, the patient not having seen one since the loss of memory following the accident. On other occasions, the dreams were more complex and related to scenes in the Pennsylvania coal district, where the patient had previously lived. Sometimes he dreamed of journeys which were actual experiences in his former life. None of these dreams were recognized as former experiences but were interpreted as strange dreams of his present life.

We have seen how dissociated experiences could appear in sleep and how the subject would interpret these experiences, on awakening, as mere idle dreams. There is another aspect of the question that must be briefly considered. In more complex cases of mental dissociation leading to multiple personality, do the waking experiences of these personalities appear during sleep? It has been shown that in sleep, there is a more or less complete synthesis of the lost memories which are interpreted as dreams. Does the same thing take place in multiple personality? Are the dreams of the different personalities the same, no matter how different the experiences of the waking life? Let us see. In the case of Miss Beauchamp,[1] who developed four distinct personalities, each with a distinct and separate mental life during the waking

[1] Morton Prince: "The Dissociation of a Personality," 1905.

state, it was shown that in sleep two of the personalities, called B. I. and B. IV., " reverted to a common consciousness and became one and the same. That is to say, the dreams were common to both; each, B. I. and B. IV., had the same dreams, and each remembered them afterwards as her own." These dreams were well remembered and recorded by " Sally," one of the personalities, who, according to her own statement, was awake the greater part of the night.

Occasionally dream states will show a peculiar periodicity, in that they are liable to occur at certain times, the interval being entirely free from dreaming. This recurrent dream state was particularly well marked in one of my cases. It related to a young woman who began to have distressing dreams in the form of nightmares, following the death of her mother. These dreams showed a peculiar cycle, in that they reappeared every few weeks and would continue for several nights. The dream never occurred in the interval. Each dream was identical, the content being about as follows:

" I dreamed that I was out walking with my mother, near the place where she died. I walked to the top of the hill, looked around and came down, holding on to my mother's arm. Suddenly my mother fell fainting. I tried to cry out, but could not make a sound. I ran to the house to get assistance, but I came back alone and found that my mother had grown old and haggard-looking and was dressed in black. Then I woke up."

Hysterical paralyses and contractures sometimes follow a dream. Under these conditions, the subject dreams of the identical paralysis or contracture which comes on after awakening. Whether the dissociated state of a purely imaginary dream is projected into the waking life or whether an emotional shock occurs during the awakening, is dissociated in sleep and reproduced as a dream, is a question that connot be answered with certainty until we have more data on these curious phenomena. In a case reported by Janet, the patient developed a contracture of the hands following a vivid dream of piano playing. In another the subject dreamed that he was falling and awoke to find a beginning paralysis of the right arm and leg. That his paralysis was purely functional in nature was demonstrated by further investigation. In a case of hysterical paralysis which came under personal observation, the following curious condition was present. While walking, the patient would suddenly experience a sense of severe weakness in the legs, then there would follow a sensation "as if I had no legs," and she would fall. These episodes would occur a number of times during the day, but only when the patient was walking. On further analysis, it appeared that there was no history of an emotional shock, but during the week previous to her first attack, she dreamed that she was walking down a hill, then suddenly fell down and landed full length on her face. This sensation of falling did not awaken the patient at once, but when she did awaken, she felt perfectly normal. The dream was not repeated, but a week elapsed before the weakness of the legs developed. Here we have a condition almost identical with the cases reported by Janet.

Let us now take an ordinary dream and attempt to trace out a portion of the elements which enter into the dream consciousness. As an example, I take the following dream related by one of my patients: "I dreamed that I was walking through the snow with L. The snow was up to my knees. I went into a house to get a hat made, and I went into another house near by. When I came into the house, I saw two bedrooms; one was my room and the other belonged to some one else. These two bedrooms were off the hall. As I went into my own bedroom, I passed by the open door of the other. An old lady lay in bed—dying. I went to bed and slept in my dream. Then the dying woman's mother, who appeared to be already dead, came to me in my sleep. She was dressed in white and had long claw-like nails. The hands and fingers were pure white. She awakened me by clawing at me and I awakened in my dream. Then she grinned at me, but I was very sleepy and only opened my eyes for a moment and tried to raise my hand and beckon her to go away."

In tracing the principal elements of this dream, the following instigators are found. These instigators were woven into the dream fantasy and their analysis will enable one to fathom the external causes of the dream, but not the unconscious or latent thoughts giving rise to the dream.

"Walking through the snow": The weather was very warm on that day, the patient had read a poem on snow in a newspaper, with an editorial comment on the contrast in the weather.

"To get a hat made": The sister of the L. dreamed about was a milliner.

"An old lady lay in bed dying": The mother of the patient had recently been ill in bed, following a surgical operation.

"Long claw-like finger nails": The patient had been recently interested in antique furniture with claw legs.

Dream-like hallucinations are the frequent accompaniment of the intoxication by certain drugs, particularly alcohol, opium, and hashish. The distorted state of consciousness produced by these poisons bears a strong relationship to ordinary dreaming. Under these conditions, also, the dreams are merely distorted experiences. Readers of De Quincey will remember how all the minute incidents of his life, his studies in literature and philosophy, furnished the key to "that tremendous scenery which afterward peopled the dreams of the opium eater." The same fact holds true of the dreams of the hashish habitué, as related in the Artificial Paradise of Baudelaire. One of my patients furnished me with a very vivid written account of his dream-like hallucinations, on recovery from an attack of delirium tremens. The fantastic and shifting character of this narrative and its distortion of actual experiences is practically a dream, but a dream experienced during an abnormal alcoholic delirium and not during a normal sleep. In part it is as follows—"There was a face at every post and every time I'd go by they'd swear and gibe at me for what I had done during life. These faces made me a promise that if I'd shake hands with a certain fellow, they'd give me peace and wouldn't torment me. So finally this fellow came along and I remember shaking hands with him, and after that those voices asked me if I wanted to stay on earth and work or go with them to the Father above. So they finally persuaded me to follow them. Then they asked me to relate all my life and I started to tell them from the cradle to the grave. I wouldn't have to speak or talk, before they'd divine it. Two spirits conversed with each other. One was supposed to be God. As soon as I'd try to hesitate on any part of my life that I wouldn't like exposed, they seemed to say 'Now he hesitates.' All during this time there was a mumbling sound, as if we were riding in a chariot, and we heard electrical music on all sides, and I related my history from the cradle. I felt moving all the time. Every moment or so, a friend or a face that I had forgotten appeared and greeted me, until finally an angel opened a trap above and showed us something grand beyond—music, angels, flowers, and every one seemed clothed in a garb of gold. Then all became darkness again and spirits appeared. We felt them in the vacuum around us and voices kept telling us that our journey was getting shorter, and at a certain stage I was shown my mother, and she told me that we would soon meet to part no more. So we reached a place where our friends all gathered around us and they said that on the morrow we would see eternal light. But the angel said that moments were counted in thousands of years. All our flesh and blood was to fade away. The spirit of a girl that I had been going with was there and she was to take my place when I faded away. During this time the gasps of the dying could be heard and I was left alone with the spirit of this girl. Finally a voice shouted, 'Tom, you'll be there to-morrow. Throw away your earthly possessions.' Then the darkness disappeared and then, as though by magic, the Wonderland of Heaven appeared to me. The sky was sapphire blue, studded with diamonds and there was a vast amphitheatre and beings clothed in gold, emerald, and precious stones."

The dreams of the blind have furnished us interesting proof of the dependence of dreams on waking sensory experiences. It was shown by Jastrow that if the blindness took place before the seventh year, the dreams were never of the visual type; if after the seventh year, the dreams were very likely to be the same as those of a seeing individual. In Laura Bridgman, the blind deaf mute, sight and hearing were as absent from her dreams as from the waking world. For instance, if she dreamed of an animal she became aware of its presence only when it touched her. The value of educational experiences in dreams is well exemplified in the accounts of the dreams of Helen Keller, prepared for Professor Jastrow. For instance, she says, " My dreams have strangely changed during the past twelve years. Before and after my teacher first came to me, they were devoid of sound or thought or emotion of any kind, except fear, and only came in the form of sensations. . . . I dreamed of a wolf, which seemed to rush towards me and put his cruel teeth deep into my body. I could not speak . . . and I tried to scream; but no sound escaped from my lips. . . . Occasionally I dream that I am reading with my fingers, either Braille or line print." Later, when oral speech was established through education, talking in the finger alphabet disappeared from her dreams.

CHAPTER VII

FREUD'S THEORY OF DREAMS

FREUD states that the dream furnishes the royal road to a knowledge of the unconscious and thus the psychology of dream stands out in the center of the psycho-analytic theory and of the mechanism of unconscious mental states. In fact, Freud's investigations of dreams furnish the chief technical procedures for psycho-analysis. Dream interpretation is very difficult, however, it is not only a science, but also an art. Without previous training one cannot hope to succeed in the analysis of dreams. Freud was led to the scientific study of dreams, because in the earlier stages of his analytic treatment of the psycho-neuroses, or as it was then termed the cathartic method, he found that his patients frequently related strange, distorted and bizarre dreams. Further investigation demonstrated that these dreams had the same roots in the unconscious mental life of the patient as the psycho-neurotic symptoms themselves, and consequently, the technique for the analysis and meaning of dreams was elaborated.

In other words, the same unconscious mechanism was responsible for the creation of both dreams and symptoms and thus the dreams furnished the best means for the analysis and treatment of the symptoms.

What, then, is the mechanism through which the logical, unconscious thoughts become transformed to an illogical and apparently meaningless dream? In answer to this question, the technique of the dream analysis was elaborated and its mechanisms were investigated. The interpretation of a dream may thus be compared in accuracy and even in difficulty to the decipherment of a hieroglyphic or a cuneiform inscription. For as these latter are merely symbols of phonetic values and consequently of a once living language, so the dream is a symbol of the active and even remote unconscious thoughts of the dreamer. As a hieroglyphic cannot be read without the aid of a special technique and knowledge, so the interpretation of dreams requires an equally well-equipped training. In the dream we are dealing with several elements, such as unconscious repressed impulses and wishes, dating back at times to the earliest years of childhood and usually of a sexual nature, interwoven with events of the day or with physical stimuli arising during sleep. The unraveling of the complex dream phenomena, and discovering a certain law and order in the heterogeneous fantasy of the dream, presupposes a high degree of technical skill which can only be acquired through long experience.

Therefore, on the surface, the dream as remembered in the morning does not say what it means. The dream itself as remembered (called the manifest content), is formed from the underlying unconscious thoughts (called the latent content) of the subject. Thus what we recall of a dream in the morning is the illogical manifest content and not the orderly unconscious thoughts or latent content, which latter alone betrays the true nature of the dream. Thus the real dream forming mechanisms, the unconscious thoughts of the dreamer, can only be disclosed by psycho-analysis because a dream may express, as it so frequently does, painful or repressed thoughts, which are sent in disguised and unrecognized form into the consciousness of the sleeper. Because of this disguise the underlying dream thoughts are unrecognized and do not disturb the dreamer, and thus the dream becomes really the protector and not the disturber of sleep. This is due to the action of what is termed the censorship of consciousness which acts on the unconscious thoughts, and forces them, for the protection of the sleeper, to adopt a distorted or symbolized form.

The mechanisms by which the manifest content of the dream is developed for the underlying (unconscious) dream thoughts for the purpose of disguise and symbolization, may be grouped under four headings, viz.—condensation, displacement, dramatization, and secondary elaboration.

A dream is brief, even its elements are brief and certain figures of a dream may be fused together, like the faces in a composite photograph. Sometimes this fusion is very elaborate and hence, when the figure is analyzed, one finds that it represents an entire series of underlying thoughts. For instance, a subject dreamed that he was walking in a public square with a girl whom he failed to recognize. Analysis of the girl in the dream, showed her to be a condensation or a blending of several male and female friends—namely:—

1. The subject's fiancée.
2. A recent female acquaintance.
3. One of his boy friends whom he had not seen for years.
4. A photograph of an actress whom he had recently seen.

Therefore, this fragmentary dream condensed or blended a number of the subjects, thoughts, and mental processes. For instance, a dream itself may occupy merely a couple of lines or half a page, while the analysis may take several or even a dozen pages, so marked does the condensation frequently become. In addition this condensation is also shown in that the dream which we remember on awakening may represent only a remnant of the total dream. Sometimes the condensation may express a profound wish of the subject or again, it may be a pun. This condensation of several subjects shows that the dream is over-determined, —in other words one figure or word in a dream may denote a manifold representation of the dream thoughts. A rather pretty example is the following dream. The dreamer seemed to see a new book upon the table with the title "Bragmatism" and under it, the name of a friend who was the author of the book. Analysis of this dream showed the following. The friend had planned to write a book on "Pragmatism" and had frequently spoken of the book at length. Thus the title on the book was obviously a condensation of two words "Brag" and "Pragmatism," which by a process of displacement of the letter P, by the letter B, had been transformed and expressed the attitude of the author of the projected book. Condensation, therefore, is a mechanism by which similarity or identity between several elements in the latent content of the dream, finds its expression in the manifest content, probably for the purpose of evading the censor. Thus in this dream, we see the same mechanism at work as Freud postulated in his theory of wit—namely a condensation leading to a play upon words.

The second distorting mechanism is termed displacement. Condensation and displacement are the two principal distorting mechanisms taking place in dreams in the passage from the latent to the manifest content. Dream displacement is one of the chief means for producing disfigurement of a dream. Displacement changes important unconscious thoughts or wishes to something insignificant, conceals the reasons of the dream and this tends to render more unrecognizable the connection between dream content and dream thoughts. The changing of the letter P to B in the dream analyzed above, is a pretty example of displacement as well as of condensation. In certain dreams showing the Œdipus-complex, the figure of the parent is sometimes displaced by an indifferent individual due to the action of the censor. When Alice in "Alice in Wonderland" refers to studying "mystery" and "seaography," we have again an example of dream displacement.

The third mechanism of dream distortion, termed dramatization, is the process by which the dream thoughts assume a dramatic form, in other words, in a dream, past, present, and even future wishes may be unrolled in a most dramatic manner.

The fourth mechanism, termed secondary elaboration, arises more from the unconscious mental processes than from the underlying dream thoughts. It tries to make sense and connection out of the dream or it may make a concession to conscious thinking. This concession to conscious thinking is often seen in a dream within a dream, as when the dreamer says to himself, "Why, it is all a dream." The best examples of this are seen in so-called self-interpreted dreams. For instance, in one case, a patient dreamed that he took a certain dream to me and I analyzed it (all in the dream). It so turned out, that the analysis given in the dream was the one which the patient himself desired, in other words, the wish of the dreamer was completely fulfilled.

Thus a dream is a many-sided and complex conscious and unconscious process. Not only do these mental processes take part in the elaboration of a dream, but external stimuli during the night (such as pressure of the bedclothes or the exposure of certain portions of the body) and recent, even insignificant episodes and conversations enter into and are woven into the dream. Likewise in many dreams an analysis will disclose many of the remote happenings, mental conflicts, and wishes of early childhood. The transformation of all these adult and infantile unconscious thoughts into the dream, combined with the conscious thoughts and external stimuli, the so-called process of dream-making, is a complex mental process and not a mere physiological automatism. The entire psychical complex may thus be reconstructed through the data furnished by the psychoanalysis of dreams and all its apparently heterogeneous phenomena thus fall into certain law and order. It is here that the validity of determinism comes in, as demonstrating that a dream, like an hysterical symptom, is not a chance phenomenon, but is conditioned or made by a group of psychical and physical stimuli, often unknown to the subject. Thus a dream represents processes of great psychical significance to the subject, for within the dream itself as remembered there is hidden the latent dream material, which may be roused to activity through various stimuli.

We now come to the central point of Freud's theory, the point which has aroused the greatest amount of discussion and antagonism, namely, that the dream represents the fulfillment of a wish. This wish may be very clear in children's dreams, since children are not actuated by severe mental conflicts and have no desire, from moral or ethical standpoints or for social conventionalities, to hide the wish elements in their dreams. In their waking moments likewise, children do not attempt to hide or symbolize their thoughts and therefore their language and actions, like their dreams, is free from disguise. For instance, a little girl who was living under conditions of poverty, dreamed one night of having a magnificent dining-room in her home and the dining-table was filled with dishes of fine china loaded with eatables. Here the wish element was clear and undisguised. It is for this reason that fairy-tales appeal to children, for the child's imagination is essentially and pre-eminently a wish-imagination and the child's wishes are fulfilled by the fantasy of the tales. In fact the central content of most fairy-tales (for instance the tale of Aladdin and the wonderful lamp or the fairy godmother in Cinderella) are wishes and subserve the purpose of fulfilling the child's imagination. Primitive races are essentially like children in this respect.

In adult dreams the wish fulfillment of the dream forms its central nucleus, provided the dream be sufficiently analyzed or the resistance of the subject is such that an analysis can be carried out. In fact, the wish in adult dreams is hidden within the manifest content of the dream. The wish in adults may be a recent one or may extend far back to the earliest years of childhood, such as the dreams of nakedness or those of the death of near or dear relatives. It is not necessary that the wish be present now, it is sufficient if it existed, even temporarily, at some remotely early period of the individual's life. For this reason a dream is often referred to as a child slumbering in the adult unconscious. Stammerers, for instance, will often dream of talking freely in company or making speeches. In another case, the subject had recently read a newspaper account of how a certain acquaintance had married his wife's nurse, the wife having died about a year previously. The news awakened an emotion of disgust in her and that night she dreamed that the wife was alive and well and that she no longer needed the services of this particular nurse. This is an example of a pure wish dream, although that wish was at no time in the consciousness of the dreamer, yet it existed in her unconscious thoughts and fulfilled itself in the dream.

Mercutio's Queen Mab speech in Romeo and Juliet, is a beautiful example of a poet's insight into the wish mechanism of dreams. The parson, the soldier, the lover, fulfills in his dreams the wish fantasies of his waking life. The instigator of each dream is individual and is transformed by the sleeper into his characteristic dream wish.

" In this state she gallops night by night
Through lovers' brains, and then they dream of love;
O'er courtiers' knees, that dream on court'sies straight;
O'er lawyers' fingers, who straight dream on fees;
O'er ladies' lips, who straight on kisses dream,
Which oft the angry Mab with blisters plagues
Because their breaths with sweetmeats tainted are:
Sometime she gallops o'er a courtier's nose,
And then dreams he of smelling out a suit;
And sometime comes she with a tithe-pig's tail
Tickling a parson's nose as 'a lies asleep,
Then dreams he of another benefice:
Sometime she driveth o'er a soldier's neck,
And then dreams he of cutting foreign throats,
Of breaches, ambuscadoes, Spanish blades,
Of healths five fathom deep: and then anon
Drums in his ear, at which he starts and wakes,
And, being thus frighted, swears a prayer or two,
And sleeps again."

(Romeo and Juliet—Act I., Scene IV.)

A patient suffering from an anxiety neurosis who came under my treatment, had one night the following fragmentary dream.[1]

[1] For obvious reasons in none of the dreams analyzed in this chapter, can the various steps of the psycho-analytic technique be given.

Dream—He seemed to be losing his hair and becoming very bald and he was attempting to overcome this baldness by the use of a hair tonic.

Analysis—In the dream, he was greatly disturbed emotionally over the loss of the hair, because he felt that this would make a marked change in his appearance. It could be shown, however, after the analysis had been carried further, that this emotional reaction in the dream was all out of proportion to the idea of baldness, in other words, it was overdetermined. The patient was a sufferer from a severe anxiety neurosis and the nervous disturbance was associated in his mind, because of the symptoms of fear characteristic of his disease, with physical weakness. Growing old likewise meant to him increasing physical infirmity and baldness and therefore the baldness in the dream symbolized this physical infirmity. The tonic in the dream was an attempt to grow the hair (in other words to strengthen that which symbolized physical infirmity and weakness). The dream, therefore, represents a concealed wish for retaining his physical power and was symbolized by the manifest content of a fear of change in his personal appearance. The latent content of the dream, however, was a wish to retain his physical strength, and in the dream there was an attempt to fulfill this wish.

One thing is noticeable in this dream analysis, namely, the resemblance of the dream to the Samson legend. Thus the symbolism of both myths and dreams has its roots in the unconscious, in one case that of the individual, in the other in the fantasies of the race. Samson loses his strength when he loses his hair; the same symbolism is found in the above dream.

The fact that the wish mechanism is the chief function of the unconscious, has, as previously stated, aroused a storm of protest. But we must remember that one of the most important elements of our mental functioning is ambition or desire, which we gratify in two different ways, either fulfilling it in reality, which is the most difficult, or gratifying it in fancies or reveries. Thus the basis of all fantasy, of all reality, is to achieve a certain end, in other words, a desire or a wish. Therefore, the Freudian term of "wish," like the term "sex," is used in a broad sense, as denoting all kinds of desires, strivings, and ambitions. If the wish is repressed and cannot be fulfilled in reality, it may break out as an hysterical symptom, which is often merely a symbolized wish fulfillment. A wish, conscious or unconscious, which cannot be fulfilled in life because of social conventionalities or ethical or moral considerations, may often appear as fulfilled in a dream.

Thus the basic characteristic of a dream, when one succeeds in penetrating through psychoanalysis from the manifest content to the latent dream thoughts, is a wish fulfillment, in many cases an erotic wish fulfillment which has undergone suppression from childhood. This is what is meant when it is stated that the wish need not be at present in the consciousness of the dreamer, but may have existed in early childhood and, either from ethical or moral or religious considerations, have undergone a suppression in the unconscious. Now the inhibitory process by which certain wishes and desires are kept in the unconscious and prevented from reaching consciousness, is termed the censorship, and to the mechanism itself the term " censor of consciousness " has been applied. In dreams, the unconscious thoughts either partially or completely escape this censorship, if the former, the manifest content of the dream becomes disguised and highly symbolized, if the latter, the dream may be literal, painful, and even wake the sleeper through the anxiety and fear which develop. Thus the censor protects sleep, by making the latent thoughts of the dreamer unrecognizable.

Dreams may originate from emotions which are common to both individuals and mankind. This gives rise to so-called " typical " dreams which are composed of wishes common to all men and it is these wishes which form the basis of myths and sagas. The typical dream is frequently an infantile reminiscence, such as the dream of nakedness or the dream of the death of a near and dear relative, usually a parent. The typical dream, then, contains wishes which our waking consciousness will not admit. Concerning the development of typical dreams and their psycho-analytic interpretation, Abraham makes the following statement:[1]

"The child, up to a certain age, is free from altruistic feelings. He lives in a naïve egoism. It is throughout erroneous to assume that the feeling of a child for its parents and brothers and sisters is from the beginning a feeling of affection. On the contrary there exists instead among the children a certain rivalry. When a second child is born the first, who had been an only child up to that time, clearly shows jealousy on account of the attention paid to it because of its helplessness. It is quite usual that a child will not give the bottle of milk to the younger, that its jealousy is stirred up when it sees the newcomer sitting on its mother's lap, which was formerly only its place. It envies it its playthings, it emphasizes its own

[1] K. Abraham: "Dreams and Myths"—New York, 1910. (Translated by Wm. A. White.)

superiority when it speaks of the younger one to adults. The younger child reacts, as soon as it is in a position to, in just such an egoistic manner. It sees in the elder an oppressor and seeks to help itself as well as its weakness makes possible. Under normal conditions these contrasts gradually disappear to a great extent. They are never wholly rooted out in spite of all educational measures.

"This hostile attitude of one child toward the other finds its expression in the wish that the other were dead. Naturally it will be disputed that a child can be so "bad" as to wish the other dead. Who says that does not consider that the idea of the child of "death" has little in common with ours except the word (Freud). The child has no clear idea of the death of a person. It hears, perhaps, that this or that relative has died, is dead. For the child that only means: that person is no longer there. Daily experience teaches us how easily the child gets over the absence of a loved person. It perhaps stretches the hand forth in the direction in which the mother has gone, it cries a little while—then consoles itself with games or food and no longer recalls spontaneously the going away. Older children of normal psychic constitution also get over separation easily. In early years the child identifies death with absence. It cannot represent to itself that anyone, of whose death it has been told, will never again return. We understand now how a child in all harmlessness wishes the death of the other (or any other person). It is its rivalry: were it not so, then the occasion for rivalry and jealousy would be removed. . . .

" New opposition arises when we consider the relation of the child to the parents from the above viewpoint. How can one assume that the child wishes the death of the father or the mother? One will at most grant that in such cases as the abuse of the child by the parents, but will add that these are fortunately exceptional cases to which the generalization is not applicable.

" The dream of the death of the mother or the father, as it occurs to everyone, contains the sought-for explanation. Freud shows from it that the dream of the death of parents is preponderatingly common concerning that one of the pair of the same sex as the dreamer, so the son, for the most part dreams of the death of the father, the daughter of the death of the mother. This behavior is explained in part as due to an early sexual preference of the son for the mother, the daughter for the father. Out of this preference grows a certain rivalry of the son with the father for the love of the mother and a similar situation between daughter and mother for the love of the father. The son rebels earlier or later against the *patria potestas,* in some cases openly, in others inwardly. At the same time the father protects his dominance against the growing son. A similar relation occurs between mother and daughter. As much as culture may soften and change this rivalry, through piety towards the parents, through love of the children, still its traces cannot be extinguished. In the most favorable cases these tendencies become repressed in the unconscious. Straightway they express themselves in dreams. Children who are disposed to nervous or psychic disease, show already in the early years a very strong love or a very strong repulsion towards the parents or towards one of them. In their dreams they show these tendencies especially clearly, not less clearly, however, in the symptoms of their later disease. Freud gives very instructive examples of this kind. He cites, among others, the case of a mentally ill girl, who for the first time, in a period of confusion, expressed violent aversion for her mother. As the patient became clearer she dreamt of the death of her mother. Finally she no longer contented herself with repressing in the unconscious her feelings against her mother, but proceeded to over-compensate for that feeling by constructing a phobia, that is a morbid fear, that something might happen to the mother. The aversion became transposed, the more the patient gained composure, into an excessive apprehension about her mother's goings and comings.

"The typical dream then contains wishes which we in our waking life will not admit. In the dream life these secret wishes find expression. These wishes, common to many or to all mankind, we meet also in the myths. The first point of comparison to occupy us is, then, the common content of certain dreams and myths. We must follow Freud's lead still further. For, as mentioned, he has first analyzed a particular myth—the Œdipus saga—from the viewpoint set forth in his 'Traumdeutung.' I cite literally the following passage from Freud.

"'Œdipus, son of Laius, King of Thebes, and Jocasta, was, as a suckling, exposed, because an oracle had prophesied to the father, that the yet unborn son would be his murderer. He was saved and grew up as a king's son in a strange court, until he, uncertain of his origin, questioned the oracle himself and received from it the advice, to avoid his home, because he would be the murderer of his father and the mate of his mother. On the way from his supposed home he fell in with King Laius and slew him in a quickly stirred dispute. Then he arrived before Thebes, where he solved the riddle of the sphinx that blocked the way, and as reward was chosen king by the Thebans and given Jocasta's hand in marriage. He reigned a long time in peace and honor and begot, with his unknown mother, two sons and two daughters, until a pestilence broke out, which caused the Thebans again to consult the oracle. Here is the material of the tragedy of Sophocles. The messengers brought the answer that the plague would cease when the murderer of Laius was driven from the land. The action of the story now consists only in the step-by-step, gradual and skillfully delayed unfolding—like the work of a psycho-analysis—of the fact that Œdipus himself was the murderer of Laius and also the son of the murdered King and Jocasta.'

"The Œdipus tragedy can affect us to-day as deeply as at the time of Sophocles, although we do not share the views of gods and fate, and the belief in sayings of the oracle. Freud concludes from this correctly that the fable must contain something that calls out in us all related feelings. For us all, perhaps, was it decreed to direct the first sexual feeling to the mother, the first hate and violent wish against the father; our dreams convict us of that. In the Œdipus tragedy we see our childhood wish fulfilled, while we ourselves have recovered from the sexual attraction of the mother and the aversion against the father in the course of our development through feelings of love and piety."

Thus because of its relation to the Œdipus myth, these types of dreams are termed the Œdipus-complex dreams. In a psycho-analytic investigation of the subject I made the following statement concerning these dreams:[1] "The complex develops only in those children who have been exposed to an over-exuberant love from the parents or who themselves have shown a parental affection of abnormal intensity. In these cases the later development of the psychoneurosis may be interpreted as the successful revenge of the nervous system upon this Œdipus-complex." I have been able to study a number of cases containing this complex and from one of these the following dream analysis may be quoted as sufficiently indicating the type of material.

Dream—He seemed to be carrying the dead body of his father and placing it on a shelf. His sorrow did not appear to be very deep,

[1] Isador H. Coriat: "The Œdipus-Complex in the Psychoneuroses."—*Journal of Abnormal Psychology,* Vol. VII, No. 3.

although his mother, who was present, seemed greatly grieved. He attempted to pronounce the burial service over his father's body, but could not seem to remember it and later, when he attempted to extemporize such a service, he likewise failed.

Analysis—The dreamer was an only child. Early in childhood, because his father once returned home intoxicated so great was the emotional shock that there had developed a gradually increasing hatred of his father and, as a result, he attempted to avoid him and blot him out of his life. In consequence the love for his mother grew greater and greater. He never wished for a brother or a sister, because, after the above mentioned episode with his father, he became very jealous and afraid that the appearance of another child in the family might deprive him completely of his mother's affection. (Children often make a threat of "killing" a new brother or sister.) For years during his childhood, he secretly wished for his father's death.[1] Although he strongly repressed this wish, yet whenever his father became ill, there arose a secret joy in the thought that perhaps he might not recover from his illness. The fact

[1] It is interesting to note, that in one patient, a psycho-analysis showed that his idea of death in early childhood meant "merely an absence after a funeral."

that he could not remember a word of the burial service in the dream whereas he could partially repeat it when awake, is an interesting example of censorship, namely, he could not remember it because he did not wish to remember it. Even before the mentioned episode, he never was over affectionate towards his father, although he never had a feeling of hostility. This he explained as arising from the fact that his father paid but little attention to him and never fondled or played with him when he was a child. There were times when his mother's attention to his father made him intensely jealous, and therefore, in his childish manner, he often thought that if his father were dead (the term death really meant to him that his father be removed, no longer in the family), the source of jealousy would be removed. Thus we see, in this dream, how a childish egotism and selfishness culminated in a childish wish. The wish, however, persisted in consciousness only during the earliest years of childhood and later, because it was incompatible with his conscious thoughts, it became repressed in the unconscious. However, the wish was never completely blotted out, for in sleep, the unconscious, yet at the same time active wish was sent into the consciousness of the sleeper in a disguised form and appeared fulfilled in a dream. Of course consciously, the subject would emphatically deny that in adult life he even entertained such a wish, in fact, he would not admit it, but a psycho-analysis of the dream proved that the wish at one time existed in childhood and was suppressed in the unconscious. Since his father was alive at the time of the dream, the fulfillment was merely a fulfillment of his childish fantasies.

Sometimes, too, a childish reminiscence or wish, if the censor allow it to pass into consciousness without distortion, becomes startlingly literal and civil, the dream then becomes hypermnesic and portrays in its naked truth the happenings of childhood. These hypermnesic dreams are free from any symbolism or distortion, in fact they are mere fragmentary memories of early childhood life produced in a most literal manner, resembling in vividness and fragmentary character my results on the experimental synthesis of lost memories in the functional amnesias. In both the dream and the experiment, the revived memories are recognized as portions of a personal experience, and in fact under these conditions, the memories are more vivid than can be voluntarily recalled or visualized under normal conditions.[1] This is

[1] See particularly my paper, "A Contribution to the Psychopathology of Hysteria,"—*Journal Abnormal Psychology,* Vol. VI, No. 1, 1911, for examples of this type of dreams.

uncommon, however, because the dream usually makes use of symbolisms to express its varied wishes.

The dream of nakedness too or of being insufficiently clothed in the presence of others, a type of dream which is so frequently experienced by normal adults, free from nervous disease, is also a childhood reminiscence dream dating from a period when the sense of shame was lacking. Freud states as follows concerning this type of dream—"This age of childhood in which the sense of shame is lacking seems to our later recollections a Paradise, and Paradise itself is nothing but a composite fantasy from the childhood of the individual. Into this Paradise the dream can take us back every night; we have already ventured the conjecture that the impressions from earliest childhood in themselves, and independently of everything else, crave reproduction, perhaps without further reference to their content, and that the repetition of them is the fulfillment of the wish."

Such data and investigations as these naturally bring us face to face with Freud's unique conceptions of the mental life of the child, particularly its psycho-sexual manifestations and the relation of these manifestations to the neuroses. Without going into details, as these must be sought for in special treatises, it suffices to state that through the data secured by psycho-analysis it can be shown that the sexual instinct long antedates puberty, and in fact may make its appearance in the earliest years of childhood. The child is not sexually neutral. As Freud so clearly expresses it—" It is not at all true that the sexual impulse enters into the child at puberty as the devils in the Gospel entered into the swine. The child has his sexual impulses and activities from the beginning, he brings them with him into the world, and from these the normal so-called sexuality of adults emerges by a significant development through manifold stages. It is not very difficult to observe the expressions of this childish sexual activity, it needs rather a certain art to overlook them or fail to interpret them." However, without entering into details, it may be stated that " sexual " in the Freudian sense, has a different connotation from the function of reproduction and is given merely to the different kinds of pleasure—sensations of the child which by imperceptible gradations pass into the sexuality of puberty and adult life.

In very young children, the sexual instinct is not, as in adults, directed towards other persons, but to the child's own body. This condition is called " auto-erotism " by Havelock Ellis. The remains of this auto-erotism may often be found in the psycho-neuroses of adults. In the unconscious mental life of all neurotics there may often be found, to a greater or less degree, perversions of the sexual instinct brought over from childhood, and neurotics often maintain their infantile or childhood attitude towards sexuality. In early childhood too, the sexual impulse may become accidentally side-tracked and attach itself to objects or actions, thus giving rise to the various sexual perversions, fetichism and symbolism. The emotion of love may be experienced long before puberty, although at a very early age the child is primarily auto-erotic and incapable of sexual choice. In cases published by Freud and Jung and also in some personal psycho-analytic investigations, it has been possible to trace the sexual emotions to the very earliest period of childhood. Unsuccessful struggle with the childhood sexual complexes, often leads to a neurosis in the adult. The theme of sexuality in dreams is often expressed in a symbolic manner, because the sexual instinct is so powerfully repressed. In fact, whole lists of phallic symbols have been worked out through psycho-analysis.

To summarize briefly, a dream is the fulfillment of unconscious repressed wishes and uses as material, either childhood episodes, adult happenings, various physical stimuli, or pre-sleeping thoughts, all of which are woven into the complex phantasmagoria of the dream. The latent thoughts alone explain the dream and this explanation can only be investigated through the special technique of psycho-analysis.

CHAPTER VIII

HYPNOSIS

WE will now take up the discussion of perhaps the most important artificially induced mental condition, namely, hypnosis. As a complete understanding of the subject can only be obtained by an insight into other related conditions we will turn very briefly to certain closely allied states, such as normal absent-mindedness, conditions of experimental distraction, and the hypnagogic state.

Hypnotism was made use of by the Egyptian priests, in the Middle Ages it became bound up by certain occult doctrines, and even to-day in India the mystic fakirs openly exhibit hypnotic phenomena in public. But it was only toward the end of the eighteenth century that the scientific world began to take hypnotism seriously. Finally through the work of a group of French investigators the phenomena of hypnosis were stripped of occultism and mysticism and became a well-recognized scientific procedure.

The theories of hypnosis have been many, and like sleep it has had its biological, physiological, and psychological interpretations. Even to-day, in spite of the immense amount of work which has been done on the subject, there is no agreement as to its exact nature, although all agree as to its multiform manifestations. It is not our purpose to go into the history of hypnosis, but rather to discuss the nature of the brain state involved in the phenomenon. We will take up very briefly the most prominent theories which have been propounded to explain the condition, and finally discuss some of the very recent investigations. Before we examine hypnosis in man it will be best to show how certain allied conditions may be found in animals and trace their evolution upwards in the same manner in which we traced the evolution of sleep.

The physiologist Max Verworn has given us very interesting descriptions of hypnosis in animals and has illustrated it by some rather striking photographs. He says, " It may suffice to recall a few well-known phenomena. The ancient experiments of the Egyptian snake charmers, which Moses and Aaron performed before the Egyptian Pharaoh more than three thousand years ago, belong to this category [*i.e.,* hypnosis in animals]. By slight pressure in the neck region, it is possible to make a wildly excited, hissing, erect asp [hooded snake] suddenly motionless, so that the dangerous creature can be put into any desired position without fear of its fatal bite. The well-known experiment of Father Kircher depends upon same causes. If an excited fowl be seized suddenly with a firm grip and laid carefully upon its back, after a few brief attempts to escape it lies motionless. Guinea pigs, rabbits, frogs, lizards, crabs, and numerous other animals behave similarly." According to Verworn, the hypnosis of human beings depends upon the same physiological mechanism, that is, an inhibition of the will.[1]

Forel, as the result of his extensive investigations in comparative psychology, particularly on the nervous reactions of ants, concludes that a number of symptoms of human hypnosis may occur in animals, not only muscular rigidity but also extreme anæsthesia. He describes the hypnosis of animals as due not to fear nor to the abnormal position in which one places the animal, but to a simplified, more automatic suggestion mechanism, which mechanism can be induced at times by fixation of the look or of the body. He claims that the lethargic sleeping condition of the dormouse and some other animals is due to a simple physiological cataleptic

[1] Max Verworn: "General Physiology, An Outline of the Science of Life."

state, which is induced by the action of suggestion, adapted to a definite purpose and inserted in the linkings of instinct.[1] Whether these experiments in animals are genuine hypnosis or mere muscular rigidity, is difficult to determine. Suggestibility increased over the normal is the most prominent manifestation of the hypnotic state, but whether this increased suggestibility occurs in animals, it is impossible to tell. Recently Claparède has been able to induce hypnosis with catalepsy in a monkey.

My personal experiments in the induction of hypnotic states in animals (crayfish, frogs, and guinea pigs) have already been given in the chapter on sleep. The condition was there interpreted as due to a cerebral inhibition, an hypothesis has also been put forth to explain hypnotic states in man.

The evolution of hypnosis offers a fascinating field for speculation and many of the same evolutionary principles can be applied to hypnosis as to sleep. Many animals seem to furnish examples of spontaneous hypnotic states, for instance the simulation of death, or still better, the fascination of birds by snakes, which seems to be a kind of hypnosis with catalepsy. Certain animals show motionless states in reaction to

[1] August Forel: "Hypnotism and Psychotherapy," 1907. (See particularly Chapter XIV.)

fear. While motionless states of the nature of genuine hypnosis or cerebral inhibition may be artificially produced in certain animals, yet probably in the evolutionary scale, such states were made possible of artificial production because spontaneously the normal defence reactions of these animals showed similar phenomena. If we assume that these motionless states arose in animals out of stationary reactions while waiting for their prey or for purposes of defence, we must also assume that this was an intelligent experiment on the part of the animal. Thus hypnosis had probably a biological origin like sleep, but since the former was unnecessary for the preservation of the species, it became only incompletely developed spontaneously and could only be artificially produced. Even then it did not appear until the animal began to show intelligent reactions, a defence or instinctive reaction on one hand and a hunger reaction on the other. These reactions, however, while of great value, did not have the biological importance of sleep, namely, a repair of nervous tissue, and therefore they did not become, like sleep, automatic and spontaneous.

Like sleep, hypnosis has had many theories offered for its explanation. The older ideas of Mesmer that the hypnotic state was due to a special magnetic fluid, and of Braid that it was caused through exhaustion by over-stimulation of the special senses, particularly sight, need only to be mentioned as matters of historical interest. Charcot, who brought his keen insight to the analysis of hypnosis as well as of hysteria, believed that the hypnotic state was nothing more than an artificial or an experimental nervous condition; a neurosis brought on by some technical device and closely allied to hysteria. This view, that hypnosis is nothing but artificial hysteria, has been insisted upon by other members of the modern French school and also in a modified form by Freud. According to this school hypnosis can be sharply divided into three distinct states: namely, the lethargic, the cataleptic, and the somnambulistic. That this division is a purely artificial one, and that subjects of hypnosis may or may not show any of the phenomena included in these states, we hope to demonstrate later.

According to Bernheim and the Nancy school hypnosis is nothing but a special form of sleep induced by suggestion. There is no relation between hysteria and hypnosis. There are different depths of hypnosis in the same manner that there are different depths of sleep, a view which is also held by Forel. Bechterew also claims that hypnosis is a special modification of normal sleep, but his theory differs from that of Bernheim in claiming that the hypnotic state can be induced by physical as well as by psychical means, without any element of suggestion.

The histological theories have been applied in the attempts to explain hypnosis in the same manner in which they have been applied to natural sleep. This theory states that hypnosis is due to the amœboid motions which are supposed, without any adequate basis, to be possessed by the nerve cells, at least by the nerve cells of the vertebrates, since it seems that in them alone hypnosis can be induced by various means. According to this theory, any obstruction, or interruption of the nerve current, due to a shrinking of the protoplasmic processes of the nerve cells, causes certain disturbances of consciousness, such as drowsiness, natural sleep, or hypnosis. The weak point in this rather fanciful theory has been the inability to demonstrate any such shrinking of the nerve processes or at least it has been demonstrated only in some of the very lowest organisms, in which it has not been possible to experimentally produce hypnotic phenomena and in which natural sleep seems likewise absent.

Disturbances of circulation have also been utilized to explain hypnosis, in the same manner as it was attempted to explain sleep. Since it is well known that anæmia or a lack of blood in the brain may cause a state of drowsiness, this anæmia of the brain has also been utilized to explain the hypnotic state. The weak point in all these theories, it appears, is the *a priori* assumption that hypnosis is either sleep or a special modification of sleep. We shall later attempt to show that hypnosis can only be adequately explained when we demonstrate analogous phenomena in a non-hypnotic state, and that these phenomena are not found in normal sleep or at least to a less extent than they are found in some phases of sleep or in normal absent-mindedness. Investigation of the blood vessels of the retina has shown no diminution in the size of the vessels during hypnosis. Besides, hypnosis can be induced after the inhalation of nitrite of amyl, a drug which causes dilatation of the blood vessels and, therefore, hyperæmia and not anæmia of the brain. Preyer postulates a chemical theory for hypnosis, claiming that the fixed attention which seems to be necessary for the inducing of the hypnotic state causes a rapid accumulation of waste products in the brain and this accumulation brings about a partial loss of activity of the cerebral cortex.

A satisfactory theory of hypnosis, then, must furnish an answer to several questions, viz.:—

1. What is the condition of the nervous system during hypnosis?

2. What is the relation between this condition and the various symptoms of hypnosis?

3. Is there any relation between the nervous system in hypnosis and the means used to induce hypnosis?

According to Claparède,[1] who has attempted to answer these questions on the basis of an extensive investigation, hypnosis is a selective form of inhibition, limited to one function, that of the initiative. By the suspension of this latter function, can be explained the increased suggestibility of the hypnotic state.

Thus the four most important symptoms of hypnosis are, loss of initiative, loss of memory, increased suggestibility, and the rapport, or state of dependence between subject and operator. The brain state which produces this condition has been the subject of much speculation, into the details of which we cannot enter here. The most prominent phenomenon of rapport on which all hypnosibility seems to depend has been explained by recent psycho-analytic investigations (Ferenczi) as due to the persistence of certain childhood complexes in the relation of the child to its parents. Thus according to the psycho-analytic theory suggestion in hypnosis

[1] E. Claparède—"Archives de Psychologie," July, 1909.

depends upon the transference of certain unconscious emotional processes in the subject's mind, usually of a psycho-sexual nature.

It seems to us that the crux of the whole question is the attempt to identify hypnosis either with sleep or as a special modification of sleep. It is true that to a limited extent hypnosis outwardly resembles normal sleep. The hypnotic state can be brought about by the same influence and conditions as produce sleep, such as withdrawal of all strong stimuli, restful position, monotonous gentle stimulation of one or more of the special sense organs, expectation, habit, banishment of certain thoughts, and the concentrating of attention on some unexciting object or sense impression. In hypnosis and likewise in sleep the subject is inert and passive. Catalepsy may occur in normal sleep as well as in the hypnotic state; in both these states the subject frequently desires to move his limbs, but is incapable of doing so. As was previously pointed out, however, this inability to move the limbs occurs only in the semi-drowsy hypnagogic state, and never in deep sleep, for in the latter condition there is complete relaxation of all muscles. This peculiar condition, which I called nocturnal paralysis, sometimes occurs also as a temporary phenomenon, when a subject is suddenly awakened from deep hypnosis. Suggestibility, however, and the presence of reactions to suggestion is absent in deep sleep but is present even in the deepest hypnosis. Unconscious reflexes without mental action, such as the withdrawal of a limb when it is tickled or pinched, occur in sleep, but never in hypnosis. Suggestions given in sleep are never carried out when the subject is awakened. The motor disturbances of certain organic nervous diseases, such as the twitching of chorea, or the tremor of paralysis agitans, tend to cease in sleep but not in the deepest hypnosis. Furthermore, the light hypnotic states even outwardly do not resemble sleep; it is only in deep hypnosis that there is any such outward resemblance. In hypnosis the subject is in touch or in rapport with the operator, and consequently there results an automatic obedience or the carrying out of post-hypnotic suggestions, a thing which is impossible in sleep. Hypnosis is a mental state brought on through suggestion; sleep is a habit, a reaction of defence on the part of the organism against fatigue. The simple command of " wake " will bring a subject out of the deepest hypnosis, because this command acts as a negative suggestion. Ordinary noise will not awaken a deeply hypnotized subject. In sleep, however, any indifferent command or noise, if made sufficiently loud, will awaken the subject. The result bears no relation to the type of command, but must be a stimulus sufficiently intense to disturb the course of sleep, and is regulated only by the depth of the condition. All intercourse with the outside world is cut off during sleep with the exception that dreams, even of a very complex nature, may arise from peripheral stimuli. But even in the deepest hypnosis the subject maintains his relations to the world about him; the subject can be made to walk, talk, or go through all sorts of complex acts; suggestions may be given which will act automatically even after the hypnotic state has been terminated. The loss of voluntary movement in normal sleep is not subject to the will or suggestions of an outside experimenter. In deep sleep it is a question how much consciousness is active, for, as we have previously pointed out, it seems very likely that dreams are absent in deep sleep and take place only as the subject is on the road to awakening. In hypnosis, however, consciousness is exceedingly active, intelligent conversation may be carried on, and even hallucinations or illusions of the special senses may be brought about through suggestion. On termination of the hypnotic state known as awakening (a term probably derived from the fancied resemblance of hypnosis to sleep) there may be no memory for this particular localized period of active consciousness. That the memories are conserved, however, but merely dissociated, is shown by the fact that they may be reproduced or restored by other special devices, such as experimental distraction, crystal gazing, automatic writing, or in a subsequent state of hypnosis.

Experiences related in hypnosis for which the subject has no memory on awakening, may also cause certain physiological and psycho-physical reactions, such as changes in the pulse rate or in the electrical resistance of the body. Changes in the personality, temporary at least, have been found to take place in hypnosis, either spontaneously or through suggestion. It is true that some complex dreams of sleep may also involve transitory changes in the personality of the dreamer, but here the assumed personality is extremely vague, and it is very unlikely that the same change will occur in a subsequent dream, whereas the hypnotic personality tends to reproduce itself spontaneously in all later hypnotic states.

We see, therefore, that there is very little if any resemblance between normal sleep, or at least between the deeper grades of sleep, and hypnosis. There is, however, a portion of sleep which in many ways bears a striking resemblance to the artificial hypnotic states. As we fall asleep there is always an intermediate state which hovers between sleep and awakening. It is called the hypnagogic state. This hypnagogic state occurs as a transitory phenomenon in all individuals, but it becomes markedly protracted in those subjects of insomnia who complain of an absolute loss of sleep. This hypnagogic state takes place at both ends of sleep, when the subject is falling asleep and when sleep has been either artificially or spontaneously terminated. Consciousness in this state is either a little hazy or is completely retained. For instance, one of my subjects who was afflicted with nocturnal paralysis, was able to judge the length of time in which she was unable to move by gazing at a watch which hung over the foot of the bed. We have already pointed out how this condition of nocturnal paralysis may be observed in subjects who are gradually or suddenly awakened from a deep hypnosis as well as from natural sleep. Now the transition from waking to sleep or from sleep to waking is never sudden, but may be of varying duration, from a few seconds up to fifteen minutes. In both the spontaneous hypnagogic state and in artificial hypnosis there is increased suggestibility, a tendency to transitory paralysis, catalepsy of the limbs may appear, and even hallucinations may arise. In fact the post-hypnotic palsy which is sometimes observed is in every way identical with these conditions of transitory nocturnal paralysis. The phenomena in both cases appear after the hypnosis has been terminated by suggestion or after the subject awakens from sleep and is in a semi-drowsy hypnagogic state.

But the most striking presence of phenomena analogous to hypnosis is found in normal absent-mindedness. Now these absent-minded states have awakened a great deal of interest because they occur in everyday life and, therefore, can be easily studied, and because they seem to be the normal analogues to many pathological processes. But whether these absent-minded acts are mere accidental chance dissociations, or whether they are due to unconscious memories or the transformation of dormant complexes into co-conscious activity, or dormant physiological experiences which have become dissociated, is still a much discussed question. For each theory a certain amount of experimental evidence can be urged in support. Indeed, Freud claims that no absent-minded acts are due to chance or accident, but are directed by the automatic influence of unconscious or subconscious memories, usually of a painful character and which may be revealed by some form of psycho-analytic technic.

We saw in the first chapter how absent-mindedness is a state of increased suggestibility; in fact during this state absurd suggestions will be accepted by the subject, an acceptance from which the subject would revolt under normal conditions. In absent-mindedness there may be a decrease of motor control, the subject may stand still as if suddenly petrified, the same as in the ecstasy of hypnosis. Temporary losses of sensation may take place in the absent-mindedness so that a person may be pricked or pinched without apparently any sense of pain. The subject may be oblivious to his surroundings; a thoughtless "don't know" or "yes" or "no" may take place in reaction to questions, the meaning of which is not fully appreciated. In the large majority of cases there is a loss of memory for absent-minded acts. The absent-minded acts in these cases remain not only dormant but likewise dissociated. That they are conserved in the unconscious or subconscious is shown by the fact that a later reproduction of the act is possible through certain technical methods. This was well shown in a certain personal experience of the writer. One day I had occasion to refer to some notes which I had made in the course of preparation for a certain technical paper. Prolonged search failed to discover these notes, although I distinctly remembered having made them on a particular kind of blue paper. It then occurred to me that perhaps it would be interesting by means of crystal gazing to see if I could recover any trace of the lost notes. The result was peculiarly interesting and successful. I distinctly saw myself in the crystal, sitting at my desk, and caught myself in the act of tearing up these particular notes in connection with some other data which I had finished using, and throwing the torn pieces into the waste-paper basket. A search in the basket discovered the lost and torn notes, which I was able to piece together. Now the tearing of these notes was evidently an absent-minded act; and yet an act which was preserved in the unconscious and later fully reproduced through the technical device of crystal gazing.

In absent-mindedness, as well as in hypnosis, negative hallucinations may occur, such as in the frequent experiences of certain persons who cannot find objects which are immediately in front of their eyes. Now all absent-minded acts are temporary; absent-mindedness is a special condition of consciousness, for we do not habitually go about in an absent-minded state. All absent-minded acts seem to be spontaneously dissociated experiences. This is shown by the fact of increased suggestibility, of the possibility of the recovery of the memory of absent-minded phenomena, and of a lack of attention which the subject pays to painful stimuli. In fact this disregard for painful stimuli is a kind of a functional anæsthesia.

Dr. Prince also insists that absent-mindedness is a form of temporary dissociation. "The phenomena of absent-mindedness, or abstraction, a normal function, indicate both dissociation and automatism. It is not difficult to demonstrate experimentally that auditory, visual, tactile, and other images which are not perceived by the personal consciousness, during this state may be perceived subconsciously. Thus under proper precautions I place various objects where they will be within the peripheral field of vision of a suitable subject, C. B. Her attention is strongly attracted listening to a discourse. The objects are not perceived. She is now hypnotized and in hypnosis described accurately the objects, thus showing that they were seen subconsciously and producing subconscious states. Dissociation is plainly a function of the mind and brain."[1]

[1] Morton Prince: "Do Subconscious States Habitually Exist Normally, or Are They Always Either Artificial or Abnormal Phenomena?"—*The Psychological Review,* March-May, 1905.

It seems, therefore, that although hypnosis is *not* identical with sleep, yet it presents many points of similarity to a certain phase of sleep, namely, the hypnagogic stage. It bears the closest resemblance, however, to absent-mindedness. But unlike absent-mindedness hypnosis is a special condition, in that the former is a spontaneous phenomenon, while the latter must be artificially produced through suggestion. Most hypnotic states are merely conditions of more or less intense abstraction, in which the subject can either open his eyes with ease or with some difficulty, and in which memory is clearly retained. The deeper hypnotic states, with catalepsy, automatism, and amnesia, usually occur only in hysterics or in highly suggestible individuals. Absent-mindedness is a temporary dissociation and terminates suddenly whether we will or no, while hypnosis can be indefinitely protracted by the operator, until a suggestion is given to awaken. Hypnosis, therefore, seems to be a special mental state, an artificial dissociation of consciousness strongly resembling, and in some cases absolutely identical with, normal absent-mindedness, but more intense and protracted, induced by suggestion and readily terminated by suggestion.

All normal individuals are subject to temporary absent-minded states. This absent-minded state is really a mental dissociation and in it there is a temporary increased suggestibility. This suggestibility ceases, however, as soon as the condition has terminated. If some device could be arranged whereby this absent-minded state could be produced at will and terminated at will, we would then have an ideal soil on which ideas planted through suggestion could grow. Fortunately we have such artificial devices in the states of hypnosis, and in the conditions of experimental distraction. In both these artificial conditions the memory is broadened, the mind is more or less completely dissociated, and suggestions are uncritically accepted. But unfortunately we cannot keep a subject in one of these artificial conditions for an indefinite length of time. Here the most important principle of all comes to our aid. Briefly it is this. Suggestions given to a subject during either of these artificial states tend to remain in the subconscious, and to act themselves out independently after the artificial state has been terminated. It makes no difference whether the subject remembers the suggestion or whether he does not remember it, the effect is the same.

These two artificial devices have a certain range of therapeutic value. They can be used to correct or to cure abnormal sexual perversions, chronic alcoholism, obsessions, recurrent states of fear, abnormal shyness, and conditions of abnormal self-consciousness. Hysterical symptoms may be made to disappear, fixed ideas which interfere with the welfare of the physical organism may be overcome, and experiences which the subject cannot recall in his normal condition may be restored. However, in many of these conditions, only certain symptoms are removed by hypnotic suggestion: In the ultimate cure of the disorder—that is, a breaking down of unconscious emotional complexes—psycho-analysis must be utilized.

Hypnotic suggestion has secured some of its best results in chronic alcoholism. Here the negative suggestion against drink, combined with the positive suggestion of increased will power to resist the temptation, has often such a far-reaching effect that it might almost be said to reconstruct the personality. Sometimes insomnia may be due to a fixed idea on the part of the subject that he cannot sleep. This fixed idea may have had its origin in a sleepless night in the past, due to some indifferent experience. But after this experience the subject expects that he will again have a sleepless night, and little by little this fixed idea produces an actual insomnia. Now the obvious treatment of this condition would be to change this fixed idea through some form of psychotherapy. Sleep-producing drugs would be useless, as the subject would sleep only during the period of drug administration.

CHAPTER IX

ANALYSIS OF THE MENTAL LIFE

THE exploration of the subconscious in abnormal mental states has furnished data which are of great value for both diagnosis and treatment. This exploration, on the one hand, can bring to light the mechanism by which a pathological mental state has been produced, and on the other, furnish hints for psychotherapeutic procedures. It has been shown that certain abnormal mental states usually arise from an emotional shock. This may be either the slow accumulation of emotional experiences, or a rapid mental change after an emotional injury. The abnormal mental experience once started tends to recur or to reproduce itself automatically, particularly in states of fatigue or through association of ideas. An idea related to the original experience will often set going all the mental and physical phenomena which had occurred at the time of the original experience. This forms what is known as an association neurosis. In many of these functional cases, the mental injury, or so-called psychic trauma, is either consciously suppressed by the subject or the subject may be unable to recall voluntarily the original experience in memory. In the first case, we speak of the experience as suppressed or dormant; in the second, we say that the experience is subconscious or dissociated. Now these suppressed or subconscious experiences may do considerable harm, and bring about a severe pathological mental condition. Such experiences may cause hysteria, double or multiple personality, or they may give rise to peculiar convulsive attacks of a purely functional nature, simulating epilepsy (psycho-epileptic attacks). Therefore, it frequently becomes necessary that we have an account of the experience which we believe responsible for the observed pathological phenomena. Yet in many cases the subject is either unwilling to make a full confession and so suppresses the incidents, or he may be utterly unable to recall them because they are subconscious or dissociated. We then must have recourse to some technical procedure. These methods of tapping or exploring the subconscious mental life are known as psycho-analysis. These technical procedures are hypnosis, the states of abstraction, free association procedures, either voluntary or induced, crystal gazing, automatic writing, the word reaction (association) tests, the electrical phenomena (psycho-galvanic reaction), the changes in the pulse rate (psycho-cardiac reflex), and finally the analysis of the dream life. When one or several of these methods is successfully applied, we can often arrive at some definite result, such as a complete confession on the part of the subject, and thereby a breaking down of certain resistances, the synthesis of certain split portions of consciousness, the working out of certain suppressed feelings, and finally an insight into emotional experiences. When these experiences, whether dissociated or dormant, are brought into full consciousness, they lose their baneful influence because they cease to have any further independent activity. The resistance has been broken down. This is a long step toward the cure of the patient. If the experiences are dissociated and the cleavage between the conscious mental life and the subconscious experience can be permanently bridged (synthetized), here again the dissociated experience can be freed from any abnormal activity. In dormant experiences, a full confession, a talking out of all the details, also acts as a therapeutic measure, by relieving the subject of his secret.

These psycho-analytic methods require for their successful practice not only a technical knowledge of abnormal psychology, but presuppose a certain amount of personal skill on the part of the operator. They require time, patience and experience, and an ability to correctly interpret the conditions found. No fragment of memory, emotion, dream, or symptom can be ignored; we must follow the mental life of the subject through all the ramifications of the psycho-pathological maze. If the abnormal experiences have left sufficient traces on the nervous system, it ought to be possible to recover them through the various technical devices.

In order for any line of treatment to be successful, it is necessary that we have a clear understanding of the mental processes which underlie the diseased condition and of the patient's physical state. Unless we have these data at hand, no form of suggestion can be successful. Suggestion is unable to dogmatically assert that such or such symptom can disappear, neither can it blindly replace the normal for the abnormal.

The emotion aroused by a painful experience is accompanied by some bodily symptoms which are expressive of the mental aspect of the emotions. This emotion may then fade from the patient's consciousness, either because the patient voluntarily suppresses it or because it is incompatible, painful, out of harmony with his character. In some conditions, the subject remains utterly unable to recall the original experience, although the phenomena which accompanied the experience may persist and take on an automatic activity. Thus the physical expression of the emotional experience, whether a state of fear, a convulsion, or a disturbance of sensibility, continues to live in the consciousness of the patient. Now the mischief that has been caused by these experiences may be annulled if the emotions are allowed to work themselves out through a full confession. The casting out of these demons from consciousness is accomplished by what is known as the cathartic method. This cathartic method is nothing more or less than a full confession. Nothing is withheld, all the gaps in memory, all the painful emotions and associations, all the disagreeable feelings, the patient is urged to bring vividly before his mind and tell them. Whatever method is used in this procedure, whether hypnosis or abstraction, is merely a matter of technic, whose object is to extract, as it were, the mental thorn which is causing the mischief. The original emotional experience is thus sidetracked and for it there is substituted a healthier mental attitude. In other cases, if the experience is dissociated and not merely dormant, a procedure must be used to enable the subject to recall the experience in consciousness. This is called a synthesis of the dissociated mental state.

Freud, however, formerly claimed that the necessary condition for the use of his cathartic method was the hypnotizability of the patient, although in his later work he gave up hypnosis as a therapeutic procedure and used simple abstraction and free association. The method is based upon the broadening of consciousness that takes place during the hypnotic or the abstracted state. From the standpoint of treatment, the method aimed to remove the symptoms of the disease by making the patient return to the mental state or experience in which the symptoms manifested themselves for the first time. According to this theory, the patient must have been in a peculiar semi-waking (hypnoidal) state at the time of the original emotional experience, and it was this abnormal mental state which prevented a complete synthesis of the experience with consciousness. In the hypnotic state or in abstraction, memories, thoughts, and ideas emerge and, after these mental processes with their attached emotions have been communicated to the physician, the symptoms could be overcome and their recurrence prevented. Thus, when the psychic process that was causing the trouble reached consciousness, it became "converted." In other words, the hitherto pent-up emotions, which had become attached to certain experiences, were liberated.

In any psycho-analytic method, it can be noted that the patient naturally tends to repress what is painful due to what is termed resistance. Hence gaps in the memory arise, and it can be found that these gaps relate to experiences having a strong emotional meaning. By persistence, however, these gaps can be filled, and when once the emotional experience is "talked out," liberated, a sense of relief is experienced. No psycho-analytic method is as simple as it appears, because many of these abnormal mental conditions are caused, not by one, but by an entire series of emotional experiences. Until all of these are brought to consciousness, the analysis is not complete, neither is the cure permanently established. So we see that these psycho-analytic methods not only give us an insight into the abnormal mental life, but have a decided therapeutic value. These methods of psycho-analysis have their parallel in everyday life in perfectly normal individuals. We all feel better when we tell a secret to a friend. A sense of relief is experienced when one is depressed and gloomy and has the "cry out." Even suppressed laughter is painful if one is in a situation where laughter would be indiscreet or inadvisable. In spite of the stress laid by the various investigators upon hypnosis, abstraction, or automatic writing, these methods are mere technical devices. Any method which will enable one to reach suppressed experiences or to synthetize a detached state of consciousness, would be equally effective. Through the association tests, and by means of the psychogalvanic and pulse reactions, we can often trace the memory of an emotional experience.

It is to Professor Sigmund Freud of Vienna that we are indebted for the psycho-analytic methods in certain functional neuroses, particularly in hysteria. Professor Freud recently visited this country and gave an account of his theories at Clark University. Dr. Putnam has furnished us with an excellent description of the evolution of these psycho-analytic methods in Freud's mind.[1] He says:

" In brief, the history of Freud's investigations and opinions is the following: In 1881, an older colleague, Dr. J. Breuer, of Vienna, had occasion to treat an intelligent young woman suffering from hysteria in a serious form for which he tried the usual means in vain. At length, after a long and tireless searching, he found that the facts offered by the patient in explanation of her illness, although they were freely furnished and represented her entire history so far as she consciously could furnish it, constituted only a tithe

[1] J. J. Putnam: " Sigmund Freud and His Work."—*Journal Abnormal Psychology,* Vol. IV, No. 5-6.

of the story which, in the end, her memory succeeded in drawing from its depths. Under the influence of a special method of inquiry, many hidden facts, representing painful experiences long ago forgotten, came one by one to light and were as if lived over, attended by the emotions that originally formed a part of them. And just in proportion as this happened, in proportion as the dense barriers were overcome that separated this hidden portion of the patient's past from that of which she had remained consciously aware, one and another of her distressing symptoms dropped away and disappeared forever. The details of the long and significant history of this case cannot be given here. Let it suffice to say that although no further investigations based on it were undertaken for ten years, yet the facts observed had made a deep impression upon Dr. Freud and were meditated on by him during this decade, a part of which he passed as a student of Charcot's in Paris, and that on his return he begged Breuer to take the matter up again. After this, for a considerable length of time, they worked together; later Freud alone. It became gradually more and more clear to them that the childhood of this patient had been in an unsuspected degree and sense the parent of her later years. For not only had it been found that many of the events which counted for so much in the production of her illness dated back to days of early youth, but the later experiences which had come upon her, one after another, and which were the ostensible and apparently sufficient causes for her illness, were discovered to owe a large portion of their power for harm to the fact that they reproduced in a new shape old emotions of childish form and substance, of which, before her treatment, she would truthfully have professed herself to be entirely unaware. Only when these emotions were reached and the experiences corresponding to them lived over, in memory and in speech, was the recovery complete. . . . It became clear to Breuer and Freud, further, and in harmony with the principle just expressed, that this patient's painful memories of the past, which at first had seemed as dead to her as if the experiences which they stood for never had occurred, represented in reality living and acting forces. And not only this, but that the very barriers which had to be overcome in reproducing them represented living and active forces too, all vibrating with significance for the present moment and for the details of the illness. In other words, the term 'barrier' as used for the 'forgetting' of the hysterical patient, was shown to be a misnomer. Indeed, the forgetting of persons in normal health is largely repression, an active process of lending oneself to the task of learning how not to dwell upon a subject now painful but which perhaps had once a powerful interest. It has often been remarked that the conscious memory picks out the pleasant items of life and rejects the rest. We remember the charms and novelty of an ocean trip, of foreign travel, and conveniently 'forget'—in reality turn away from—the seasickness, the dirty inns, the sleepless nights. It was the significance of this species of forgetting and its relation to sickness and to health that Freud was led to study, and to which he has devoted all the powers of a keen and well-trained mind for twenty years. In the course of these investigations Freud and Jung and their followers have dived more deeply than any one before into the mysteries of the unconscious life. These investigations were inspired, primarily, not by theory but by the recitals of patients who had been helped to search out their memories and their motives to a degree that never before had been made possible. New evidence has thus been brought to show that this hidden life, if technically 'unconscious,' is anything but inactive. On the contrary, it is the living supplement of our conscious and willed existences, the dwelling-place and working-place of emotions which we could not utilize in the construction of the personality that we had shaped and rounded and that we longed to think of as standing completely for 'ourselves.'"

Thus psycho-analysis is dependent upon the Freudian conceptions of the unconscious. The gaps and defects in memory which appear in every psycho-analytic procedure are due to repression, and the repression itself to the resistance which sets itself against the revival of unconscious memories. Thus the resistance opposes reproduction of the unconscious thoughts often extending back to the earliest years of childhood and so distorts these memories that they appear only in a disguised and symbolic form in consciousness, either as the dreams of the patient, or in the form of various hysterical and obsessional manifestations. The greater the resistance, the more pronounced the distortion. A psycho-analysis cures, therefore, by overcoming these resistances and thus by means of the special technique brings the unconscious thoughts to the full consciousness of the subject. All psycho-analytic treatment is a constant struggle against newly-appearing resistances, because it is the content of infantile repressed memories or abnormal emotional fixations or reactions which occur in early childhood, which are responsible for the development of a psychoneurosis in adult life. A psycho-analysis strikes complexes and forces an expression of repressed feelings, in the same way that the play within the play in Hamlet forces a confession from the guilty King, and thus subserves the purposes of a psycho-analysis. Psycho-analysis works by both breaking down resistances and by a mechanism called " transference " which is really a free yielding up to the psycho-analytic treatment. Into these important factors, whose management constitutes the most difficult part of psycho-analysis, it is impossible for us to go, without leading too far into technicalities.

Psycho-analysis has had its opponents and modifications, in an attempt to break away from the radical conceptions of Freud. However, these modifications, while introducing several new hypotheses, have left the fundamental principles unaltered. The most recent modifications have come from Adler and Jung. According to the former, psycho-neuroses develop only in those whose organism, from the functional standpoint, has shown a defective development. The neurosis arises as a compensation for this defect, rather than on the basis of a repression.

Jung starts out with the proposal to liberate the psycho-analytic theory from the purely sexual standpoint. He considers all psychological phenomena as manifestations of energy, which energy is conceived as a desire or a libido in the widest sense of the term, thus making it synonymous with vital energy in general or with Bergson's élan vital. He then goes on to state:[1] "The first manifestation of this energy in the suckling is the instinct of nutrition. From this stage the libido slowly develops through manifold varieties of the act of suckling into the sexual function. The pleasure in suckling can certainly not be considered as a sexual pleasure, but as a pleasure in nutrition."[2]

[1] This and the other statements of Jung are quoted from his report on Psycho-analysis to the International Congress of Medicine—London, 1913 (Symposium on Psycho-analysis).

[2] In order that this conception may be understood, it must be stated that Jung is at variance with the Freudian conception, which asserts that the suckling instinct in babies is a manifestation of infantile sexuality and may be independent of its relation to hunger.

While he admits that infantile sexual fantasies may determine the form and development of a neurosis, he does not believe that this fantasy *originated* the neurosis. They are, however, frequently exaggerated and put in the foreground of the neurosis, because of the activity of the stored-up energy previously referred to not being applied in a suitable manner.

Thus a nervous disease usually breaks out at a critical moment when a new adjustment or adaptation is demanded. The failure of the adaptation causes the neurosis, and in the neurotic this lack of adaptation is more important than abnormal fixations dating from childhood. However, Jung is forced to admit the strong part played by childhood fixations, particularly the Œdipus-complex. He modifies this viewpoint by claiming that while fixation is persistently active, it is only under certain conditions that it becomes disintegrated and thus produces a neurosis. This disintegration usually occurs when new psychological adjustments or adaptations become necessary or are demanded, a feature which has been noted by every neurologist and is usually referred to in popular language as a "nervous breakdown." The stored-up energy cannot meet the new obstacles, there is a return to more primitive ways of adaptation (fixation), in other words, a regression has taken place. Thus sexual regression and not sexual repression is the cause of an outbreak of a neurosis.

This altered view of the etiology of the neuroses does not in any way invalidate the procedures of psycho-analysis. Jung states for instance as follows, concerning this standpoint —" Here the question arises whether it is still advisable to bring to light all the patient's fantasies by analysis, if we now consider them as of no etiological significance. Psycho-analysis hitherto has proceeded to the unraveling of these fantasies because it considered them as etiologically significant. My altered view concerning the theory of neurosis does not change the procedure of psycho-analysis. The technic remains the same. We no longer imagine we are unraveling the final root of the disease, but we have to haul up the fantasies because the energy which the patient needs for his health, i.e., for his adaptation, is attached to the sexual fantasies. Through psycho-analysis you re-establish the connection between the conscious and the libido in the unconscious. Thus you restore this unconscious libido to the command of conscious intention. Only in this way can the formerly split-off energy become again applicable to the accomplishment of the necessary tasks of life. Considered from this standpoint, psycho-analysis no longer appears to be a mere reduction of the individual to his primitive sexual wishes and it becomes clear that psycho-analysis, rightly understood, is a highly *moral task of an immense educational value.*" [1]

The only modification in Jung's theory of the neuroses, so far as I am able to determine, is an etiological one, the fundamental principles of the relation of the unconscious to the conscious remain unchanged. It is merely a difference in definite causation and not in therapeutic procedure.

A brief report of a simple case will make the subject of psycho-analysis clearer. This case was analyzed by means of the abstraction method and the association tests. A woman complained to me of a headache, fatigue, depression, inability to make up her mind to do things, and numbness, stiffness, and a decided weakness of the left hand. This latter she first noticed while attempting to put on a pair of gloves. An examination disclosed some physical signs of hysteria, such as diminished sensibility and muscular weakness of the left hand, and a limitation of the field of vision. When the patient was placed in a quiet, relaxed position, and encouraged to tell everything concerning her illness, the following story was obtained:

[1] The italics are Jung's.

Her sister-in-law had died suddenly, some two months previously. At the funeral, the patient was much depressed and considerably overcome by emotion. On taking off her gloves that night, on her return from the funeral, she found that the left hand was numb and weak. Both the numbness and the weakness covered the exact area of the glove. The association tests showed a distinct lengthening of the reaction time when test words relating to the emotional experience were used (such words as funeral, sister, flowers).

For fulness of record and psychological insight, Dr. Prince's case of Miss Beauchamp is an example of what may be accomplished through psycho-analysis. The record of this case also emphasizes the fact that the psycho-analysis is neither a mere euphuism nor a synonym for a kind of psychological "third degree." It means mental analysis gained through the utilization of all sorts of psychological devices, long patient observation, the careful sifting of material and the unprejudiced interpretation of all the data gained. The secret of Miss Beauchamp's several personalities lay unrevealed until it was discovered that the Miss B. who applied for treatment was not the original self. After long observation the problem was solved through the sudden appearance of a strange individual who went back to an emotional experience six years earlier. It was this experience which led to the complex mental dissociation that formed the various personalities. The neurasthenic Miss Beauchamp who sought medical advice was but one of this group of personalities. After the details of the experiences are given the narrative goes on to say, "Then she began, according to Sally's account, gradually to change in character. She became nervous, excitable, and neurasthenic. All her peculiarities became exaggerated. She became unstable and developed aboulia.[1] She grew, too, abnormally religious. There was no serious objection then to regarding B. I.[2] as a quasi-disintegrated somnambulistic person, in spite of the continuity of her memory."

In one case of nocturnal paralysis, it was possible, through psycho-analytic methods, to trace the pathological condition back to an emotional shock which had occurred several years previously.

Psycho-Analysis of a Case of Hysteria

We are now prepared to give the detailed analysis of a complex case of hysteria, with the aid of some of the technical devices already

[1] Weakness of will power.

[2] One of the personalities, in fact the personality who applied for treatment on account of her neurasthenic symptoms.

enumerated. In the interpretation of this case, the problem will be approached from the standpoint of the theory which states that hysteria represents a state of mental dissociation. This theory has given us a clearer understanding of the psychical mechanism underlying the various hysterical manifestations than any other theory with which we are acquainted.

Miss F. for a number of years had suffered at various intervals from peculiar attacks consisting of headache, palpitation of the heart, and twitching of both arms, particularly the left arm. Each attack was of several months' duration. In the intervals between the attacks she was perfectly well. Sometimes the twitching was so severe that the patient was compelled to go to bed for a week at a time, and on one of these occasions, she was in a stuporous condition for two days. The attacks are said to have followed an emotional experience when the patient was eight years of age, a fright at seeing her cousin disguised in white to resemble a ghost. While the patient had heard of this experience in general, she has never been able to recall it in detail. Sometimes in the attacks she feels peculiarly, as if she were not herself; on other occasions there is no sensation of the left side of the body, so that she is able to strike and bite her left arm without pain.

A physical examination showed some of the physical signs of stigmata of hysteria, such as loss of sensation on the left side of the body, weakness of the left arm, and a limitation of both fields of vision to between 35° and 40°.[1] In this case, however, as in most hysterical conditions, the mental state was the most important phenomenon as presenting a type of disintegration of the personality. An analysis of this mental state showed many interesting phenomena, such as extreme suggestibility, instability of character, abnormal emotionalism, amnesia, illusions of memory, and the presence of subconscious mental states, in which episodically the almost complete disintegration of personality became very marked. Furthermore it was possible to show that these protean symptoms followed an emotional experience, which became subconscious and assumed an independent activity.

Analysis through Hypnosis

Miss F. was very easily hypnotized, with amnesia (loss of memory) on awakening from the hypnotic state. In this artificial condition, she was able to recall vividly all the details of the emotional experience, but on being awak-

[1] The field of vision in normal individuals varies between 90° and a minimum of 60°.

ened, she again became amnesic for this experience. While hypnotized and asked to relate the ghost experience, she gives the account as follows in laconic sentences and in a very dramatic manner. " Seem to see it all now. The door opens. He is coming out of the room. I see the white over him. He makes a noise. He comes near me. It is dark. All I can see is the white, and I scream. He tells me it is he and not to cry. I was taken to the bed. I don't remember from that until the doctor came." In the same hypnotic state she also gave some further details of her experience, in which she struggled, bit, and was finally rendered unconscious through the use of chloroform. The emotional shock occurred when the patient was only eight years of age, and we hope to show that the dissociating effect of this emotion was directly responsible for the mental and physical aspects of her hysterical condition. While relating these experiences in hypnosis, the emotional reaction was quite dramatic. She sighed, shivered, grated and gnashed the teeth, the whole body trembled, the left arm twitched, and the facial muscles became distorted into an aspect of agony and fear. Occasionally she would scream " Ghost," " white," " that smell." In other words while hypnotized, the patient lived over again the harrowing experiences of years previous. On being awakened from hypnosis even in the midst of the state of fear, all abnormal symptoms would cease at once (except the twitching of the left arm). The patient had no recollection of either the peculiar phenomena during hypnosis or of her narration of the experiences. The loss of sensation on one half of the body persisted even during the hypnotic state.

On several occasions, while she was hypnotized, the dissociation became more marked. When she was carried back to a period antedating these experiences she did not know where she was, had never heard of the ghost episodes, and denied all knowledge of contemporaneous current events. In fact she was living over her early school days again, and once gave a vivid account of a fire at school during these early days of childhood. While in this latter state of her early childhood personality, it was noted that the loss of sensation had disappeared and all abnormal emotional reaction had ceased. If while in this state she was again carried forward to the time of the experience, the sensory disturbances not only returned, but the same attack of emotional reaction would take place. Here we seem to be dealing with the birth of a new but temporary personality. Through this method of analysis of the mental condition in the hypnotic state, it was furthermore demonstrated that the twitching of the arms first occurred at the time of the emotional shock. The fact that this twitching was absent when the hypnotized subject was carried back to a period antedating these experiences, and appeared immediately when she was carried forward to the experiences again, is a proof of the hysterical mechanism in this particular condition. The abnormal hysterical phenomena were therefore caused by a certain emotional experience, which was responsible for the dissociation.

Analysis by the Association Method

This case was also analyzed by the association method, with the following results:

In order for retardation to take place in the association tests, the emotional experiences which cause the mental retardation or slowness must be present in the memory of the subject, although it may be suppressed or dormant. However, after a cure, retardation does not take place, even though the experiences are present in memory, because the emotion aroused by the test word then finds a normal path of discharge. The application of these tests to the case of Miss F. gave interesting results and showed the effect of the emotional experiences upon the workings of her mind. In the waking condition, painful test words caused no retardation, because the patient could not recall her experiences. When these same words were used while the patient was in an hypnotic state, where the memory of the experiences could be recalled, the retardation became very marked. The test words were chosen from the emotional experiences and the reaction to all the words showed a marked slowness of reaction. These tests demonstrated that the experiences acted as a strong emotional factor in the hysterical dissociation, otherwise a slowness of reaction could not have taken place.

Association Tests Before Recovery:—In the waking state, in which there was no memory of her experiences.[1]

Test Word	*Reaction Word*	*Reaction Time (in seconds)*	*Test Word*	*Reaction Word*	*Reaction Time (in seconds)*
White	Rose	0.8	Hand	Body	2.8
Food	Eat	1.4	Smell	Scent	3.2
Bite	Feeling	0.8			

It will be noted in the above series, that the reaction time is very short, although the words used refer directly to the experiences which caused the hysterical state. In hypnosis, asso-

[1] Only the words referring to the experiences are given. Some of the words were taken from details of the emotional experience, which it was not thought necessary to relate here. The reaction time in this particular case for indifferent words such as "hungry," "street," "book," varied from eight-tenths of a second to three seconds.

ciation tests were again tried, with identical words. If the reader will compare this list with the one previously given, he will notice that it took the patient much longer to give the associated word and furthermore, the reaction word itself, instead of being an indifferent one, related closely to the experiences.

In the Hypnotic State in Which the Experiences Could Be Recalled

Test Word	*Reaction Word*	*Reaction Time (in seconds)*	*Test Word*	*Reaction Word*	*Reaction Time (in seconds)*
White	Ghost	6.4	Hand	Thing I saw	4.
Food	Eat	12.4	Smell	Handkerchief	6.4
Bite	What I did	6.8			

After the patient was cured through a synthesis of the dissociated states, the retardation time disappeared, both in the waking state and in hypnosis. At this place it might be well to point out, that after the cure the patient was able to recall all details of her experiences while in the normal waking condition, whereas previously this could only be done when the patient was hypnotized.

Association Tests in Both the Waking and Hypnotic State After Recovery

Test Word	*Reaction Word*	*Reaction Time (in seconds)*	*Test Word*	*Reaction Word*	*Reaction Time (in seconds)*
White	Pink	2.2	Hand	Body	1.6
Food	Eat	1.	Smell	Handkerchief	4.
Bite	Feeling	1.8			

Analysis by the Pulse Reaction Tests

When the patient was placed in a state of abstraction [1] (not hypnotized), by listening to a monotonous sound stimulus and asked to think of words connected with the experiences for which she had no memory, the pulse rate would become more rapid, the increase varying from four to twelve beats a minute. Indifferent test words caused no change in the pulse rate. [See Fig. VI.] After a cure through synthesis, this

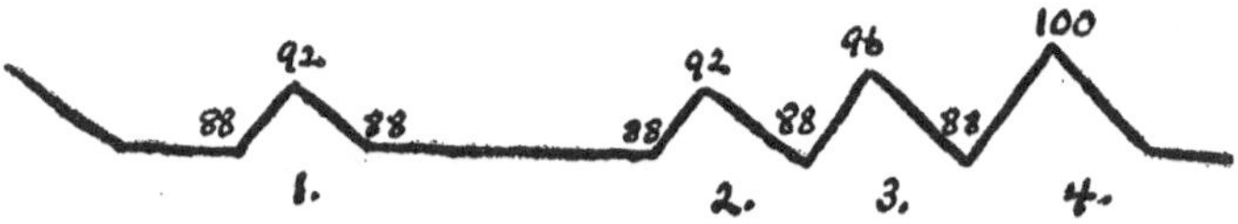

FIG. VI.—A portion of the pulse curve in the case of hysteria analyzed in the text. Note how sudden rises took place in the curve when test words relating to the subject's emotional experiences were used. These same test words also caused a lengthening of the reaction time in the association experiments.

No. 1 refers to test word *white;* No. 2, to test word *food;* No. 3, to test word *smell;* No. 4, to test word *bite.*

The numbers above the curve indicate the pulse beats per minute.

increase of the pulse rate failed to take place when the same test words were used. [See Fig. VII.] It was observed that the same test words which caused an increase in the pulse rate

[1] In abstraction, the patient could not recall any of her experiences, but could in hypnosis. Therefore, in a state of abstraction, these experiences still remained dissociated.

also caused a mental slowness in the association tests. In a case of multiple personality reported by Prince and Peterson [1] it was likewise demon-

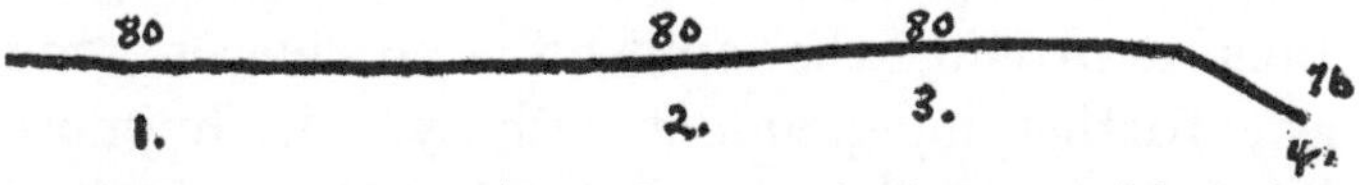

FIG. VII.—A portion of the pulse curve in the same subject given in Fig. VI., after recovery. Note how the same test words now fail to cause any increase of the pulse rate. The numbers below the curve refer to the same test words as in Fig. VI. The numbers above the curve indicate the pulse beats per minute.

strated that electrical reactions took place when test words connected with subconscious emotional experiences were used. These experiences could not be voluntarily reproduced in consciousness as memory, but appeared in dreams or could be reproduced in the hypnotic state. It would seem, therefore, that subconscious mental processes can cause electrical reactions and pulse variations in the same manner as conscious processes.

How the Hysteria Was Cured

Since it seemed evident from an analysis of this case, that the hysterical condition was due to certain dissociated emotional experiences, it ought to be possible to cure a case of this kind

[1] "Experiments in Psycho-Galvanic Reactions from Co-Conscious (Subconscious) Ideas in a case of Multiple Personality." —*Journal Abnormal Psychology,* June-July, 1908, Vol. III, No. 2.

by synthetizing or uniting these dissociated experiences with the normal waking consciousness. In other words, the hysterical mischief would stop if the split mind were made whole again, thus depriving the split-off experiences from any further independent activity. In hypnosis it was suggested to the patient that on awakening a complete memory of the dissociated experiences would persist. This was finally successfully accomplished, the treatment through synthesis covering a period of several weeks. The patient then remembered all the details of the two experiences, and in addition, the loss of sensation disappeared, the visual field became normal, and no further attacks of twitching took place. Furthermore, as previously indicated, the time for association of words having an emotional meaning became normal and no further increase of the pulse rate took place when these same test words were used. Any further narration of the emotional experiences, either in the waking state or in hypnosis, was unaccompanied by the emotional reaction previously described.

PART II

THE DISEASES OF THE SUBCONSCIOUS

CHAPTER I

LOSSES OF MEMORY

THE subject of memory is a complex one. Only its most essential points can be discussed, in order to make clear the chief subject-matter of this chapter—namely, the diseases of memory. With memory, as with sleep, the biological interpretation has been the most fruitful of results. What, then, is memory?

Memory, like irritability and reproduction, is one of the phenomena of living matter. Memory may be defined as the characteristics or traces retained by the nervous substance from previous reactions or stimuli. Of the exact nature of this trace we are in the dark: we only know that *something* is retained and this *something* is reproduced. The reproduction of stimuli is usually in the order in which the stimuli are stored up, one stimulus leading up to or calling forth the next one, in a serial reproduction psychologically known as association or associative memory. Memory, therefore, can be reduced to two simple biological phenomena—conservation or storing up of impressions or experiences and their later reproduction. Recognition and localization in the past are supposed to be a part of the act of memory, but these are merely the conscious accompaniment of the biological reaction. They are unnecessary for memory, for, as will be shown later in the course of this chapter, memory can exist without either localization or recognition. Destroy conservation and reproduction and memory ceases to exist; preserve these and destroy localization and recognition, memory is still there as a biological phenomenon, but without the psychological element.

Let us take a few simple examples of storing up and reproduction of physical stimuli and apply these to the phenomena of memory. If one talks into the plain waxen cylinder of a phonograph, then places the cylinder back to its starting point and again sets the instrument going, the words are produced in the exact order in which the cylinder stored them up. This is conservation and reproduction from a physical standpoint, based upon the laws of sound vibration produced by the human voice. Take a more complex example. Look steadily at a bright light for a few seconds, then close the eyes, and for a brief interval we perceive the sensation of light, after the stimulus which produced it has ceased to act. In this case, the retina of the eye, by virtue of the peculiar construction of its nerve elements, has stored up those other vibrations which produce light. The sensation, however, has outlasted for some little time the stimulus which occasioned it, and we have what is known in physiology as the retinal after-image. This teaches us that one tendency of the nerve tissue is to repeat physiologically its previous reactions or stimuli. Probably the same action but far more complex, takes place within the brain in the mechanism of memory. Hering has given us a vivid description of the biological aspect of memory.[1] "It is well known that sensuous perceptions, if constantly repeated for a time, are impressed into what we call the memory of the senses, in such a way that often after hours, and even after we have been busy with a hundred other things, they suddenly return into consciousness in the full, sensuous vivacity of their original perception. We thus experience how whole groups of sensations, properly regulated in their spatial and temporal connections, are so vividly reproduced as to be like reality itself. This clearly shows that after the extinction of conscious sensations, some material vestiges still remain in our nervous system, implying a change of its molecular and atomic structure, by which the nervous sub-

[1] E. Hering: "Memory and the Specific Energies of the Nervous System."

stance is enabled to reproduce such physical processes as are connected with the corresponding psychical processes of sensations and perceptions."

For the act of memory two essentials are necessary: first—a nervous system in such a stage of development that a brain is present, and secondly, the absolute integrity of such a nervous system or brain. Without the first, memory is impossible; if the brain be totally or partially destroyed, either through disease or for the purpose of physiological experiment, there is either a total or partial loss of memory. For instance, in the destruction of a certain portion of the brain of man through disease, we may have a partial loss of memory for words, known as aphasia. On the other hand, a brainless animal is absolutely without the slightest vestige of memory. Take two frogs, one of which has been blinded and the other without brain. Place both in positions of danger, the blinded frog attempts to escape, the brainless frog remains quiet, although the danger has reached the point of death, because the brainless frog possesses no memory of its previous positions of danger. Furthermore, it cannot learn anything new, because memory is necessary for the act of learning. In Goltz's famous experiment of the dog, from which he removed the brain, the animal showed no spontaneous movements, neither did it recognize its master. In certain states of dementia where the brain is profoundly diseased there is always a marked disorder of memory. In some experiments on cats and monkeys, it was shown that, when the frontal lobes of the brain were destroyed, recently formed habits and associations were lost.

It has been shown that normal memory consists of several elements, some physiological and some psychological. Essential are conservation and reproduction; non-essential, yet entering into the act of memory and completing it, are recognition and localization in the past. Conservation and reproduction are the physiological elements, and for these physiological elements or sensations to leave their traces in the nervous system it is necessary that they endure a certain length of time. These sensations as a rule outlast for some little time the objective stimulus which occasioned them. This is the explanation of retinal after images to which we previously referred and it is also this physiological mechanism which forms the basis of habits. Habits are memories, but unconscious memories, because unaccompanied by thought.

The non-essential elements in memory are recognition and localization in the past. All localization of past experiences undergoes what we may call "foreshortening," due to the omission of large numbers of events by which the present is bridged with the past. Without these omissions, recollection would be a tedious act; for instance, before we could recall the events of a holiday a year ago it would be necessary to fill up in consciousness all the details of the intervening gap. We do not do this, however. We simply jump the gap.

In abnormal memory, one or several of its elements may be disturbed, producing some form of what is known as amnesia. Amnesia is an inability to reproduce memories for certain events. This inability of reproduction may be due to actual destruction or to mere dissociation. If the former, the memory cannot be restored through special psychological devices. If the latter, restoration in most cases is possible. For instance, in certain organic brain diseases, after epileptic or hysterical attacks or convulsions, sometimes following severe blows to the head, or after emotional shocks, the memory for a certain period may be either destroyed or dissociated. In an epileptic who came under personal observation, a series of convulsive seizures was followed by an amnesia of five years. In another epileptic, a very slight dizzy attack was followed by a loss of memory for eighteen days. The memory for this period was never spontaneously recovered, thus proving an absolute destruction and not a mere dissociation.

While in an intoxicated condition a man received a blow on the head while resisting arrest. Following the injury he was unconscious for eight or ten hours, and on regaining consciousness found that he was unable to recall any events of the week previous. The memories of the amnesic period have never spontaneously returned, although a period of several years has elapsed. His only knowledge of the events of that week comes through information gathered from friends. None of the memories returned in dreams.

The destruction or dissociation of memory in amnesia usually comprises those impressions which are least highly organized. According to well-recognized laws of association it is just such elements which immediately precede the physical or psychical injury which are destroyed in amnesia, making a condition known as retrograde amnesia. These particular groups of memories are involved because they are loosely organized. Sometimes conservation primarily is disturbed; the impressions vanish as soon as received, making what is known as continuous amnesia, a condition which is very marked in senile dementia and in certain cases of alcoholic brain disease. It may be, however, that this form of amnesia is only an apparent one—the residuals may persist in the nervous system, but cannot be consciously reproduced. In Janet's case of Mme. D.,[1] for example, the continuous amnesia followed a severe emotional shock. The patient forgot the experiences of her everyday life as fast as they occurred. During sleep, however, she called out the names of the physicians who attended her during the day, thus proving that her dreams had their origin in her waking experiences, which must have been stored up and left their traces.

In other cases of amnesia the power of reproduction alone is at fault. The experiences or impressions are stored up, but voluntary reproduction is impossible, a dissociation has taken place, although the experiences may be reproduced or synthetized through special devices. Most cases of amnesia are of this latter type.

That localization in the past is not a necessary concomitant of the act of memory is shown by several cases of extensive amnesia, particularly in the case of Miss Beauchamp and in the case of Susan N. In these cases, isolated memories would suddenly flash into consciousness without any concomitant time association or the recog-

[1] Pierre Janet: "L'Amnesie Continue."—*Nevroses et Idées Fixes*, Vol. I.

nition of the memories as portions of the personal experience. They were mere scrappy and fragmentary automatisms, not synthetized with the personal consciousness and, therefore, looked upon by the subject as strange, unfamiliar, and isolated ideas.

If both recognition and localization are disturbed, there results a distortion or an illusion of memory, known as paramnesia. The interesting subject of paramnesia will be briefly discussed in the course of another chapter. If memory for particular concepts is at fault, for instance the memories of the sounds of words or for the names of things, we have what is known as aphasia.

Amnesias are systematized when they comprise all the memories of a period, localized when they take in memories of a certain epoch of life, and general when the subject has no recollection of any of his previous life. Cases have been observed that confirm all these types.

It will be impossible to give an extended account of the various cases of amnesia that have been studied and published. The reader who is interested in the subject may consult the bibliographies appended to my papers in the *Journal of Abnormal Psychology*.[1]

[1] Isador H. Coriat: "The Experimental Synthesis of the Dissociated Memories in Alcoholic Amnesia."—*Journal Abnormal*

The Lowell Case of Amnesia throws light on many obscure problems of amnesia. Susan N., an intelligent middle-aged school-teacher, left home on a certain day in March, 1906. Until she was later recognized by her relatives in August of the same year, her family had absolutely no explanation of her disappearance. During this time, however, a number of rather startling dramatic episodes occurred, for which she later had no recollection. She wandered from place to place, adopted various fictitious names, such as "Mrs. Sarah Wilson," "Mrs. Alice Walker," "Margaret Kelly," and on several occasions came into collision with the police under rather sensational conditions. Finally an attempt at suicide by drowning in the Merrimac River, and her rescue in a semi-comatose condition, led to her being placed in a hospital. On her person were found several memoranda, in which she gave a fragmentary account of her wanderings under the various names she had assumed.

After her rescue from the river, she remained in a stupor for a week, and on awakening from this state it was found that the memory of the events of her whole previous life, from the date

Psychology, August, 1906; "The Lowell Case of Amnesia."—*Journal Abnormal Psychology,* August-September, 1907; "The Mechanism of Amnesia."—*Journal Abnormal Psychology,* 1909.

of her birth, was completely obliterated. A similar condition of stupor, followed by an extensive loss of memory, has been reported in other cases. For instance, in the Mary Reynolds case, there was a profound sleep from which the patient awoke "to all intents and purposes as being ushered for the first time into the world." Likewise in the case of Susan N., the educational memories, the names of objects, persons, scenes, knowledge of events were gone. She retained, however, the knowledge of reading, writing, sewing, and automatic movements. The extensive amnesia seemed, therefore, to have affected chiefly the higher psychic memories and spared the lower and more automatic acquisitions. After awakening from the stupor she learned things anew with an astonishing rapidity, thus showing that the mechanism of associative memory was not actually destroyed, but merely dissociated. This rapidity of acquiring knowledge made it very difficult to distinguish between what the patient actually remembered and what she had learned since awakening from the stupor. Everything she read or saw appeared to her as if perceived for the first time. For instance, she said, "When I first saw trees and houses, I never remembered having seen them before." It was necessary to teach her the names and uses of ordinary objects. Literature with which she was formerly perfectly familiar it was necessary for her to relearn. She recognized no one, not even her relatives. She gave her name as Margaret Kelly, and when addressed as Susan N., paid no attention.

Attempts to restore the memory led to interesting data, proving that the entire life experience was simply dissociated from her conscious perception and not irrevocably destroyed. Scrappy, isolated memories would suddenly flash into her mind, consisting of verses of poetry, strange names, visual memories of persons, places, etc. These were not recognized as memories and were not localized in the past, but were called "strange thoughts," "wonderments" by the patient. These peculiar phenomena proved that recognition and localization are unnecessary for memory. Her dreams consisted of episodes of her life from which at present she was totally amnesic. A detailed account of this dream life as a dissociated state has already been given in the chapter on Dreams. Patients afflicted with amnesia will frequently dream of the experiences which they cannot spontaneously recall in their waking condition.

A few details will make some of these phenomena clear. When the attention of the patient was distracted by a monotonous sensory stimulus, isolated flashes of memory resulted. These I called experimental distraction memories, and they consisted principally of quotations from popular poets, such as Longfellow and Whittier. As all knowledge of literature was absent in her present state the quotations must have been of the nature of dissociated memories, that is, of experiences stored up, incapable of conscious reproduction, although synthesis was possible through the devices used. Sometimes, without being experimentally induced, for instance, in normal abstraction or during reading or conversation, the same phenomena would take place, such as the reproduction of isolated names or "vivid memories" of towns and cities. These were called spontaneous distraction memories. When the subconscious was tapped by automatic writing names and quotations were again produced, but these also were strange and unfamiliar to the patient.

Fortunately I was present at the visit of an old and intimate friend of the patient. This furnished an excellent opportunity for the study of her reaction to former acquaintances. She was unable to recognize this friend, even when her name was mentioned and when she was brought face to face with her. She reiterated "I don't remember," in answer to questions relative to prominent incidents of her childhood and early life. She asked the name of some nasturtiums brought by her visitor, and did not recall having seen similar flowers before. When the name "bobbins" was used in the course of the conversation, she naïvely inquired, "What are bobbins?" although she had once worked in a mill.

An analysis of the case showed that we were dealing with a functional amnesia, in which the higher psychic memories, such as the knowledge of objects, places, events, and literature were compeltely dissociated, while the lower and more organic acquisitions, such as reading, writing, speech, co-ordinated movements, were retained. In this respect the case is unique of its kind from the standpoint of general amnesia. The experimental evidence, in this case of Susan N., proved that we were dealing with mere isolated, disconnected fragments of a wide system of experience and knowledge which, in her present condition, were entirely dissociated from the conscious mental life, *i.e.*, incapable of voluntary reproduction.

If certain memories are dissociated, it is often possible to restore them through some artificial method. The restoration of lost memories in amnesia and the sudden recollection of a forgotten name have the same mechanism in common.

For instance I attempt to recall a name, but try as hard as I will, I cannot recollect it. I give up the conscious attempt and later, while engaged in conversation or reading, the name flashes into my mind. What has happened? The name was there all the time, otherwise I could not have recalled it later. This is one of the simplest examples of dissociation of consciousness, or more strictly speaking, in this case a dissociation of memory. When the attention was distracted by conversation or reading, concentrated upon one point, the name flashed into my mind. The conscious inhibition of the name had been removed while I was in this state of abstraction and the subconscious memory of the name flashed into consciousness. In psychological terms it has become synthetized, whereas previously it was dissociated. This is the mechanism of the restoration of lost experiences in amnesia reduced to its simplest terms. It has been shown that this synthesis is possible only where there is a dissociation, not where the experiences are destroyed. In absent-minded acts where there is often a dissociation of memory for the act, the memory may also be restored. These dissociations of memory, which clinically are some type of amnesia, occur in hysteria, acute alcoholism, sometimes after blows to the head, and occasionally in those episodes of wandering for which there is no later conscious recollection, known as fugues. The practical results of the synthesis of these particular amnesic states is one of the triumphs of the theoretical part of abnormal psychology, particularly of modern investigations into subconscious or dissociated mental experiences. The results are best accomplished by having the patient listen to a monotonous sound stimulus in a quiet, semi-darkened room and while he is in a condition of perfect relaxation. After one or several trials it will be found that isolated experiences flash suddenly into consciousness, and by continued stimulation these groups become finally fused into their chronological order. My first experiments along these lines were performed upon alcoholics who had suffered from amnesic states as the result of long-continued alcoholic indulgence. In the cases which I observed it was possible to restore in its entirety the complete amnesic period. Further researches along these lines proved the soundness of the application of this theory and it was also shown that what was true of alcoholic amnesia was true of other types of amnesia. As a result of these studies, I found that it was possible to divide the amnesias into three distinct groups:

1. Amnesic states in which the dissociation

was of such a nature that a complete experimental synthesis of the lost experiences was possible. This group comprises short hysterical, epileptic, and alcoholic amnesias, protracted fugues (wandering states), and certain types of amnesia following cerebral embolism.

2. Retrograde amnesia, following blows to the head, in which the whole or a portion of the amnesic period spontaneously cleared up.

3. Amnesic states in which the memories were so completely destroyed or dissociated that neither spontaneous restoration occurred nor experimental synthesis was possible. In this group may be placed protracted epileptic amnesias and the retrograde amnesias of cerebral concussion not comprised under group 2.

The amnesia after deep hypnosis, like the losses of memory in the states of dissociation, is not a real amnesia at all, but only apparent. The events of the hypnotic state may be restored by various psychological devices, such as crystal gazing and automatic writing; or, the patient will recall the events of the hypnosis in subsequent hypnotic states. Hysterical losses of sensation and paralysis are really localized amnesias, a "forgetting" of the sensation or movements of a certain limb.

We learn from these observations, that a loss of memory is not synonymous with unconsciousness. A person may perform many natural but complicated acts extending over hours, days, or weeks and yet have later no memory for these facts. The period is a blank in the mind. During this period, the subject is not in an unconscious state, but rather in a subconscious state. For instance, cases have been reported where a subject has left home and no trace could be found of him. Later, he suddenly comes to himself, in a strange location and engaged in a strange occupation. All memory of the period since leaving home has vanished. During the period, to all outward appearances, he was in a normal condition. Yet the memory is not really destroyed, but it may be restored by appropriate methods. Examples of a loss of memory extending over several days, in one case with the apparent birth of a new personality, will be discussed in the next chapter. In both instances, it was possible to permanently restore these lost memories through a special device.

CHAPTER II

THE RESTORATION OF LOST MEMORIES

THIS chapter will be devoted to the study of two cases of amnesia in which the lost memories were successfully restored. The first case comprised the events of a delirium, while in the second case there was a change of personality, during the amnesic period. In the first instance it was possible to restore practically every episode of the lost period, although the amnesia had existed for two years before the experiments were attempted. During all this time, the patient, try as she would, could not recall a vestige of this lost period of four days. In the restored period, there was also obtained a most valuable account of the patient's mental state during this four days' delirium. At first only a few isolated fragments were obtained, then larger and larger groups without reference to their chronological order became firmly synthetized, until finally the gaps became filled and there resulted a firm and permanent restoration of the four days' period. Where before there was a gap in the patient's life, this gap became filled through these restored memories.[1]

Mrs. X. left B. by train, on a journey to the city of N. After travelling about an hour she experienced a sensation of a sudden snap in the head, after which it seemed to her as if the train began to sway from side to side and the passengers began to change to people with whom she had been previously acquainted. After this she *remembered nothing more for a period of nearly five hours.* Her next recollection *was a very hazy memory of finding herself sitting on a trunk in the railroad station* (the end of her destination), then another hazy memory of a ride in an ambulance, and finally *an entire blank of four days,* when she found herself in the ward of a hospital. Up to the time that the patient came under observation, a period of nearly two years, she had never been able to recall the events of those amnesic periods. An attempt was therefore made to restore these lost memories, on the supposition that the entire experience was merely dissociated and not destroyed. The attempt was eminently successful, as the following data will show. The memory was not

[1] The fragments are given verbatim as they were synthetized, so that the reader may have a clear idea of the mechanism of the synthesis. The numbers refer to each individual fragment, as it entered consciousness, in the order in which they were restored, without regard to chronological sequence.

only restored but with it also came an account of the mental state during the delirium.

The result of the experiments follows:

1. "I remember a picture across the wall from my room in B., a picture of an animal, a horrible, uncouth animal like a rhinoceros, with bones or stones in front of it."

2. "A music box that they played in this room—between my room and the door of the main hall."

3. "The queer things the train did. I thought it was the Asylum and before they took me out, the train crashed down a precipice, or seemed to, just like a train wreck. I saw the name on the station."

After this the memory of her own state of mind which while in the train spontaneously returned, "The state of mind was unlike anything I had before this delusion, I was always I. My personality, my identity, did not change."

4. "The first seat in the car. At first I had one in the back and it seemed later that I had a seat on the right hand side of the car looking out of the window. I don't remember changing my seat. The people were talking near me and it seemed that what they said in some terrible way had reference to me. I didn't hear it, but I thought it. I thought I mustn't speak—I knew it. I hadn't lost my identity, I could always have told my name. Yet I didn't know where I was going or why I was in that car."

5. It was on that side that I thought I saw people I knew, and in particular a friend who had died. That

was one of the things that made me sure I was insane, because I *remembered* that *he had died.*

6. "Now I remember the conductor. He came, but I couldn't give him my ticket. I couldn't use my hands at all. *I couldn't think how to.* He took the ticket out of my lap and went away. I had a horrible fear, but I thought to myself I would keep still and I think I did. I don't believe I made any outcry or disturbance on that car. I had a dress-suit case with me, two magazines, a handbag, and a box of candy. As I grew worse, I dropped all care of these things. I sat there while the train whirled on. Part of the time it was dark, but it was very early—I think it was before 5 o'clock."

7. "All the memories seem to be of sitting on the right hand side of the car with just that horrible fear —fear of everything—that some terrible thing had happened to my daughter."

8. "I came to myself on the train and gave my husband's name and address. I felt that I had committed some horrible crime and the name and address proved it. I felt as if it was some one else I was talking about. My memories are quite clear about lying on a trunk. I was violent, screamed, struggled, not to be held. There was police officers around. I thought they were there because of the terrible thing I had done.—I thought that I had killed my daughter. I felt something clutch my dress and I turned around and thought I saw a large stuffed cat. I screamed and was afraid and a woman tried to soothe me and tried to give me some medicine."

9. "I can see now the people getting off the car, but

I didn't move at all. I think some one came and told me to get off. All this time I thought someone was with me to take care of me—and so I did just as I was told. Then I walked along with my suit case and men came running up to me—I think they were hackmen—but I thought then that they were just interested in me and thought they kept saying ' C. C.'—the place where I lived, a suburb of Y."

10. "I didn't even think then where I was going or what I was going to do. I couldn't have told my name then."

11. "I was at B. Hospital from Tuesday until Friday, but it seemed like one day to me. It is hard to distinguish old memories and new ones. I remember being questioned by physicians there and asked my name and address, which I gave correctly. Then I was questioned a good while about my physical condition, but I can't remember just what. I think I tried to make myself out insane and I remember being undressed by several nurses and put into a bathtub. The nurses all seemed to be people I knew—I called them by familiar names and their voices seemed to be familiar. I was violent and it took three or four nurses to get me to bed. That was in a room to the right as the hall is entered. The room seemed to have windows like a church—stained glass with rounding tops and in the door was a place that could be opened for some one to look in. I was terrified in that room all the time. There was a vacant bed across and a sound of breathing always came from it, as if some one were in it. It was a perfectly smooth white bed, unoccupied, and that terrified me more. I heard voices most

of the time—voices I recognized—my father's and my sister's voice. Part of the time the door of my room was open and when the nurses passed I called them by familiar names, although all the time I recognized that they were nurses by their caps. In that room was the picture I spoke of—opposite the door, and the picture kept changing."

12. "I can't remember being taken from that room to the one across the hall, but I remember being in that room across the hall. I remember medicine being given to me in that room; I drank it out of a glass, I also remember drinking milk that was brought to me there. I thought there was some terrible thing that I had done and couldn't remember what it was. There was still another room on that same side and I remember being dressed and sitting out in the middle part—the hall—where the pictures were and an organ or music box against the wall. I still thought the patients were people whom I knew. But gradually that wore off and they began to look just like themselves. I remember a physical examination there by a doctor, a young man, whose hair was brown, the eyes grayish blue, and the whites of the eyes very yellow. He thumped my chest and listened to my breathing and after that he gave me different things to smell and taste. After I was dressed they took me into the anteroom and I saw my husband and daughter there. I looked at the clock—it was 9.15 A. M. Then when they took me back I was better, I didn't think any more of the horrible things I had done to my daughter, because after I had seen her I knew that she was all right, but I began to think then that other people were harming her. I

remember being taken out to my husband and daughter again and I said, after looking at the clock, 'It was 9.15 when you were here before'—it was then 5 o'clock. It wasn't the same day, although it seemed like it to me. It seems to me as though they took me to the M. Hospital after they left me the last time."

It will be noted that the memory was restored in isolated fragments without any reference to their order of occurrence. By continued tapping or stimulation of the subconscious mental life, larger and larger groups of memories entered consciousness. Finally the entire gap of the four days' loss of memory became bridged. The restored memories have remained permanent and there is no longer a blank period in the patient's mind. In this case the patient was in an abnormal mental state during the four days and she was unable later to recall voluntarily the events of this period. Hence the amnesia arose, an amnesia of dissociation and not of destruction, otherwise the lost memories could not have been restored.

In the second case, up to the time of his amnesia, the patient was always a healthy man and of strictly temperate habits. During a slight illness he remained in bed one day, but did not remember getting up or dressing. He had a faint recollection, however, that about 10 A.M. he was told by his mother that she was going out for a while and that if he felt hungry he would find some breakfast on the back of the kitchen stove. The patient remembered nothing more until he found himself in a hospital in N. three days later, and although he was well known in his own neighborhood, no one saw him leave his house on the particular morning he disappeared. When he came to himself in the hospital he did not know where he was, but he later learned the name of the hospital. He did not know whether he came to himself suddenly, or out of a normal sleep, but in the course of an hour or two he realized his condition. He left B. on Thursday, was admitted to the hospital on Sunday. Thus there was an absolute amnesic period of three days. According to the hospital report he seemed nervous and depressed on admission, and gave his name, age, occupation, and address incorrectly. Here we have an example of the birth of an apparently new personality.

I first saw the patient three weeks after his return home. During this time not even the slightest detail of the amnesic period had spontaneously returned. He would frequently lie awake at night in an attempt to recall these lost experiences, but without success; neither had there been any dreams relating to these.

Thus we see that we are dealing with a loss of memory and a change in personality in which many complicated but natural acts were performed, the whole period being dissociated from consciousness, thus producing a complete amnesia. It was only when psychological methods were used, that the lost memories could be restored. An account of these restored memories follows as given in the patient's own words:

"It seems as though I could realize the conductor or brakeman with the lantern on his arm going around for tickets, and then it is as though there was a depot and a crowd. It seemed to me as if I walked and kept on walking, not knowing where.

"I got mixed up with a cabman, he was quite a short man compared with me. I walked a long distance before I got a cab. Then I seemed to be riding with the cabman and we went over a bridge. I can't seem to remember getting rid of that cabman. It seems as though I was walking when it was coming on dark. I fully realized it was getting dark. I remember going to some place and eating. I think I ate steak and I think there were hot biscuits there and I had a glass of milk. I remembered giving the waitress a bill, and I remember buying a cigar there directly after I paid the bill. It seems as though I went out on the street and bought a newspaper—I don't know the name of it, and I put it in my pocket. I can recollect being in a theatre —there were different varieties, and I can recall one or two acts. I recollect two fellows coming out in a

German dialect and the second one was a fellow and girl in a trapeze act. I can remember looking at the paper while I was in the theatre. I can't recall what I read, but there was something startling in it about a train wreck. I remember coming out of the theatre with the crowd and I went into a barber shop with a tobacco store connected and bought some more cigars and made inquiries about a room. I didn't receive any definite reply from them. It seems as though they told me to go farther down, quite a distance, and one of the fellows came to the door and pointed in the direction. I can remember a woman leading me to a room. I could hardly understand her talk; she was an oldish woman. I remember going into another lunchroom after I left the cigar store. A crowd in an automobile came into the restaurant directly after me. It was in that restaurant that I was told where I could get a room. They all had a foreign accent as though they were Germans. The man in the restaurant pointed out the hotel to me. It was at the corner of the street. It was a kind of boarding house. I remember the old woman showing me the bathroom and asking me several questions—if I wished to be called at any certain time, etc. She explained to me the rules of the house and showed me how to turn on the electric light in the hallway. I have just a faint recollection of retiring, but I remember raising the window before I lay down to sleep. I tossed in bed nearly all night, and did not fall asleep until daybreak. I can recall the sweeping in the next room and the woman must have heard me, because she came to the door and asked if I were up and how I felt. It struck me that she must have noticed that I did not look well. I dressed myself, but felt weak and sick. I then called her and she came into the room. I asked if I appeared sick, and she replied 'yes,' and then I asked for nourishment, something to eat. She said that as soon as she was through with her work she would bring me something. She advised me to return to bed and she would attend to my wants. I can remember her coming in with some broth in a bowl, and she also brought some eggs in a glass. I can remember drinking a cup of tea. I remember then, although I felt weak, that I thought the fresh air would do me more good and I dressed. I changed my mind and undressed again and finally again I made up my mind I'd go out. I remember going out—I remember making a study of the place. I don't remember the number, but I know it was at the corner of two streets. I made a note of the name of the street on a small card, but I can't recall it now. There was a big tailoring establishment on the corner, and the house had a sort of a brownstone front. You had to go up a dozen or more steps to the door. I can recollect walking a long distance and was so tired that I felt inclined to eat. I remember going into a restaurant, but when I sat down I took only a light stew. I believe it was one of the courses served, but I felt sick and didn't eat any more. When I left the restaurant I felt tired, so I boarded a car and rode quite a long distance. I remember getting out and going into a barbar shop.

"I can recall getting into a car that night after I left the barber shop and getting off at a theatre. I got into line with a number of people and waited a long while. I can recollect buying two tickets for a fellow that was ahead of me, as he didn't think they'd sell him all the tickets he wished. He said he had friends and later he and his friends sat aside of me. I went into the theatre and I can recall some acts. There was a fight with cow-boys and Indians on an extra large stage and later a scene in which persons would dive into the water and disappear. I can recall a girl getting into a boat that already had several men in it, and the boat sank out of sight under the water. I went out before the show was over and asked an officer in the balcony of the theatre the best way to get to the address I had on the card. He told me to go to the corner and I'd find an officer there. I didn't find the officer, and so walked quite a distance until finally I did meet one and he directed me down some streets. He told me I could get a car which would bring me in that direction, but that I would have to transfer. I can remember the conductor stopping the car and giving me a check. I only waited a minute when the car came along and it brought me to the door of the house. I started to go in but changed my mind and went into a restaurant. I remember having an oyster stew and they gave me some large crackers, such as I had never seen before. From there I went back to my room and opened the window. It was raining hard. There was some talk in the room next to me, it sounded like the voices of two or three men. I remember undressing and lying down, but I did not sleep. I would get up and take a paper and read and return to bed again. In that way I passed the night. In the morning I can remember the woman rapping at the door and giving me a towel. She asked me how I felt and I told her that I didn't feel well. She said there was a doctor a short distance down the street and that she would either send for him or I could go there myself. I didn't go to the doctor, but it seems to me as though she mentioned a hospital and I left the house with one of the boarders. I think he went to the hospital with me, although they say there that I entered alone. This was about midday. I felt weaker and weaker, started to ask some questions, but they advised me to keep quiet and not to worry. They placed me to bed in a room and darkened the room. I think I saw the doctor and he examined me. I slept well that night and the following morning he came in and asked me how I felt. He then said that I needed rest for a few days or a week, and again advised me to keep quiet and not to worry. They brought breakfast to me, but every opportunity I had I would ask some questions. I remained in that room until I came to my senses. Sleep brought me to my senses and it struck me that I was in a strange place. Then my first object was to return home."

Attempts to obtain the patient's personal conception of himself during this amnesic fugue and also the reason for giving an incorrect name on entering the hospital were unsuccessful. Some portions of the revived memories were dream-like, others appeared like natural recollections.

CHAPTER III

ILLUSIONS OF MEMORY

THE memory may play us other tricks besides mere forgetting. It may make us believe, in spite of ourselves, that we had previously lived through an experience which we are certain occurred for the first time. In a previous chapter we saw that normal memory consists of several elements. These essential elements were conservation (storing up) and reproduction; the non-essential elements were recognition and localization in the past. Memory may be present without the non-essential elements, but without the essential elements it ceases to exist. In certain pathological disturbances of memory we particularly saw that neither recognition nor localization in the past was a necessary concomitant in the act of memory, for isolated memories could suddenly flash into consciousness without either localization or a recognition of the memories as a portion of a personal experience. When either conservation or reproduction was at fault, however, we could have the various clinical types of amnesia.

When localization in the past and recognition are at fault, present happenings are sometimes mistaken for previous experiences, the memory becomes distorted and plays us tricks. We refer to this trick as an illusion of memory, a false memory, or technically as paramnesia. As amnesia is due to some disturbance of storing up or reproduction, so paramnesia is a fault of recognition and localization.

We may be in doubt if we have seen a certain landscape or experienced a certain situation or sensation before, and yet all the time we may feel certain that the experience is new and could not under any circumstance have previously happened. This sense of what is called familiarity may reach a point when even absolutely new experiences seem familiar and old. The sense of time may also become disturbed, so that new experiences may be localized in the remote past. The French writers have called this disturbance of memory the "déjà vu" or the "already seen." In contrast with this feeling of the "already seen" there may be a sense of strangeness, of newness, in familiar places, a kind of a feeling of the "never seen." These illusions of memory are found not only in certain abnormal mental states, but also in everyday life, and to a greater or less extent have caught the fancy of writers and so have pervaded the literature. The late Lafcadio Hearn has also given us a most vivid account of the illusions of his memory. He says, "To the same psychological category possibly belongs likewise a peculiar feeling which troubled men's minds long before the time of Cicero and troubles them even more betimes in our own generation,—the feeling of having already seen a place really visited for the first time. Some strange air of familiarity about the streets of a foreign town or the forms of a foreign landscape comes to the mind with a sort of a soft, weird shock and leaves one vainly ransacking memory for interpretations."

The exact reason for these strange tricks of memory is very difficult to determine. These illusions of memory may recur as a transitory phenomenon in everyday life and are sometimes associated with a temporary feeling of depersonalization. They may also be present as a prominent symptom in some form of alcoholic insanity, epilepsy, the insanity of old age (senile dementia), in some paranoiac states, and occasionally in hysteria. In their occurrence in both normal and abnormal mental states, they show a striking resemblance to some subconscious phenomena. Both may be temporary disintegrations of the personal self occurring in everyday life and both may become more complex and thus become pathological mental phenomena.

What, then, is the cause of these strange illusions of memory? Many theories have been proposed, but none seems to explain the exact mechanism.[1] The whole subject is a rather confusing one, but probably the most satisfactory explanation is that the illusions are probably due to the fact that a transitory first impression of a scene or situation becomes immediately and partially dissociated from the personal consciousness. There follows a rapid recovery from this dissociated state and on again perceiving the object or scene, a sense of recognition and familiarity arises. This sense of familiarity may present all grades, from extreme vagueness to startling distinctness. Synthesis seems to be absent and it is this lack of synthesis which causes the illusion of the "already seen." For instance, in looking over a newspaper, we may give a hasty but forgotten glance at an account of a current event. But is it really forgotten? The impression produced may become immediately dissociated, pass out of consciousness, only apparently forgotten like the functional amnesias. But if we should

[1] For an account of the various theories of paramnesia the reader is referred to my paper on "Some Recent Literature on Paramnesia."—*American Journal of Psychology,* October, 1905.

happen to return again to the same account with a more complete measure of attention a synthesis will be formed. In the more attentive re-reading of the passage it will seem as if we had read of the same event before, but how or when we cannot tell.

These illusions of memory have been studied by various observers. In one case the phenomenon, as in all reported cases, was immediate and instantaneous, before the patient had time to examine the persons or objects in detail. Here the illusion followed an epileptic delirium. To anyone who approached the patient for the first time, the patient said, "I know you. I have already seen you here. I was here in the same bed and same ward. I am not able to say when this was, but I am certain I was here before. You have spoken to me the same as you do to-day." When taken for the first time into the laboratory, she claimed to have seen all the instruments at this alleged previous visit. In another case the patient claimed to have previously dreamed events which had occurred for the first time.

In a personal study of some cases of paramnesia occurring in a form of alcoholic insanity,[1] isolated events in the patient's present memory

[1] "Reduplicative Paramnesia."—*Journal of Nervous and Mental Disease,*" 1904.

were impressed upon him as a repetition of previous events. In other words, everything seemed doubled or reduplicated, and for this reason the condition was called reduplicative paramnesia. One of the patients had the illusion that another person of the same name was formerly in the same hospital, that he had visited him several times and that he bore a minute physical resemblance to him, even down to the detail of the amputation of identical fingers of the same hand. He furthermore stated that the hospital grounds, buildings, wards, nurses, etc., were familiar to him because of this former visit. Other cases showed the same duplication of events with the minutest details. The phenomenon was interpreted as due to a doubling of memory images in consciousness, but as the patients were not aware of the doubling, the illusions were looked upon as actual events.

A stenographic report of a portion of a conversation in a subject with illusions of memory, will explain better than any description, this curious disturbance. An examination of this patient's physical condition, including tests for sensation and the reflexes, had been made a week previously. The patient had never been in the hospital before and, therefore, his minute description of an alleged previous residence there, was a pure illusion. This illusion of memory was a condition due to disease, and not the result of a deliberate fabrication.

Up to the time that the illusions of memory suddenly appeared during a spontaneous remark, there had been no suspicion of any disturbance of this kind. The following is an account of the illusion:

"One day the subject spontaneously said, 'I was here in this hospital four years ago for typhoid fever' (incorrect).

Q. For how long? A. About two months.

Q. Who was your doctor? A. I don't know.

Q. Describe him? A. A little black mustache.

Q. In what ward were you? A. A hospital ward.

Q. What did it look like? A. It had photographs and battleships on the walls, and they worked the biograph on me to see how much I could stand.

Q. Did the hospital resemble this? A. Not exactly, there is a lot of new things here.

Q. Is this the same hospital? A. Yes.

Q. Was I a doctor there? A. I don't know for sure, but I think you were.

Q. Did I look the same as now? A. No, you only had a little mustache then.

Q. What is my name? A. I forget.

Q. What did I do to you? A. Cured me.

Q. Did I examine you? A. Every way, and you said you would make a good man of me. And you examined my feet and legs and arms with a hammer. You stuck me in those places. Then you swung my feet, too (referring to the physical examination a week previously).

Q. What ward were you in before? A. I guess this ward.

Q. All the time? A. No, I was in the hospital ward for awhile.

Q. Since coming here this time have you been in this ward all the time? A. No.

Q. In what other ward were you? A. Hospital ward.

Q. Did it resemble the hospital ward you were in before? A. Yes.

Q. How many nurses there? A. Four or five (three).

Q. Are you sure that you have been in this hospital before? A. I am sure of that; I was here two months."

At a later examination nothing of the above could be elicited. The patient had a vague remembrance of the physical examination, but he placed it at his alleged previous residence in the hospital. He had been in the infirmary ("hospital") ward for some time and the period during which he was in bed in the infirmary ward, and also the ward itself, he reduplicated in all his statements. In addition there was also a prolongation of the time sense.

CHAPTER IV

THE SPLITTING OF A PERSONALITY

It has been shown by numerous investigators that multiple personalities present various degrees of organization of the secondary personalities, from the simplest to the most complex. For convenience they may be divided into three prominent groups:

1. Secondary personalities may develop as hypnotic phenomena. These may be called abortive personalities. To this group also belong some of the subconscious states of automatic writing. Compared with the more fully developed forms these types are the most simple; they are really artificially dissociated groups of memories without the development of a new ego. Examples of this class are the state called "Mamie" in Prince's case of Mrs. R., Janet's cases of Madame B., Lucie, and Marceline R., and finally the case of Mrs. Y., which constitutes the present chapter. It is extremely doubtful if, in any of these cases, a new personality would have developed, if the

subject was not already in a state of partial mental dissociation.

2. The more complex forms, such as Mlle. Helene Smith reported by Professor Flournoy ("From India to the Planet Mars"), and Mrs. "Smead," studied by Professor Hyslop. Both these cases showed automatic writing with subconscious fabrications, the communications giving alleged accounts of life on the planet Mars, frequently in a highly imaginative and fabricating Martian language.

3. The most highly developed forms, with the development of a new ego resembling, outwardly at least, a normal mental life. To this group belongs Dr. Prince's case of Miss Beauchamp.

These groups are not distinct, however, for there is a decided overlapping of types. Phenomena such as automatic writing, crystal visions, and gaps in the memory (amnesia), which are present in the most simple dissociations may also be present in the most complex. Before passing to the study of Mrs. Y. it will be well for the sake of clearness to give a brief account of some of the cases belonging to group 1 of secondary personalities. We will then be able to comprehend more clearly the interesting phenomena presented by Mrs. Y. as the hypnotic dissociation pre-eminently accounted for the development of her secondary personalities.

In Dr. Prince's case of Mrs. R.,[1] there developed a hypnotic personality who called herself "Mamie." The normal self was called "Annie." "Mamie" knew "Annie," but "Annie" had no knowledge of "Mamie."

Janet[2] reports the case of a poor peasant woman, Madame B., who had been repeatedly hypnotized for years. Finally two personalities developed, a normal waking one known as Léonie, and a hypnotic personality who called herself Léontine. Léonie was serious, sad, calm, slow, and timid, while Léontine, on the contrary, was restless, gay, vivacious, and noisy. In a deeper hypnotic state, a third personality appeared, known by the name of Léonore. Of the same class is Janet's Marceline R., who suffered from severe hysterical vomiting in her normal state, but when the patient was hypnotized the vomiting ceased.

In our case of Mrs. Y. it was possible to demonstrate four distinct personalities. For several years she had suffered from an hysterical paralysis which had resisted all forms of treatment, and it was finally determined to try

[1] Morton Prince: "Some of the Revelations of Hypnotism."—*Boston Medical and Surgical Journal,* 1890.

[2] Pierre Janet: "L'Automatisme Psychologique."

hypnotic suggestion, in the hope of effecting a cure. At first there was no suspicion of the presence of the interesting phenomena about to be described. Suddenly and spontaneously, however, during the course of treatment, a new personality developed in one of the hypnotic states and on further hypnotization three other distinct personalities were added to this one, making four in all. The unravelling of the three last personalities was altogether as unexpected as the development of the first. These new personalities persisted only during the hypnotic state. When the patient was awakened she immediately reverted to her normal condition without memory of the hypnotic personalities. The case also showed other interesting phenomena of dissociation of consciousness, such as the presence of crystal visions, subconscious perception of stimuli, and the development of hallucinations while the patient was half asleep and half awake (hypnagogic state). In order that the reader may clearly grasp the evolution of these spontaneous hypnotic personalities, it is absolutely necessary that the main events of the patient's life be given in full detail. Otherwise, much that is clear and definite will remain obscure.

The patient was born in England and came to America when she was fourteen years of age.

Two years later she entered college and remained there several years. At the age of eighteen she married a man whose conduct towards her was brutal and neglectful. The patient had six children, one of whom (E.), her favorite daughter, died in November, 1901, after a protracted illness. During ten years of her married life (from 1889 to 1899) her husband was in the hotel business in the city of P. He deserted her shortly after the death of her favorite daughter. The following two years she was superintendent of a certain society in L., and later became matron of an institution, a position which she retained until February, 1904. During this time she also did some literary work. Both sources of income being insufficient to sustain herself and her children, she was compelled to place them later in an asylum. Immediately afterwards she became ill and it was necessary to undergo a severe surgical operation by Dr. J. of L. On the night of her daughter's funeral the patient was taken suddenly ill and remained in bed for three weeks, experiencing a severe sense of exhaustion. The exhaustion continued, the right arm would occasionally become numb and cold and the limbs grew weaker and weaker. Thus we see that a series of severe emotional shocks extending over several years was followed by a group of symptoms very suggestive of neurasthenia. Instead of improving, these symptoms gradually became worse and were aggravated during the next few years by her financial condition, overwork, and worry about her children. She was finally admitted to a sanitarium in July, 1905. During the first few months in the sanitarium she suffered from sleeplessness, depression, weakness, severe and almost continual headaches, and pains in the limbs, in fact, nearly all the classical symptoms of neurasthenia or nervous exhaustion. In addition, she had several fainting spells. Six months after admission there developed complete paralysis of both lower extremities and of the right arm, with complete loss of sensation (anæsthesia) in all the paralyzed members. Nausea and vomiting were almost persistent. The field of vision in the right eye became much limited. She became irritable and cranky and made unreasonable demands of the nurses and of her physician. At times she was delirious and suffered from hallucinations of hearing and a fear of receiving personal injury at the hands of imaginary individuals. After remaining in the sanitarium for a year, she was removed to a private home, and from there she was taken to the hospital where I saw her, and where the following experiments and studies were made:

The patient was a bright, intelligent woman,

without any defect of intellect or memory. Both lower limbs and the right arm were paralyzed and completely anæsthetic. It will be unnecessary to give the other details of the physical examination. It is sufficient to state that everything absolutely pointed to the fact that the patient was suffering from a functional (hysterical) paralysis. Hypnosis was used in an attempt to cure this paralysis. On the first few attempts, the patient went into a deep hypnotic state with total amnesia (loss of memory), for this state, on awakening. In the waking state, when the anæsthetic arm was touched or lightly tapped a definite number of times (three, four, and six), the patient's eyes being meanwhile tightly closed, and the patient was asked to state the first number that came into her mind, in every case this corresponded to the number of taps or touches made. Although the experiment was frequently repeated, in order to avoid error and coincidence, the reaction remained the same.

Here we have a pertinent example of the persistence of subconscious perceptions. In other words, the severe anæsthesia was merely a functional one, and the patient subconsciously counted the number of stimuli, although consciously unable to feel them. After the patient had been hypnotized a number of times, the first of the hypnotic personalities suddenly and spontaneously developed under the following conditions. On a number of previous occasions when the patient was addressed while in the hypnosis, she always gave relevant answers, had a perfectly clear comprehension of her surroundings, knew the date and where she was. On this occasion, however, while the patient was in the hypnotic state, a new personality had developed, which we shall designate by A. In this personality the patient believed she was in England, shortly after her marriage. The details follow in the form of questions and answers, the form in which the notes were taken, as indicating more clearly than any description, the peculiar mental state which had developed.

Personality A.

Patient in a deep hypnosis.

Q. Where are you? A. With mother in London.

Q. Is this London? A. Yes.

Q. What month is this? A. December—when I was married.

Q. What year? A. 1887.

Q. How old are you? A. I was married at eighteen

Q. Are you eighteen years old now? A. Yes.

Q. Have you any children? A. I am to have a baby soon.

Q. Where are you living? A. In a beautiful home.

Q. In what city are you living? A. D.—— on the south coast—in a pretty cottage there.

Q. What is your name? A. It is Mrs. Y., now.

Q. How long have you been married? A. Since last December.

Q. How old are you? A. Eighteen. I told the minister that I ran away from home and school.

On being awakened the patient remembered nothing of the above conversation, gave her correct age and the age of her children, and when confronted with some of the facts elicited from personality A., seemed surprised at the physician's knowledge.

Personality B.

Several days later the patient was again hypnotized. In this state which we call B. the patient believed that she was living in the city of P. (United States) during the years 1889 to 1899. There was no knowledge of subsequent events.

Q. How old are you? A. Just married.

Q. But how old are you? A. My father will tell you (irritably).

Q. Are you in good health? A. Oh, yes.

Q. Is your arm paralyzed? A. Of course it is not. You know it is not.

Q. Then move it. A. I can move it as well as my other arm. (She makes a vain effort to move the paralyzed right arm.)

Q. What city is this? A. P. (sighing).

Q. Did you ever hear of —— Hospital in B.? A. Why, no (referring to the hospital where the patient is at present).

Q. How many children have you? A. Two.

Q. How old is the eldest? A. Three years.

Q. What month is this? A. The twelfth of May.

Q. How old are you? A. Twenty years.

Q. What are you doing in the city of P.? A. In the Hotel.

Q. Who is the proprietor? A. My husband, of course.

Q. Were you ever a patient in any hospital? A. No, I was always too well to be a patient anywhere.

Q. Did you ever hear of President McKinley? A. No—but I remember Garfield, who was assassinated.

Q. Who is the ruler of England? A. Queen Victoria.

Q. Ever hear of the —— Sanatarium? (The Sanatarium where the patient was ill during the years 1905—1906.) A. Never.

Q. How long have you been married? A. Three or four years.

At this point the patient awoke suddenly, with no recollection of the above conversation. She was hypnotized two days later and the B. personality again appeared. At this time she was irritable and cranky, refused to talk at first, stating that she did not talk to strangers, saying, "I don't recognize your voice." In neither of these personalities did the paralysis or loss of sensation disappear, a phenomenon which was observed in other cases with the development of hypnotic personalities.

Personality C.

In this personality, the patient believed she was in the Institution during the years 1902-1904.

Q. Where are you? A. This is the Institution.

Q. In what city? A. B.

Q. What are you doing here? A. What am I doing here? (surprised)—I came from another institution in L.

Q. But what are you doing here? A. I am superintendent.

Q. How long have you been here? A. Two years.

Q. Are you in the Institution at present? A. Yes.

Q. Who am I? (Dr. C.) A. I think you are Dr. J.

Q. Were you a patient in a sanatarium? A. Never.

Q. Did you ever hear of —— Hospital? (where the patient is at present.) A. Yes.

Q. Have you ever been there as a patient? A. No.

Q. What year is it? A. I don't know.

Q. Do you know the month? A. I can't tell if it is summer or not. (In reality it was February.)

Q. Are you in good health? A. Always well, but I am tired, I don't go to bed until morning.

Q. What time is it now? A. It is night—about three o'clock. (Incorrect.)

Q. What are you doing now? A. I am writing, I can't be bothered talking (irritably), I have no time. I write for a domestic column in a paper.

Q. Are you in your room at the Institution? A. Yes.

Q. Are you awake? A. Of course I'm awake (surprised). I could not write if I were asleep.

Urged to make an attempt to write with the right hand, she is unable to do so.

Q. What year is it? A. I think it is 1904.

Q. Isn't it 1907? A. No.

Q. How many children have you? A. Six, E. is dead.

The patient was hypnotized several days later and on this occasion Personality C. reappeared, although some further details developed. She believed that she was in the city of L., in the office of Dr. J., the physician who had performed several surgical operations on the patient. Only the more important details of this other phase of Personality C. will be given, in order to show how vividly this particular state was enacted and how dominant was the dissociation. All the answers were given quickly and in a tone of voice which showed that the patient was hurried and resented any effort to detain her. Further, when speaking of her husband's conduct towards her, the attitude was one of hate and disgust, mingled with surprise that Dr. J. should be ignorant of all the facts. It is well to state that at this time she mistook me for Dr. J.

Q. How do you feel now? A. Tired, I've been on a case all day. Dr. J., you know all about the case. Oh, Dr. J., will you give me something for that pain? Do you think I've taken cold?

Q. Who am I? (Dr. C.) A. Why—Dr. J.

Q. What city is this? A. L.

Q. What place is this? A. Dr. J.'s office. Oh, Dr. J., give me something, please. I must catch that four o'clock train.

Q. For where? A. B.

Q. Where are you located in B.? A. At the Institution.

Q. Are you with your husband? A. Why, Dr. J., you know all about it. You ask such silly questions. Don't you remember?

Q. What time of day is it? A. It is ten to four. Didn't you say so? I don't want you to take me down to the train. I can walk myself. There is an awful blizzard going on now, everything is blocked up. I have to catch the four o'clock train.

At this point the patient suddenly awoke with a start. There was absolutely no recollection of what had taken place during hypnosis. This personality, more than the others, was full of activity. The patient actually seemed to live over again certain incidents of her past life. Immediately after the patient awoke from this last hypnotic state, some experiments in crystal gazing were carried out, with results as detailed in the chapter on crystal gazing. Some of the experiences detailed in this hypnotic state were reproduced as a crystal vision.

Personality D.

Hypnotized several days later and Personality D. appeared, in which the patient believed she was in the same Sanitarium where the hysterical paralysis developed. This was during the years 1905-1906.

Only a few of the most essential details will be given, but here again as in Personality C. the realism of the hypnotic state was marked and the patient mistook me for the physician in the Sanitarium.

Q. Where are you? A. In the Sanatarium.

Q. Do you know me? A. Yes, Dr. M. (Physician in the Sanitarium).

Q. How long have you been here? A. Don't know.

Q. Why did you come here? A. Why, doctor, I came here because I was tired and I haven't been sleeping. But don't let the young doctor take my history.

Q. How long do you intend to remain here? A. Three weeks—then I will take my position again.

Q. What is your position? A. Why, doctor, I told you. Didn't I show you all my testimonials (in a surprised tone of voice)?

Q. Is your arm paralyzed? A. Why, no—I have been sitting out on the veranda to-day.

Therefore, as will be clearly seen from the data given above, the original Mrs. Y., a sufferer from a severe form of hysteria, when hypnotized spontaneously developed four successive personalities or rather multiple hypnotic states. In none of the states was there any change of character, other than demanded as a reaction to her surroundings.

These four personalities may be summarized as follows:

Personality A. In England in 1887, when eighteen years of age, just after her marriage.

Personality B. In the city of P. during the years 1889 to 1899.

Personality C. In the Institution at B. during the years 1902-1904.

Another phase of the same personality developed in a later hypnotic state, viz.:—an episode in the office of Dr. J. in L.

Personality D. In the Sanitarium during the years 1905-1906, during which time the hysterical paralysis developed.

All these states may be called hypnotic personalities, to which we have referred above. The mental organization in each personality was simple, there was no development of a new ego, and no change of character. We are dealing, strictly speaking, with a complex group of memories. The four personalities are really the original Mrs. Y., yet each personality is Mrs. Y. at a particular period of her life. The individual hypnotic personalities had no knowledge of subsequent events in the life of Mrs. Y. Thus the A., B., C., and D. states are each ignorant of Mrs. Y. and her present hysterical paralysis. In her waking condition, however, the original Mrs. Y. has a knowledge of all the past events of her life, but does not know that she reverts to these events in her hypnotic trances and develops an incomplete hypnotic personality. Each of the hypnotic personalities had a knowledge of the patient's entire life previous to the date which the personality comprised, but not subsequent to it. Thus we are dealing with a peculiar amnesia or gap in the memory occurring in a subject in whom mental dissociation easily took place.

Janet has formulated a law, that in the development of secondary personalities anæsthesia, or loss of sensation, and amnesia, or gaps in memory, go together. Amnesia is invariably present in cases of multiple personality, particularly in the more complex types. But losses of sensation do not always take place when one personality changes to another and when one of these personalities is combined with an anæsthesia. It certainly did not occur in Mrs. Y., as all the hypnotic personalities preserved the anæsthesia and paralysis which were present in the original Mrs. Y. This was probably due to the incomplete form of dissociation which took place when the patient was hypnotized.

CHAPTER V

HYSTERIA

We are now prepared to take up one of the most interesting of functional diseases, a disease which in whole or in part may be taken as a type of the pathological dissociations of consciousness. We refer to the disease hysteria. The study of this disease has thrown a flood of light upon the mechanism of dissociation. Hysteria is one of the most complex of functional neuroses, and although the work of recent investigators has helped to an understanding of it, yet many of its phenomena still offer some of the most baffling problems in psychopathology. Certain functional neuroses seem to be caused by mental dissociations. These fall into several groups, as follows:

1. The neurasthenic state, which frequently shows phenomena which lead one to believe that it is a form of mental dissociation caused by fatigue.

2. The more complex psychasthenic state, with its peculiar obsessions and fears, its epi-

sodes of unreality, and its frequent far-reaching effects upon the personality.

3. The periodic changes of personality with losses of memory for each personality. These are known as double or multiple personality according to the number of groups which are formed.

4. The systematized functional losses of memory or amnesia.

5. The condition known as hysteria, in which the dissociation comprises all the motor, physical, and psychical activities which make up the complex personality.

It appears from recent investigations that the disease hysteria, the phenomena of multiple personality, and the artificial hypnotic state have many of the same symptoms and much of the same mechanism in common.

In the chapter on the analysis of the mental life a brief account of the disease hysteria was given. In the report of a case we saw some of the elements of which the disease was composed. We are now prepared to discuss the subject at length. Hysteria is of paramount importance, not only from the medical standpoint, but because many of the famous characters of history showed the disease in a well-defined form. Many of those who have been blind or paralyzed for years, or in whom tumors appeared and then suddenly disappeared without surgical aid, were cases of hysteria.

We often hear people say that such or such a person is hysterical. When this term is used in popular language, it means unstable, ill balanced, erratic, easily moved to laughter or to tears. The word "hysterical" in a popular sense is used as loosely as the word "nervous." As a matter of fact, while hysterical persons may be unstable or ill balanced in manner, yet uncontrollable laughter or crying but seldom accompanies true hysteria. So widely does hysteria depart from the popular idea of the disease, that the layman frequently fails to recognize it. In hysteria we are dealing with a world in itself. It is the most protean of all nervous diseases, its symptoms are multitudinous and it can stimulate many functional and indeed some organic diseases. The manifold symptoms of hysteria have no organic basis; such symptoms as paralysis, sudden losses of sensation, or sudden losses of the voice, blindness, convulsions, contractures, peculiar mental disturbances, being, when they occur in hysteria, purely functional in nature. Hysteria bears no relation to the etymological definition of the word, for we have hysterical men as well as women. In fact, some of the most marked cases of hysteria have occurred in strong, athletic men.

This brings us to the various theories of the disease. The older idea, that it had something to do with the womb, has been, of course, entirely discarded, its only survival being Freud's theory of the sexual mechanism of the hysterical state, which will be discussed later.

The modern work on hysteria may be said to have started with Charcot and his pupils, of whom Janet is the most prominent of the later representatives. Indeed the latter has given us a working basis for the mechanism of hysteria which has born the most fruitful and practical results. Previous to the work of Charcot and his pupils the French school had directed a certain amount of attention to hysteria, and their ideas on the subject paved the way for the more modern theories. France has led the way for the work on this disease, probably, on account of the abundance of clinical material which may be found in the French hospitals. It would lead us too far to give a detailed account of all the French investigations on a disease which Janet says has a beautiful history. In 1859 Briquet defined hysteria as a general disease which modifies the whole organism. This definition, in a way, resembled a later one given by the German neurologist Möbius, who stated that hysteria was a condition in which ideas controlled the body and produced morbid changes in its functions. Now it is to the merit of Charcot and the earlier French school to have given us what in time became later designated as the classical picture of the disease hysteria, although, as we shall see later, their description of the disease is open to certain changes, modifications, and even criticisms. Charcot had no theory to offer for the mechanism of hysteria, other than it occurred in highly suggestible subjects in whom ideas could control functions of the entire body.

Heredity is the great predisposing factor in hysteria, the disease occurring particularly in the offspring of hysterical and neuropathic parents. While the larger number of the cases of hysteria are seen in adult women and men, the disease may also occur in children, even in very young children. Juvenile types of hysteria have been reported in children varying from three to twelve years of age. Probably in the very early cases the child imitates the symptoms of some other child, or some adult, who is suffering from either a functional or an organic disease of the nervous system. I have seen children who have imitated the convulsions of genuine epilepsy and also of an organic paralysis of the legs or arms. Here the child seems to have become the victim of a fixed idea or of a deeply-rooted obsession. Hysteria in children may be treated as Jung and Freud have done, through psycho-analytic methods, or through what are termed the methods of surprise and disregard. It is best, however, in these cases to combine any form of psychotherapy with purely physical methods of treatment. When hysteria occurs in children the manifestations of the disease are usually limited to one or to a few symptoms, such as transitory paralysis of a limb, hysterical pain limited to a joint, losses of voice, convulsive attacks, blindness or mutism.

Emotions of various sorts, particularly fright and terror, or the suppression of painful experiences are among the chief direct provoking agents of hysteria. In adults, as well as in children, outbreaks of hysteria may arise from imitation. Then we have hysterical epidemics, as in the dancing mania of the Middle Ages. Fatigue may also bring on an hysterical condition, and the neurasthenic state that is produced may be one of the principal mental signs of a disease which, on close analysis, is found to be hysterical in nature. So we see that it is not necessary for a subject to have all the classical symptoms in order to be a sufferer from hysteria. A few only of either the bodily, or the mental symptoms, or both, may suffice for the diagnosis. What, then, are the so-called classical symptoms of this disease as they have been established by Charcot and the French school of investigators? We will briefly pass these in review, although, as we have previously stated, they are open to certain modifications and corrections.

The symptoms of hysteria may be divided into two principal groups, physical and mental. The former will be first discussed, as they are somewhat easier of comprehension and will pave the way for a better understanding of the more complex mental state of the disease. It is the mental state of the hysterical, however, which is responsible, in a great measure, for the physical symptoms. The most frequent physical symptom is hysterical paralysis. This paralysis may comprise a single limb or an entire side of the body, or it may be limited to one muscle of the eye, or to the vocal cords. When the eye muscles are involved the patient sees images double; when the vocal cords are involved there is produced a hysterical loss of voice known as aphonia. These paralyses usually appear quickly and disappear quickly, either spontaneously or as a result of treatment. In one of my cases, that of a hysterical boy, a paralysis of the leg with complete loss of sensation for the affected limb could be made to appear, and to completely disappear, by means of mere waking suggestion. One of the most frequent forms of hysterical paralysis is that in which the patient is unable to walk, although the limbs may be freely used and moved when the patient is lying down. This is known as hysterical astasia-abasia. In one of our cases this hysterical paralysis of the legs followed a dream in which the patient thought that she was falling down a steep hill. In another case the condition developed in a highly emotional and suggestible woman who happened to be placed in a bed next to one occupied by a patient with complete hysterical paralysis of both legs. Now these hysterical paralyses only outwardly resemble the real organic paralyses of the nervous system. In cases of hysterical paralysis of the limbs there are no changes in the reflexes or in the reaction of the paralyzed muscles to electricity, and no matter how long the paralyses may persist, no wasting of the paralyzed muscles follows, such as would take place in an organic paralysis.

Sometimes a limb is not actually paralyzed and yet there may be an inability to move the limb, due to a certain muscular contracture which takes place, usually at the joints. The fingers, the hands, the feet, or even an entire limb may be involved. As a rule these contractures follow the pain of a slight injury, after which the patient feels unable to move the limb and finally becomes possessed with a fixed idea that all active or spontaneous movements are impossible. These hysterical spasms may also involve the neck muscles, thus either twisting the head or bending the head either from the left or right, producing what is known as hysterical wry-neck or torticollis. Occasionally the muscular spasm may involve the diaphragm and produce disturbances of respiration or persistent hiccough. An hysterical tremor has also been described, which may resemble chorea or very closely simulate a tremor of some organic disease of the nervous system.

Another very prominent feature is the disturbances of sensation. It is frequently noted that hysterical patients may be unable to feel a light touch or even a pin-prick in certain parts of the body. That these sensory disturbances are not due to lesions of any particular nerve, but are purely functional in origin and nature, is shown by the fact that they do not follow the usual anatomical distribution of the nerve trunks, and that they can frequently be made to disappear by means of some form of suggestion. The hysterical sensory disturbances may involve and be sharply limited to one side of the body, and may even involve the mucous membrane of the mouth and tongue. This latter type forms what is known as hysterical hemi-anæsthesia and it is one of the most frequent so-called physical stigmata of the disease. Sometimes the anæsthesia may cover the hand or leg, like a glove or a stocking. Not only are these sensory disturbances not caused by a nerve lesion, but the lack of sensation is only apparent and not real. This is shown by the fact that the subject may have a subconscious perception of the number of times the limb is touched or pricked, as in our case of Mrs. Y. Sometimes the most amazing contradictions may arise in the testing of sensations of hysterical anæsthesia. For instance, one of Janet's patients who was anæsthetic on one side of the body, on being tested was requested to answer "Yes" when she felt the touch and "No" when she did not feel anything. The patient did so and in this curious contradiction we must not interpret the matter as one of simulation, but seek deeper for its psychological basis. Sometimes, also, another curious disturbance of sensation may take place. A touch on one side of the body is not felt at that particular spot, but on exactly the opposite side of the body. Technically this is known as allocheiria.

In some recent investigations on the psychogalvanic reflex, it has been pointed out that stimulation of the skin in areas in which there is a loss of sensation (anæsthesia) results in only a slight electrical reaction. In hysterical anæsthesia, however, the electrical reaction from stimulation of the anæsthetic area is as strong as though no loss of sensation existed. Here we seem to have another experimental proof that hysterical anæsthesia is not real, but only apparent, and that the impressions are subconsciously perceived.

The special senses may also be involved in hysteria. Disturbances in taste, smell, or hearing may arise; there may be complete inability to distinguish sound or music, or to tell the difference in odors or in the taste of food. Sometimes there may be hallucinations of hearing in the delirious state of hysteria; occasionally there may be a persistent hallucination of smell with a clearly retained consciousness, as in Freud's famous case of the patient who was troubled by the odor of burnt pudding. To a detailed account of this case, which in a way has become classical, we will return later.

The most important of the disturbances of the special sense in hysteria are those referable to sight. The field of vision may be limited in all directions, forming what is known as the concentric limitation of the visual field. This limitation of the visual field in hysteria applies equally well to all colors, whether white, red, or green. Now the visual field in normal individuals extends from about 60 to 90 degrees in all directions. In hysteria this may be moderately or markedly retracted in all directions down to 30 or 40 degrees, or as in one case which recently came under observation the visual field did not exceed 10 degrees. Of course, in this case the patient was practically blind in the affected eye. Hysterical blindness may also occur, usually appearing and disappearing suddenly. In all these hysterical disturbances of sight the optic nerve is found to be absolutely normal, a fact which speaks strongly for the purely functional nature of the condition. Hysterical patients whose visual field is markedly narrowed will be observed to intelligently avoid all obstacles, which shows that the disorder of sight, like the disturbance of sensation, is not real but only apparent. In fact, subconscious persistence of vision takes place in the same way as the subconscious persistence of lost sensations to which we have already referred. This has been very well pointed out by Janet in the recent work on the "Major Symptoms of Hysteria." He says:

"Hystericals who have an exceedingly small visual field, run without in the least troubling themselves about it. This is a curious fact to which I remember having attracted the attention of Charcot, who had not remarked it, and was very much surprised at it. I showed him two of our young patients playing very cleverly at ball in the court yard of La Salpetriere. Then having brought them before him, I remarked to him that their visual field was reduced to a point, and I asked him whether he would be capable of playing at ball, if he had before each eye a card merely pierced with a pin-hole. It is one of the finest examples that can be shown of the persistence of subconscious sensations in hysteria.

Besides, I had shortly afterwards the opportunity of making a still more precise experiment on the same point. A young boy had violent crises of terror caused by fire, and it was enough to show him a small flame for the fit to begin again. Now his visual field was reduced to five degrees and he seemed to see absolutely nothing outside of it. I showed that I could provoke his fit by merely making him fix his eyes on the central point of the perimeter and then approaching a lighted match to the eightieth degree."

As a rare symptom there have also been reported peculiar illusions of vision in which objects appear either abnormally large or abnormally small. The peculiar fact in the various disturbances of vision, particularly in the narrowing of the visual field, is that the patient is indifferent to it. He believes his vision to be normal, in the same manner that the anæsthetic subject believes his sensation to be normal.

A group of other peculiar phenomena may

appear in hysteria, such as sudden swelling around the joints, high fever without any apparent cause, persistent vomiting, disgust and distaste for food, sometimes leading to absolute refusal of food, and occasionally bleeding from the mucous membrane of the mouth, which may resemble a hemorrhage from the lungs.

Another frequent set of symptoms are the various convulsive attacks. These convulsive attacks strongly resemble genuine epilepsy; in fact, so strong is the resemblance that frequently a correct diagnosis can be made only after prolonged observation and study. The convulsions may be general in nature or limited to one limb, but are less inco-ordinate than in epilepsy. As a rule the attack begins with a sense of constriction in the throat and the patient has no memory for the attack. Sometimes the memories for a period antedating the attack are apparently completely obliterated (retrograde amnesia). We say apparently, for by proper artificial devices the lost memories may be completely restored. We have already referred to some of this work in a previous chapter. In the attack itself there may be a complete unconsciousness, or the patient may alternately laugh and cry. Peculiar attitudes are taken, the body being sometimes arched in half a circle, the patient resting on the head and heels. Other motor phenomena are the attacks of stupor and of sleep; occasionally a condition of catalepsy may arise, so that the limbs may be moulded in any position as though they were made of wax. Sometimes periods of sleep wandering may take place, known as somnambulism.

More important, however, than the physical symptoms are the mental states of hystericals. These mental states are legion. There may be malingering, unstable emotions, loss of memory, weakness of will, increased suggestibility, delirium or stupor, subconscious acts, fixed ideas, and finally, severe modifications and changes in character, leading to double or multiple personalities. Hallucinations of the various senses may arise, and also peculiar dreamy states of consciousness. The mental state is far more important than the physical side of hysteria, but it probably has the same underlying mechanism.

We have thus very hastily and in a very fragmentary manner reviewed the principal mental and physical symptoms of hysteria as they have been outlined by the French school. Hysteria may take one or any of these forms, or it may widely depart from the usual classical description. What, then, is the cause of these multiform symptoms, how are they to be explained, and how does the hysterical mechanism work? Many theories have been propounded for the cause of hysteria, and although these theories may differ in some minor points, yet their essential ideas remain the same. In other words we seem to be dealing with a peculiar mental state, but whether this mental state is one of increased suggestibility, or an effort on the part of the subject to get rid of painful ideas or of suppressed emotions, the result seems to be the same, namely a dissociation of consciousness leading to mild or severe changes in the personality. We shall now review these theories somewhat in detail.

The work of Janet may be taken as a type of the leading theories of the French school.[1] After dismissing anæsthesia and falsehood as a necessary accompaniment of hysteria he states that the most fundamental stigma of the disease is increased suggestibility. He insists on the marked resemblance between experimental suggestion or hypnosis and spontaneous suggestion or hysteria, thus agreeing with the recent conception of Grasset. Suggestion is the development of an idea, while abstraction is a form of exaggerated absent-mindedness, and both exist to an astonishing degree in hysteria. The subconscious phenomena of hysteria are the results of this disposition to an exaggerated absent-

[1] Pierre Janet: "The Mental State of Hystericals"; "The Major Symptoms of Hysteria."

mindedness; the mind is too narrow to take in a number of ideas at the same time and certain perceptions do not enter consciousness. To this condition Janet applies the phrase " retraction of the field of consciousness." In anæsthesia, it is sensation which escapes personal perception; in paralysis it is movement; in amnesia the storing up or conservation of impressions is entirely disregarded by the patient and hence reproduction of these impressions is at fault. Ideas are very important factors in the symptoms of hysteria. These ideas are all-powerful and dominating, and act upon the body in an abnormal manner. The retraction of the field of consciousness either gives too much power to certain ideas or certain ideas may temporarily drop out of the field of conscious perception. Hence, on the one hand there arises the exaggerated motility of hysteria, and on the other hand, the peculiar amnesia, anæsthesia, and paralyses. Hysteria, therefore, according to Janet's interpretation, is a disease of personal synthesis, a form of mental depression, characterized by a narrowing of the field of personal consciousness and a tendency to the dissociation and emancipation of the systems of ideas and functions which constitute the personality. Its starting point is a depression, an exhaustion of the higher functions of the brain. The dissociation seems to follow several laws; it reacts most powerfully on a function that was weak and disturbed. The most complicated functions disappear first and that particular function is inhibited which was in full activity at the time the emotion or fatigue had its dissociating effect. According to Janet most cases of alternating personality are hysterical in nature. Hysterical anæsthesia is a certain species of absent-mindedness; the sensation itself has not disappeared but is merely dissociated, that is, not connected with the totality of consciousness. In the normal absent-mindedness of everyday life there is also, temporarily at least, a condition of anæsthesia and amnesia, and sometimes even increased suggestibility and a decrease of motor control. In absent-mindedness, too, we may pay little or no attention to a pinch or a pin-prick, we may assume an attitude in which we seem temporarily devoid of all ability to move the limbs, or we may perform absurd actions which can afterwards be recalled in memory only through a special device. Thus we see how many of the phenomena of the hypnotic state or even of the disease hysteria may be found in an abortive and temporary form in normal absent-mindedness. In the hysterical amnesias there is no real oblivion or destruction of memorial images; it is not conservation that is at fault, but merely the impossibility of spontaneous reproduction, yet frequently the memory may be restored by artificial devices. In hysterical paralysis it is the idea of the motion of the limb that is lost or dissociated and not the motion itself. Sometimes this loss comprises an entire system of images of movement as in astasia-abasia. In hysterical blindness or hemianopsia there is no real blindness, the visual images or stimuli being merely suppressed.

Thus we see how both Charcot and Janet laid great stress upon a state of increased suggestibility, as forming one of the principal mental stigmata of hysteria. On this basis another French neurologist, Babinski, has recently brought forth another theory of the disease. He denies the invariability of all so-called hysterical stigmata, claiming that they are all produced by the suggestion, conscious or unconscious, of the examiner. According to Babinski, when great care is taken to exclude any form of suggestion during the medical examination, these stigmata do not appear. This view thus makes use of a state of increased suggestibility as a basis for the production of an entire range of mental and physical symptoms. Emphatically and almost dogmatically he affirms that the common stigmata of hysteria, such as limitation of the field of vision and hemi-anæsthesia, never occur in the patients under his control, since he studiously avoids any element of suggestion in the examination. Hysteria has two prominent characteristics; first, the possibility of producing some of the symptoms of the disease through suggestion, and, secondly, the effect of suggestion in making the symptoms of the disease disappear. It might be asked pertinently, does he also make the abnormal mental state of increased suggestibility disappear, a mental state through which he claims all the symptoms are reproduced? The suggestion theory of Babinski cannot certainly be accepted without considerable criticism or without great caution. It is true that no hysterical symptoms develop without suggestion, either on the part of the examiner or as the result of unconscious autosuggestion on the part of the patient. Babinski says nothing as to the ultimate nature of the disease. According to him hysteria is not a pathological state, but is always the result of a simulation or of suggestion. What Babinski has done is not to explain the mechanism of hysteria, but to lay emphasis upon one of its prominent mental stigmata—namely, a state of increased suggestibility, which, acting from within or from without, can produce a long line of morbid symptoms. Certainly many of the most prominent symptoms of hysteria cannot be explained by Babinski's theory.[1] If a subject is so abnormal as to be open to such a great degree to suggestions of paralysis or loss of sensation, it must logically follow such a subject is in a diseased mental condition.

Sollier[2] has given us a physiological theory for the disease, in contradistinction to the usual psychological interpretations. He claims that hysteria is a peculiar going to sleep of portions and at times of the whole brain. He says, "Hysteria is a physical, functional disturbance of the brain, consisting in a torpor or sleep, local or general, of the cortical (brain) centres, and manifesting itself, according to the centres affected, by vasomotor or trophic, visceral and sensory, motor and psychic disturbances, and, according to its variations, its degree and duration, by transitory crises, permanent stigmata or paroxysmal accidents. Confirmed hysterics are only somnambulists whose state of sleep is more or less profound, more or less extensive." Of this physiological theory of hysteria, it can only be said, that somnambulistic episodes are very rare in the disease, and when they do occur, it is an effect rather than a cause.

In America Dr. Morton Prince has given

[1] J. Babinski: "Ma Conception de l'Hystérie et de l'Hypnotisme." *Archives Général de Medecine,* 1906.

[2] Sollier: "Genèse et Nature de l'Hystérie."

us the most complete study of the hysterical mechanism, interpreting the phenomena from a purely functional and psychological standpoint. He applies his theories to all forms of this protean disease, from the slight disturbances of sensation to the classical picture of the deeper dissociations, such as paralysis, hemi-anæsthesia, amnesia, and the changes in the personality. According to Dr. Prince, one of the most prominent mental stigmata of hysteria is the so-called neurasthenic state, which may be one result of a mental dissociation. He finds the same symptom complex in the so-called dissociated or multiple personality, as in the disease hysteria, and both conditions are merely manifestations of a dissociated personality.[1] He says, " The alternation in mass of an hysterical state with the normal condition allows it to be seen that the hysterical symptom complex is not only a disintegration of the personality, but, from one point of view, a phase of multiple personality. The changing back and forth of the two states, with amnesia on the part of one or the other, or both, brings out the contrast between the hysteric and the normal. The hysteric stands out plainly as a different personality, in the sense of a disintegrated

[1] In addition to other publications previously cited, see " Hysteria from the Point of View of Dissociated Personality."—*Journal Abnormal Psychology,* October, 1906.

personality with a well-organized, though pathologically deranged nervous system. There is a doubling of personality, a normal and an abnormal one, and the abnormal hysteric is seen to be a phase of this double personality. Before the phenomenon of alteration was established, this doubling was obscured by the gradual transition from health to disease and by the retention of memory. There was no contrast. Nevertheless at this period the pathological condition was in every way identical with that which existed after alteration occurred. The conclusion to which our analysis of the case brings us, is that certain symptom complexes which commonly pass under the name of hysteria, with or without amnesia, are from another point of view to be regarded as disintegrated or multiple personality, and if taken in connection with the normal condition, may be regarded as a phase of multiple personality. That is to say, the previous or later acquired normal state may be regarded as one personality, and the disintegrated hysteric as another. As the hysteria, ordinarily developed insidiously, and equally gradually returns to health, retaining a continuous memory through the whole cycle, the splitting of the personality and the multiple characteristics are disguised. One condition slides into the other so gradually that, in the absence of any loss of memory, there is nothing to mark the division of the personality. But when, as is sometimes the case, a sudden restoration to health is effected, bringing with it an amnesia on the part of the hysteric or of the restored normal person, then the duality of personality becomes plainly recognizable." This identity of the hysterical state with multiple personality was clearly brought out by Dr. Prince in two carefully studied cases, that of Miss Beauchamp and that of B. C. A.

Miss Beauchamp was a classical picture of hysteria, and yet, when she first came under observation, B. I. was the only personality in existence. This B. I. had typical neurasthenic symptoms, such as fatigue, insomnia, and pains without any physical basis. These neurasthenic symptoms were proven to be merely one phase of the hysterical dissociation. When the other personalities developed, many of the various hysterical stigmata could be established, the weakness of the will, instability, abnormal suggestibility and limitation of the field of consciousness. When a relapse occurred after restoration by treatment to the normal healthy individual, there was found to be a loss of memory of the developed, hysterical condition for the normal individual.

The case B. C. A. could also be interpreted

as one of hysteria. Like Miss Beauchamp, when first seen she also presented the picture of ordinary neurasthenia, such as fatigue and the usual physical symptoms. This phase was described as state A. Later another state, suddenly developed, which was described as B. A., had no memory for B. but the latter not only possessed a full knowledge of A., but persisted co-consciously when A. was present. This latter phenomenon was well shown by the psychogalvanic experiments. B. was, therefore, both an alternating and a co-conscious state. Besides differences in memory, both A. and B. had distinctly different characteristics. While A. was neurasthenic, B. showed a state of exaltation and complete freedom from neurasthenia. It was shown after long study, that neither A. nor B. represented the normal, complete personality. The normal state was finally obtained in hypnosis, and on being awakened from hypnosis, a personality was found to have developed which possessed the combined memories of A. and B., and was free from the abnormal symptoms which characterized each. This normal personality called C. had, therefore, split into the two abnormal personalities, A. and B.[1]

[1] See "My Life as a Dissociated Personality."—*Journal Abnormal Psychology,* Vol. III.

We are now prepared to take up a theory of the mechanism of hysteria which has recently attracted much attention—namely, the studies of Dr. Sigmund Freud of Vienna. Beginning with certain temporary dissociations which take place in normal individuals, called by Freud the psychopathology of everyday life, he gradually applied his theories to the study of the complex pathological state of hysteria and found that the same mechanism underlay both conditions. In normal cases, however, this mechanism was temporary and isolated; in the hysteric it was protracted and acted upon the entire mental physical life. In his studies of the psychoneuroses he claimed that all hysterical symptoms were manifestations or expressions of a wish fulfilment, particularly of a sexual nature. In normal everyday life disagreeable or painful thoughts are always forgotten; we intentionally, or even unconsciously push them out of consciousness, so as to free ourselves from disagreeable feelings or pain. This may be called a mental protective mechanism. In some of the ordinary dreams of everyday life, its purposeless actions or its absent-minded acts, its forgetting of names and places, slips of the tongue, or mistakes in writing remain temporary because we are able to crowd out these disagreeable feelings or ideas at will. Sometimes, however, a disagreeable incident remains in our unconscious memory, forming what Freud calls a complex. Then, because we have no control over it, this complex acts in a pathological manner. It cannot run its normal course and, therefore, becomes converted or changed into the condition which we designate as hysteria. The method of digging out this buried complex and bringing it to light or consciousness and, therefore, to conscious control, is called psycho-analysis. Now this psycho-analysis may be performed in a number of ways as has already been indicated.

An abstract of the analysis of one of Freud's cases will make this clear. The patient, a governess, was sent to Freud, because she was troubled by the persistent hallucination of the smell of burnt pudding. When the patient was placed in abstraction (here abstraction was the device used for psycho-analysis) and she was asked to recall the occasion on which she first was troubled by the odor, she gave the following account, " It was about two months ago, two days before my birthday. I was with the children in the schoolroom and was playing with them at cooking, when a letter was brought in, which had just been left by the postman. I knew from the postmark and handwriting that it was from my mother, and was about to open and read it when the children rushed at me and tore the letter from my hand, saying, ' No, you mustn't read it now, it's sure to be a congratulatory letter for your birthday, we'll take it away from you.' While they were playing about me a strong odor suddenly spread through the room. The children had left the pudding which they were cooking, and it was burnt. Ever since the smell has pursued me." Further examination, however, revealed the fact that the patient had occasionally secretly cherished the hope of taking the place of the children's mother, and it was only with great difficulty that she was able to get rid of this idea. The psychical excitement, the birthday, and the sexual emotion had become symbolized, converted into the hallucination of smell. Here we see how, at the bottom, the sexual element, or rather the sexual repression was a controlling factor in this process.

It could be shown, that the forgetting of events which were brought out only by analysis was intentional and desired. Concerning the peculiar site of the hallucinations in this case, Freud states, " It is quite unusual to select sensations of smell as memory symbols of traumas, but it is quite obvious why these were here selected. The patient was afflicted with a purulent rhinitis, hence the nose and its perceptions were in the foreground of her attention."

Painful experiences, usually having a sexual coloring, which may or may not be accompanied by a physical expression, may occur. The imprint or experience may fade out of consciousness, but the symbolic emotion which first attended it remains and continues to recur. For this to take place Freud postulates at the time of the original emotion, that the patient was in a state of abstraction called by him an hypnoidal condition. He works out his principles and theories with great detail and with consummate literary skill. These repressed emotions are the mischief-makers at the bottom of all hysteria. If they are given an opportunity to complete themselves, if the patient in a state of relaxation and passivity (abstraction) is asked to talk out these painful experiences, to bring them vividly before his mind, they " cease from troubling " and a decided therapeutic effect is the result. It is the unconscious experiences, the experiences which we cannot recall, of which we are unaware, that cause the trouble. By certain technical devices we may become aware of them, showing that they were dissociated, preserved in the subconscious mental life.

According to Freud, there are several distinct types of hysteria, which he designates as defence hysteria, hypnoid hysteria, conversion hysteria, anxiety hysteria, and retention hysteria. He criticises Janet's theory that a splitting of consciousness is the primary feature of the hysterical alteration, and yet is forced to admit that this splitting exists in a rudimentary form in every hysterical case. Freud defines the defence hysterias as those types of cases in which the splitting of consciousness was an unconscious arbitrary act on the part of the subject. The subject sought to banish a painful emotion or experience from his mind. In the hypnoid hysteria there is a dreamy state of consciousness, in which the abnormal ideas are isolated from communication with the rest of consciousness. In the retention hysterias, as he was able to demonstrate by the psycho-analysis of intelligent patients, the splitting of consciousness plays an insignificant part, perhaps no part at all. The hysterical symptoms in these cases arise as the result of an absence of reaction to a painful experience, usually of a sexual nature. In the conversion hysterias there is a replacement of a mental by a physical manifestation, for instance, either the hysterical paralysis of a limb or an hysterical loss of voice. The anxiety hysterias or the phobias are characterized by attacks of fear in certain situations, such as in open or closed places. The attacks of fear are protective mechanisms to prevent an attack of anxiety. For instance, an individual with a fear of closed places will avoid these places and therefore the fear acts as a preventive of an anxiety attack. Many of the same mechanisms of unconscious repression, censorship, and wish fulfillment as occur in dreams, are at work in the production of hysteria. Therefore, many of the symptoms of hysteria, on careful analysis, can be shown to be a symbolized wish fulfillment.

A few quotations from Freud's original contributions will make his complex theories more intelligible:

"Nevertheless, the causal connection between the provoking psychic trauma and the hysterical phenomenon does not perhaps resemble the trauma which, as the provoking agent, would call forth the symptom which would become independent and continue to exist. We have to claim still more, namely, that the psychic trauma or the memory of the same acts like a foreign body which even long after its penetration must continue to influence like a new causation factor. We found, at first to our greatest surprise, that the individual hysterical symptoms immediately disappeared without returning if we succeeded in thoroughly awakening the memories of the causal process with its accompanying emotion and if the patient circumstantially discussed the process, giving free play to the emotions. Emotionless memories are almost utterly useless. Those memories which become the cause of hysterical phenomena have been preserved for a long time with wonderful freshness and with their perfect emotional tone. As a further striking and later realizable fact we have to mention that the patients do not perhaps have the same control of these as of their other memories of life. On the contrary these experiences are either completely lacking from the memory of the patients in their normal psychic state or at most exist greatly abridged. . . . The splitting of consciousness, so striking in the familiar classical cases of double consciousness, exists rudimentarily in every hysteria, and the tendency towards the appearance of abnormal states of consciousness which we comprehend as 'hypnoid states,' is the chief phenomenon of this neurosis." (Psychic Mechanism of Hysterical Phenomena.)

In a later contribution Freud claims that the voluntary incursions of daydreams into consciousness, or in other words, the fantastic reveries of youth, are the normal, psychical prototypes of hysterical symptoms:

"The hysterical symptoms are nothing other than unconscious fancies brought to light by conversions. . . . The technic of psycho-analysis gives the means of finding out for the symptoms the unconscious fancies and then of bringing them back to the patient's consciousness. (Hysterical Fancies.) Therefore, the hysterical's symptoms may be a memory symbol of certain experiences, the expression of a wish realization or the realization of an unconscious fancy serving as a wish fulfillment."

Considerable stress is laid upon the fact that many hysterical symptoms represent a portion of the sexual experiences of the individual.[1]

Such is a brief account of Freud's dynamic theory of hysteria. For more detailed study, the reader is referred to the original publications.[2] It will be seen that the modern tendency is to disregard the usual classical physical symptoms of hysteria as necessary for a diagnosis and to interpret certain types of mental dissociation as an hysterical complex. Sometimes the condition acts on the whole organism; at others, a few isolated symptoms may be the only manifestations of the dissociation, such as a loss of sensation limited to a portion of one limb. In either case, the underlying mechanism is very complex. It is certainly a step in the right direction to lay more stress on the mental state of hystericals than on the time-honored, so-called physical stigmata. It seems, therefore, that, according to Janet, any sudden emotion may cause hysteria while, according to Freud,

[1] The quotations from Freud are taken from a translation of some of his work by Dr. A. A. Brill. ("Selected Papers on Hysteria and other Psycho-Neuroses," 1909.)

[2] See chapter on the "Analysis of the Mental Life," where a more detailed account of psycho-analysis may be found.

only those emotions or ideas cause hysteria which are painful, and which the subject has difficulty in expelling. Evidently any emotion, if severe enough, can have a selective action in causing a mental dissociation.

Let us follow the ramifications of two cases of hysteria, one with the symptoms in full bloom,—the other, what we may call abortive hysteria, or hysteria in the making, in which the neurasthenic complex was the predominating symptom, until the searchlight of psycho-analysis revealed what lay at the bottom of the hysterical disturbance.

In some of the previous chapters we have already seen different types of hysterical cases, such as sudden losses of memory associated with a wandering impulse, what is called a hysterical fugue, and later restoration of these lost memories by means of certain technical devices; a case showing multiple hypnotic personalities, and a hysterical paralysis and loss of sensation; another case of hysteria with a localized anæsthesia and weakness of the arms occurring after the emotional shock of a funeral, and analyzed by means of the association tests; and finally the case of a young woman in whom the various devices of psycho-analysis were able to bring to light the cause of her hysterical attacks and finally to effect a cure. So we see that the disease hysteria is not confined to any one type or to the classical description. In fact we may have all forms of hysteria, from the slightest disturbance of sensation and motion to complete changes in the personality. It seems best, therefore, to speak of the hysterias rather than of hysteria.

A subject of great interest and importance is the evolution of hysteria, its study in the earliest stages, or what may be called hysteria in the making. At the very outset of the disease, Janet found that his subjects were free from any anæsthesia. He established, however, a remarkable indifference and absent-mindedness to all the phenomena of sensibility. This absent-mindedness to sensations was interpreted as a phenomenon which precedes anæsthesia.

The best examples of hysteria in the making are found among primitive races and in the hysteria of children. In savages the processes of thought are simple, and hence their hysterical symptoms are simple, the same as in the hysteria of children, in whom the objective manifestations are principally mono-symptomatic. There is a certain resemblance likewise between the mental life of the savage and the neurotic, for instance in the relationship of the taboo and neurotic obsession or obsessional prohibition, a comparative feature which is best seen in the fear of touching certain objects (délire de toucher). Suppression is the result of our complex civilization. Savages, like children, have not learned to suppress, and as the dreams of children are perfectly transparent and show little or no symbolism or effort at concealment, so in the savage the hysterical attacks are primitive emotional reactions following almost immediately upon the emotional injury. In other words, there is a complete absence of suppression and unconscious incubation. Their hysterical attacks are merely sudden outbreaks with little or no conversion of unconscious mental states into physical symptoms. These primitive emotional reactions occur in the disease called piblokto of the Eskimos or in the latah or amok of the Malays. In children, too, the hysterical attacks or symptoms are simple conversions of their repressed wishes.

Sometimes in the very earlier stages of hysteria the only symptoms are those of a state of neurasthenic depression. The neurasthenic depression may be a newly developed personality, or it may be the result of an effort to banish a painful experience from consciousness. An example of this latter condition I once had the opportunity to observe. It related to the case of a young woman, a school-teacher, who some weeks after her return from her summer vacation suddenly stopped teaching. She became depressed, claimed that she was not equal to the work, everything seemed dreamlike to her, there was a marked sense of fatigue, and her head ached and felt heavy. Sleep was poor and broken by dreams of her school work. She became seclusive, anti-social, unable to concentrate her mind, and claimed that her thoughts were scattered and wandering. Literature with which she was formerly well acquainted now seemed strange and unreal to her as if she had read it for the first time. None of the so-called physical stigmata of hysteria were present. Psychoanalysis, however, brought out the fact that during her vacation period a certain affair had taken place. Certain experiences in this affair finally led to the whole matter becoming painful and distasteful to her. On her return to work the effort to banish these experiences from consciousness led to the symptoms already detailed. If we interpret this case from Freud's standpoint, it would seem as if the mechanism involved in the effort to put a painful experience out of mind had led to a state of mental dissociation, which in this case took the form of hysteria. It is true that the condition here described did not conform with the usual description of the disease, but we have already pointed out how wide is the conception of hysteria, and how many forms the disease may take.

So important is the subject that even at the risk of repetition we will report another case of hysteria. This case will show how an emotional disturbance finally acquired a separate and independent activity and how it led to a dissociation, manifesting itself by losses of memory, disturbances of sensation, and narrowing of the field of vision. Finally typical hysterical attacks developed through mere association. The case showed that hysterical anæsthesia was not real anæsthesia, that hysterical losses of memory were not real losses of memory, and that the basis of the condition was an emotional experience which became dissociated from consciousness and took on an independent and automatic activity. A young woman had suffered for two years from the following attacks, which were sometimes repeated several times a week. The attacks began with severe headaches, then she would commence to scream, at times violently striking at those about her or breaking objects. There was no memory of these attacks, the amnesic period sometimes comprising several hours. On one or two occasions she had a typical fugue, would wander through the streets for several hours at a time, and then would suddenly come to herself without any memory for the period of wandering. Examination showed complete loss of sensation over the entire right side of the body involving the tongue and mouth, a limitation of the vision to 35 degrees in all directions, loss of taste and smell in the right nostril and on the right side of the tongue, and a diminution of hearing on the right. During one of the attacks of excitement she was very violent to several members of the household; on another occasion she attempted suicide by drinking carbolic acid, on still another occasion an attack followed attendance at a wedding. The patient was easily hypnotized and had complete amnesia for the hypnotic state. In hypnosis the anæsthesia disappeared spontaneously, to return again when the patient was awakened. In her waking condition she could not explain the attacks nor account for their origin. In hypnosis, however, she stated that two years previously, shortly before her sister's wedding she was awakened from a sound sleep one midnight, by the voices of her two sisters quarrelling in the next room. As this was an unusual circumstance in her household she immediately went into a state of great fear and trembling and was unable to sleep the remainder of the night. Three days later she had her first attack of screaming and violence. One of the later attacks at a wedding can easily be explained on the basis of associating her first attack with her sister's wedding. Furthermore, both in hypnosis and in states of experimental distraction I was able to completely restore the lost memories, although the experiences were revived in a rather fragmentary manner. This fragmentary return of the dissociated experiences is well indicated in the isolated synthesis as follows, "All that came to my mind, is—that I'd like to go away." (The patient frequently repeated this latter phrase in the attacks.) "Two weeks ago I had a dream, in which I thought that I would like to kill my father and mother." (In her last attack she actually did refuse to allow her father and mother to enter the room and spoke of killing them.) "I remember I had a big bottle of carbolic acid and drank some, and a smooth-faced doctor came in and gave me something to drink and put hot water to my feet" (correct). "I know how I broke the plate now. The plate was standing on the stove and I broke it with my left hand" (correct).[1]

In the treatment of hysteria, two things must be taken into consideration. First, the tendency

[1] For a more detailed account of the conservation of memories in hysterical amnesia see "The Mechanism of Amnesia."—*Journal of Abnormal Psychology*, Vol. IV, No. 1, 1909.

to increased suggestibility and emotionalism should be combated; second, an attempt should be made to unify the split states of consciousness. Re-education of the emotions is of great importance, but whether this re-education should be accomplished by isolation, persuasion, the personality of the physician, or ignoring of symptoms or psycho-analysis is merely a matter of individual technic. The individual symptoms such as the paralysis, anæsthesia, convulsions, contractures, pains, tremors, require appropriate treatment, particularly electricity, massage, and special baths. The psychic treatment of hysteria, which may be carried out by any of the modern psychotherapeutic methods, requires training and skill. Any element of abnormal suggestion must be carefully avoided, otherwise the ends of treatment might be defeated, by unconsciously substituting a new hysterical symptom for one which has disappeared. Some hysterical cases require psycho-analysis; in others, isolation is indicated; in still others, purely physical therapy is called for. There is no one line of treatment for the disease. The treatment must be modified according to the cause of the disease, its evolution, its particular symptoms, by the social condition and age of the patient, and finally, by the patient's personality.

The psycho-analytic treatment of hysteria represents the latest advance in the efficient therapeutics of the disease. Through this method, the unconscious mental processes which produced the hysterical symptoms are uncovered, and thus the resistance which prevented the unconscious thoughts from entering consciousness, is broken down. The pent-up emotions thus become discharged, are diverted into useful channels instead of into pathological symptoms and thus lose their intensity and baneful influence. The unconscious complexes are brought under the influence of the mind, whereas previously they were inaccessible and led an independent automatic existence. The dissociated elements thus become reassociated and conscious, and the hysterical symptoms, which were caused by a deflection of these dissociated elements, tend to disappear.

CHAPTER VI

PSYCHASTHENIA

For a number of years it had been observed that states of pathological fear or anxiety, obsessions, and fixed ideas, were associated with a peculiar mental state. These various symptoms were formerly thought to be a part of neurasthenia, and hence arose such phrases as neurasthenia with fixed ideas, neurasthenia with fear, etc. In 1903, however, Janet[1] attempted to show that these multiform symptoms were part of a distinct nervous disease, which he termed psychasthenia. This psychasthenic neurosis, while in many cases it bore some resemblance to neurasthenia, hysteria, and epilepsy, yet had many symptoms which occurred in it alone and enabled it to be clearly recognized. These symptoms were partly mental and partly physical. They will be described in the course of this chapter and may be thus enumerated:

1. Obsessions of various kinds, such as obsessions of sacrilege, crime, disgrace of self and body, and hypochondriacal obsessions.

[1] Pierre Janet: "Les Obsessions et la Psychasthénie," 1903.

2. The various mental agitations, such as manias of interrogation, doubt, precision, precaution, repetition, conjuration, and arithmetical manias.

3. Motor agitations or tics.

4. Emotional agitations, which comprised the various phobias or fears, such as phobias of objects (délire du contact), phobias of situation (agoraphobia or fear of open places, and claustrophobia or fear of closed places), and the states of anxiety. Like hysteria, which has so many so-called physical and mental stigmata, various stigmata were likewise found in the psychasthenic state and served to distinguish it from hysteria. These stigmata are the feelings of incompleteness in action, in all intellectual problems, in the emotional sphere, and in personal perception. Under the latter are grouped the strange feelings of unreality and of depersonalization, called by Janet psycholeptic crises. Other stigmata of psychasthenia are disorders of the will, of the intelligence, and of the emotions. Many psychasthenic states also present physical symptoms such as headache, digestive and circulatory disturbances, sleeplessness, and exhaustion.

Psychasthenia has also, by the German school, been termed a compulsion neurosis, because the mental processes of the disease are associated with a feeling of compulsion. The mechanism of the compulsion is very complex and it will suffice to state here that psycho-analytic investigations have shown that the compulsion represents a transformed self-reproach from childhood. This reproach is buried in the unconscious and its disguised form in the consciousness and actions of the individual, constitutes the compulsive act, which is, in some cases, merely an overcompensation for the unconscious reproach. Likewise according to psycho-analytic investigations, the states of fear are termed either anxiety neurosis or anxiety hysteria.[1]

A detailed account of a psychasthenic case will make the condition more comprehensible. This case is taken because it presents in a fairly typical form the headache, gastric symptoms, tics, phobias, depression, lack of energy, and feeling of unreality, which occur in so many psychasthenic states. The patient was a young man whose mother had been a neurasthenic and suffered from sleeplessness for years, and whose sister had nervous dyspepsia. (Neuropathic heredity.) As a boy he stammered badly, suffered from severe one-sided head-

[1] The anxiety neuroses will be discussed in the chapter on neurasthenia. The anxiety hysterias have already been described in the chapter on hysteria.

ache (migraine), and on one occasion, lasting for nearly two years, there was twitching of the face and the eyelids (tics). Ever since reaching adult life, certain words could be pronounced only with great difficulty, and synonyms were often substituted (stammering as a form of mental tic). Whenever he becomes excited, there arises a feeling of distress in the stomach (unstable emotional state). For a number of years there has been a feeling of mental depression associated with digestive disturbances, and although the stomach contents have been repeatedly examined, they have been found normal. When he was about fourteen years old, he remembers having had an attack of unreality, which lasted about twenty minutes. Two years before he came under observation he was sitting in a theatre one evening, when suddenly a feeling of faintness took possession of him. This lasted three or four minutes, but he did not lose consciousness. Within a month this feeling recurred three or four times, usually in church, theatre, or a public place, and he felt that if he did faint, it would be exceedingly embarrassing for him. As a result, he developed a fear of crowds and closed places (claustrophobia) and has almost entirely avoided any public gathering. Sometimes the head feels dazed, and he is depressed and fatigued a great deal of the time. Occasionally he is subject to peculiar nervous crises with a sense of unreality. A vague fear will take possession of him, then headache, eructations of gas from the stomach, then suddenly for a brief period, objects about him appear as if in a haze, dim, small, far away, "as if I am looking through the wrong end of an opera glass." (Psycho-epileptic crisis.)

These psychasthenic conditions, which seem to be related on one hand to hysteria and neurasthenia, and on the other to epilepsy, are of great clinical and psychological interest. There is but little doubt, however, that psychasthenia forms a clinical entity, for the disease picture has symptoms which occur in no other functional neurosis, at least in such fully developed and intense forms. This psychasthenic neurosis is a very complex mental state and comprises the entire range of obsessions, impulses, mental manias, tics, agitations, phobias, states of anxiety, feelings of inadequacy, and the peculiar feelings of strangeness, unreality, and depersonalization. According to Janet, these multiple phenomena are the result of what he called a lowering of the psychological tension, just as hysteria was to him a narrowing of the field of consciousness. Some of the German writers, in particular Freud, interpret the condition on a purely sexual basis and look upon the obsessions, fixed ideas, and phobias as the result of the substitution or reproach for certain suppressed sexual ideas and emotions. An effort to keep this sexual complex or reproach in the background of consciousness causes various abnormal ideas and fears to appear in its place.

Now according to Janet, any variations or disturbances in what he calls the psychological tension, or the normal mental level, that effort of complex mental synthesis, can lead to a psychasthenic state. In many psychasthenic cases a state of mental dissociation follows on this interference with the psychological tension. The peculiar feelings of unreality and depersonalization, during a portion or the whole of the disease, are an evidence of this mental dissociation. These changes in personality in psychasthenia are, however, incomplete, in contradistinction to the hysterical dissociations, where they are often total in their character. One psychasthenic patient offered a very clear example of this incomplete mental dissociation. In one of the states she felt as if she were "a bloodless nothing," a sense of tension, everything seemed out of harmony, she experienced darting pains all over the body and had difficulty in breathing. "I feel as if I were going to pieces. My neck is brittle, I feel as if I were a piece of chalk and would break in pieces. I seem to have no personality. I am rigid and brittle. I am nothing and float along. If I shut my eyes I do not think or feel." In the second state she had a sense of being "solid and good, like a living plant," ideas came without a feeling of effort, there was a sense of physical well-being, of cheerfulness, "I feel I am something, I know what I am. I am an entirely different person and these other things seem unreal to me." These different states of personality would alternate with one another and were of several hours' duration.

Psychasthenia may be either hereditary or acquired. In the hereditary cases, there is usually a history of some mental or nervous disease, either in the direct family or in some of its collateral branches. Many psychasthenic patients have been shy and timid, from childhood up, blushing on slight occasions and subject to day-dreaming, imaginative lying, and mental rumination, a tendency which is also noticeable in some hysterics. In the acquired cases, the disease is usually brought about through an emotional shock. The incidents of this emotional shock, by a kind of an unconscious auto-suggestion, tend to repeat themselves automatically, and thus there arise the various obsessions and the recurrent attacks of fear. When the memory for the original episode enters consciousness it usually does so automatically and suddenly, to the exclusion of everything else. Hence arises the mental torture of the obsessions and phobias with their various physical symptoms. One woman developed a fear of closed places because on one occasion, while in a state of fatigue, during a visit in a small, close room, there arose a slight fainting attack. In still another case there developed a fear of crowds, because some time previously at a crowded school celebration, the patient became slightly overcome by heat and felt like screaming. Now in conditions like these, the recurrence of the fear is automatic, and the mental state of fear that develops is accompanied by its usual physical symptoms, such as trembling, palpitation of the heart, dryness of the mouth, a dazed condition of the mind, and cold perspiration. Sometimes the original incident cannot be voluntarily recalled, because it is dissociated. Under these conditions, the emotional state alone enters consciousness periodically. These so-called fear neuroses are really psychasthenic states.

The obsessions are intellectual phenomena of the highest order, are ideas usually of a pathological character. They are frequently very abstract and complicated ideas. They are called obsessions because they *obsess* or *possess* the mind of the subject to the exclusion of nearly everything else. The obsessions are characterized by their absence of usefulness in practical life; in fact, they may be interpreted as pathological and not as normal ideas. They are usually divided into five classes, which again may have numerous subdivisions and variations, and relate to all the acts of everyday life. These five classes are, in general, obsessions of sacrilege, crime, disgrace of body, disgrace of self, and hypochondriacal ideas. In spite of their variation and multiplicity of symptoms, the obsessions have many common characteristics. They are usually automatic in their action and dominating in character, and while at times they may be less insistent than at others, yet during the course of the disease, they are usually more or less present in the consciousness of the subject. Thought is always directed towards peculiar behavior, and extremes of behavior and actions are marked. There is a strong tendency to action, with a very marked absence of execution, hence obsessions are usually associated with a certain weakness of the will. In spite of this weakness of the will, some patients will perform acts having some relation to the obsession, or even contrary acts may be the result of the dominating idea, a kind of a reaction of defence. Sometimes these obsessions are associated with hallucinations, the hallucinations are always vague, thus differing from the same phenomena of the insane. The visual image seems to be without color, and in the auditory type the words are without sound; they have not the characteristics of exteriority, they lack reality, they are merely symbolic of the dominating idea. Frequently these obsessed patients are forced to think in an exaggerated and unnatural manner, their head " works " in spite of them, they feel compelled to accomplish useless movements and have violent, irresistible emotions.

One of the most common of these obsessive states is what is known as the obsession of self-consciousness. Here the subject becomes abnormally self-conscious in everything he does, a distinct embarrassment and timidity arises, particularly in the presence of strangers, sometimes the hands tremble, and blushing is quite frequent. This pathological blushing is known as erythrophobia and it is really only a symptom of a pathological self-consciousness.

One patient became obsessed with the idea that perhaps he had done something wrong during a certain examination. He analyzed his mental state as follows—" All this time there was hardly a quarter of an hour when I was free from the obsessing ideas. At first I laughed at the idea. Then I remembered that some one had once shown me some dates and asked me if they were correct. I feared that I had seen some dates and used them. Then I remembered that once I was given a foreign text without notes or vocabulary, in order to translate a passage at sight. One word puzzled me and I turned over some leaves to see if I could find it in another context which would indicate its meaning. I remember saying to myself, 'No, I won't do that, some one might think I was cribbing.' I stopped, although, of course, the thing was entirely proper. Then I began to think that while, of course, I could never have taken help with me to the examination, yet I might have copied off the paper of some one near me. I couldn't remember doing such a thing, but I couldn't remember *not* doing it. Then I began to think, that perhaps the reason I couldn't remember copying was because it was so habitual that it made no impression on my mind. I wrote to the school and discovered that the distance between the desks was so great that it was impossible for a man to copy. That eased my mind, but then came the idea that perhaps I had taken help into the class. This was strengthened by the discovery that I had forgotten so many incidents in my life." The above shows in an admirable manner the peculiar manner of thinking and the abnormal logic of an obsessed patient and how he will go to extremes of action in the attempt to either prove or disprove his obsessing idea.

Obsessions are compulsory ideas, and from these obsessions it is but a step to other peculiar compulsory thoughts, known as mental manias or agitations. Here the mind of the subject swings or oscillates hopelessly between certain given ideas, never reaching a normal mean, but going from one absurd extreme to the other. These unfortunate subjects can never arrive at a final decision or a complete conviction. Shakespeare's *Hamlet* is a type of this condition of indecision.

In the mania of interrogation, the questioning relates mainly to the subject's personal appearance. One patient was constantly troubled by a fear of growing old, frequently looked at herself in a mirror, and constantly repeated to herself, "Why are these men working? Why is this woman happy? Why is this house pretty? Why do people buy pretty things? I can't keep from getting old, and this is on my mind all the time. Everything I see reminds me of getting old. I noticed a couple of wrinkles under my eyes and then I wondered if other people had them, and then I kept looking and looking at myself."

In the mania of hesitation and deliberation

the doubts which assail the mind of the subject prevent the execution of all normal acts. Sometimes the patient is troubled with a mania of omens and then seeks the determination and carrying out of his actions in certain mystical and religious symbols. This type of mania can be found in the confessions of certain writers, like Rousseau, and in the pages of certain mystics, like John Bunyan.

After a time, these manias may react in ways called by Janet the "manias of going to extreme." Here we have a multitude of subdivisions whose symptoms are sufficiently indicated by their names. These manias are precision, verification, order, symmetry, contrast, contradiction, cleanliness, micromania, the arithmetical and symbolic manias, explanation, precaution, repetition, perfection, etc. The arithmetical manias are very curious and a number of these have as their basis superstitions which attach to certain numbers, for instance, three, seven, or thirteen. Some patients will avoid certain numbers; in others, a number becomes a fixed idea. One patient felt compelled to count, in spite of herself, the number of fingers with which she touched an object, and for nothing in the world would she touch an object with seven fingers at a time. If she happened to touch an object completely with three fingers and lightly with the fourth, this light touch would count as half a finger. This, if multiplied by two (because there are two hands), would equal seven, and hence the terrible number would again arise.

The motor agitations or tics frequently accompany certain psychasthenic states. These are peculiar muscular contractions, either shaking of the head or twitching of the face, in fact, any sort of muscular activity of which the human body is capable may enter into a tic. Tics are systematized muscular movements produced regularly and automatically, thus differing from the irregular muscular movements of chorea or St. Vitus' dance. The movements are useless and inopportune, however. Consciousness is always clear during these movements, but the will feels forced into their accomplishment. If there should arise a feeling of resistance, there always accompanies this more or less mental anguish, until the act is accomplished. When the subject thinks of it, or when there is increased attention, there is likewise an increase of the tic. Distraction has a contrary effect; it leads to a diminution.

Under the emotional agitations are comprised the various pathological fears (phobias) and states of anxiety which usually accompany these fears. The number of these fears is legion, but for convenience they may be divided into four groups, viz.:—phobias of bodily functions, phobias of objects (délire du contact), phobias of situation (agoraphobia and claustrophobia), and phobias of ideas.

These fears are always abnormal in character and, like the obsessions, are automatic. They may arise gradually, but their more frequent onset is through some emotional shock in a certain place, which later tends to recur when the subject is in an identical place or anticipates being in such a place. So we see that auto-suggestion is an important fact in the production of these pathological states of fear. The attacks of fear are accompanied by a mental state of anxiety; sometimes the mind becomes a little cloudy; sometimes there arises a transitory feeling of unreality. These mental accompaniments of fear form true psychasthenic crises. Psychasthenic fears are usually intense, systematized, and may attach themselves to any object or idea. Among the more common fears, are the fear of being alone (monophobia), fear of closed places (claustrophobia), fear of open places (agoraphobia), fear of dirt or germs (mygophobia), fear of the number thirteen (triskaidekaphobia), fear of railroads (siderophobia), etc. Stage fright is also a condition of pathological fear. In addition to the mental state of anxiety that accompanies the attack of fear, there are also associated the usual physical accompaniments of fear, such as trembling, pallor, sweating, dryness of the mouth, increased heart action, and occasional disturbances of the stomach and intestines, all of which have already been sufficiently described in the chapter on the emotions. Most of the fears can be traced to an emotional episode which has been conserved in the unconscious; in a few cases, the original episode has become dissociated.

In these states of abnormal fear, when the original experience which caused the fear has become dissociated from consciousness, it is necessary to form a synthesis before a cure can take place. This is well indicated in the following personal observation. After a period of fatigue, incident to some rather strenuous social duties, a young woman had a peculiar attack one evening, just as she was about to fall asleep. She suddenly awakened from a drowsy state with a sensation as if she were going insane, her thoughts seemed confused and jumbled, the head whirled, the heart palpitated, and she felt in a panic. This attack was of about ten minutes' duration. The attacks repeated themselves nearly every night thereafter and tended to become longer and longer. An examination showed that the patient was free from any signs of hysteria. She was unable to explain the origin of the attacks. Here, undoubtedly, we are dealing with a recurrent state of fear, probably due to some experience in the past, but which, by reason of the physical exhaustion, had become dissociated from the personal consciousness. Psycho-analysis led to the following interesting results. When the patient was placed in a state of experimental abstraction, a record of experiences was obtained, fragmentary at first, but they finally could be grouped into a logical order, in the same manner that the lost memories appear in functional amnesia. These dissociated experiences showed briefly that following a period of fatigue incident to the entertainment of some friends, the subject shortly afterward went on a visit, without complete recovery from the fatigue. While on the train, she became greatly interested in a novel. In this novel there was given a vivid description of fear in one of the principal characters. In general this character became panic-stricken under certain conditions which it is not necessary to explain here. That same night the patient had her first attack of fear, and this was indefinitely repeated as detailed above. While in this state of experimental abstraction, in which the submerged memories were brought to the surface of consciousness, when asked to think of this experience, there was an immediate increase in the pulse rate. [See Fig. VIII. A.]

These details are very instructive and emphasize the following points. During a state

Fig. VIII.—Pulse curves in a psychasthenic subject, who had peculiar attacks of fear.

A.—Increase of pulse rate when requested to mentally recall the original emotional experience.

B.—No change in pulse rate after recovery when requested to think of the same emotional experience.

At 1 in each case the test was made.

of fatigue certain incidents of a novel impressed themselves with great force upon her mind. While reading she was probably in one of those states of normal abstraction which have been already described. In this state of abstraction and fatigue, certain impressive incidents became immediately dissociated from consciousness and she could not voluntarily reproduce them. Hence a mental state of fear arose, with its accompanying physical symptoms, a mental state which exerted its baneful influence because it had an activity independent of the subject's consciousness.

In a condition like this, if the dissociated experience were synthetized with consciousness and thus brought under control and censorship, the attacks ought to cease. This, in fact, was the case, and the patient recovered after this synthesis was accomplished. Coincident with the recovery, no further quickening of the pulse took place, when she was again asked to think of the original experience. [See Fig. VIII. B.] The physiological reaction of the pulse increase and the mental state of fear ceased because the emotions could now run a normal course.

Sometimes, too, a recurrent attack of fear will take place, due to an association with some of the elements of the original attack. Here the psychasthenic state becomes what has been termed an association neurosis. In these conditions, if an analysis be made according to the association method, it will be found that a slowness of reaction will take place with test words related to the original experience. In one case of this class, for instance, it was noted that while the reaction time for indifferent words varied between two and three seconds, yet for words relating to the emotional experience, the reaction time was increased from seven to twenty-five seconds. Here the emotional factor caused not only the recurrent attacks of fear, but also the inhibition of thought.

While the phobias are classed under the head of systematized emotional agitations, the diffuse emotional agitations may be termed states of anxiety. Yet this latter is merely the mental and physical anguish that accompanies the phobias and obsessions; they are really the psychical and physical correlatives of the emotional state of the obsessed or fearful subject. In the same manner a state called mental rumination accompanies the manias, a sort of pathological "to be or not to be," in which the subject accumulates ideas, piles question upon question, and finally loses himself in an inextricable maze of symbolism.

A brief account of two cases will show the nature of these psychasthenic fears. The first patient, on one occasion, two years previously, while riding horseback, suddenly came to an open field. Immediately he became frightened, thought that he was going to fall off the horse, felt faint, the heart beat rapidly, he perspired freely, and trembled all over. He felt, to use his own expression, "as if the end of the world was coming." Since then he has been afraid of open places, or public squares, fields, and parks. If he goes into an open space, there results a repetition of the first attack of fear. Later he also developed a fear of closed places, such as cars and subways. In a closed place he becomes uneasy, develops a marked sense of anxiety, and feels like fainting. Here we have a typical example of the fear of both open and closed places (agoraphobia and claustrophobia).

In another patient, these crises of anxiety due to fear became very intense and led to a sense of partial depersonalization. The patient expressed his condition as follows: "I am horror-stricken. I am in a horrible daze all the time. There is nothing to me. I can't think or do anything. When I go out in the street, I am in constant fear of people. I feel panic-stricken. I have a frightful time getting home. I feel all contracted and cannot move, you can see my heart thumping all over, and I seem to feel disjointed, I have no legs or arms or hands, my sensations are gone. My limbs seem to belong to some one else."

There are two symptoms which frequently occur in psychasthenia and which in many ways are characteristic of the disease. These symptoms are the feeling of unreality and the sense of depersonalization. The latter, in particular, shows that in many psychasthenics we are dealing with a form of mental dissociation. While these symptoms may also occur in certain mental diseases, such as melancholia, yet in the latter condition they are mere episodes, while in psychasthenia they result from the nature of the disease process itself. The feeling of unreality relates either to the outside world or to the subject's own mental or physical personality. When the mental or physical personality is involved in the feeling of unreality, there follows that marked sense of depersonalization or the peculiar change in the identity of the subject. The explanation of this sense of unreality has given rise to many conflicting theories. Into these psychological explanations we cannot enter in detail, further than to state a few of the main facts of two of the opposing theories. Some German investigators claim that the symptom is due either to a disorder of the organic sensations, particularly the muscle sensations, or to an alteration in the feeling of recognition. Janet calls the phenomenon a psycholeptic crisis and claims that the symptom has nothing to do with organic sensations, because a careful search for changes in sensation in his case revealed nothing. Still others consider these strange feelings of unreality as a kind of diluted or lengthened epileptic attack which, if compressed into a shorter length of time, would result in unconsciousness. As a rule, the sense of unreality comes on very suddenly and just as suddenly ends. Sometimes it is of only a few minutes' duration, at other times it may last for days and weeks, and then it is accompanied by intense anxiety because of the inability of the subject to properly grasp either the external world or his own personality.

The external senses act only in an accessory and secondary manner in the "feeling" of the personality. All sensory perception is made up of two elements, the specific or sensorial element and the organic or myopsychic element. This latter is made up of sensations of muscular activity, and the memory images of this activity are intimately united to the images of organic sensations of the internal or visceral organs. Their totality contributes to what is called the cenesthesia, the sense of our bodily existence, of our physical personality, the vague feeling which we have of our being, independently of the evidence of our senses. Now when this cenesthesia is disturbed in any of its parts, the feeling of unreality or depersonalization arises, due, according to one school, to changes in the organic sensations, and according to the other to a lowering of the mental level which interferes with the normal sense of reality.

Now this sense of unreality may be of several varieties. The personality may appear changed, so that the subject loses his identity, either in part or in whole; the external world may appear strange, dreamy, misty, phantom-like, unreal; familiar objects may appear as if seen for the first time; finally, the personality may change from time to time, a real multiple personality occurring in a psychasthenic; in a few cases, even the thoughts may appear unreal, not a part of the subject's self, and finally there may be a sense of entire negation of self and of the universe. So we see that this sense of unreality may present varying degrees of intensity, from the very mildest forms to a complete sense of negation. A few details from cases will make this strange phenomenon clear.

In the first patient, the attacks came on suddenly and were of only a few minutes' duration. The patient would suddenly feel strange, a sensation would take possession of her as if she were "pushed away," as "though my real self were away off there, and I didn't belong to myself. Things did not seem to belong to me, as if I were not a part of the surroundings. Things did not look natural. I wondered how I got there, and to whom all these things belonged."

Another patient described her condition as follows: "I can't form a mind picture of where I live. I am all alone in my mind. Things change every day. The looks of my house and the street seem to change every day. It seems as if I lived long ago, as if I did everything before. It is all past, there is no present and no future. I am not conscious of sleep. I just open my eyes. I don't know who I am,—I've lost my identity. My mind is all gone, it seems as if there was nothing there. The *feel* of things is unnatural. I look at my body and wonder if it is mine, and I wonder if my mind is in my body. Everything looks large and magnified, and everything in the distance appears close."

A third patient felt that "nothing is right. I don't feel like myself. I think I have a Dr. Jekyll and Mr. Hyde existence." Still another patient expressed herself as follows: "I feel as if I move in a great space of the world, I am not related to anything in the world. I feel that I am not myself, that only a part is myself. I that *was*, am I no longer."

The treatment of these psychasthenic states is distinctly psychotherapeutic, either by direct suggestion in certain artificial states, through synthesis, or by means of psycho-analysis. Re-education of the emotions is of particular value in psychasthenia. In all conditions, the physical element of treatment through baths, electricity, rest, and drugs must not be neglected.

CHAPTER VII

NEURASTHENIA

Hysteria, psychasthenia, and neurasthenia may be called the great triad of functional neuroses. The last, however, is by far the most common of the three. The subject of neurasthenia is a vast one, not only because of the wide distribution of the disease, but also from its complex symptoms. The history of the disease bears a curious analogy to that of hysteria. Whereas, both diseases were formerly considered to have a physical basis, hysteria as being dependent on some uterine disturbance and neurasthenia as a form of genuine nerve exhaustion, modern investigations have shown the purely functional character of both these diseases. With the exception of Freud's recent theories on the part played by sexual emotions in the genesis of hysteria and some obsessions, the only survival of the old sex idea is in the etymology of the word, in the same way that " nervous exhaustion " persists as a popular term for the extremely complex psychological phenomena of neurasthenia. Although neurasthenia is the most common of all the functional neuroses, particularly in modern times and in our large cities, yet there is no word in medicine which has been so loosely or so vaguely used. How many patients are conventionally labelled with this disease because of slight depression and fatigue symptoms, when in reality, in some of these cases, the neurasthenic state is an outward expression of another functional disturbance. Sometimes a severe organic nervous disease may tend to resemble neurasthenia. In other cases, mild forms of dementia præcox are sometimes mistaken for neurasthenia. The psychical condition of certain mild forms of depression resembles the mental state of neurasthenia, but close analysis will bring out several prominent features which clearly differentiate the condition from the neurasthenic state. These mild depressions, which are usually periodic in character, are termed cyclothemia. Freud tends to distinguish between the "actual neuroses," in which the causative agent is usually active at the time of the first appearance of the symptoms, as in neurasthenia, and the psycho-neuroses, in which the symptoms arise from unconscious, repressed thoughts in childhood, such as hysteria and psychasthenia. In this chapter we can discuss only the most essential points of the disease from the standpoint of abnormal psychology.

In other words, we shall attempt to show that, like hysteria and multiple personality, neurasthenia is but one of the many expressions of a dissociation of the personality. It is thus the psycho-genetic viewpoint which is of value in elucidating neurasthenia, rather than an attempt to correlate the neurasthenic symptom-complex with a physiological substratum. The two principal factors producing this neurasthenic dissociation are the emotions and fatigue. In a previous chapter we have already seen how certain depressing emotions may lead to dissociation of consciousness, while, on the contrary, the emotion of well-being and exaltation has an opposite synthetic effect. Before we take up the subject of neurasthenia as a functional, fatigue neurosis, we will briefly direct our attention to fatigue itself, in its physiological, psychological, and pathological aspects.

Fatigue is one of the phenomena of over-stimulation. If living tissue be subjected to long-continued or oft-repeated stimuli of any kind, after a time it passes into a condition which we call fatigue. In fatigue there is a decrease of the irritability of living substance, and even if the intensity of the stimulus remains the same, the results of the stimulation gradually become less and less. In addition, it will be found that it takes a stronger and stronger stimulus to bring about any reaction at all, until, finally, a point is reached where even the strongest stimuli are ineffective. If an isolated muscle of a frog be stimulated until it becomes incapable of further work and then the muscle is flushed or washed out with normal salt solution, it will again respond to stimulation. The Italian physiologist Mosso has shown that the introduction of the blood of fatigued dogs into the veins of fresh, healthy dogs, will give rise, in the latter, to definite symptoms of fatigue. These experiments demonstrate that in fatigue certain deleterious products accumulate which act as poisons, and that these products prevent any further reaction of the living tissue to stimulation until they are removed. In normal tissue these fatigue products disappear after rest and sleep. Here we have an explanation, partial at least, of the beneficial results of rest and sleep in normal and pathological fatigue. Since most neurasthenic states are only partially benefited through rest, and in some cases not at all, we must interpret neurasthenia as only partial fatigue neurosis. In fact, fatigue is only one of the factors in the production of neurasthenia as certain emotions can also cause the disease. The neurasthenic state appears to be but one of the many expressions of a dissociation of the personality.

Certain definite mental symptoms may also appear in fatigue. These are restlessness, diminution of attention, lack of energy, emotional instability, leading to apparently causeless laughter or crying, disturbances of association of ideas and difficulty in recalling words (amnesia). In addition, sensations which enter consciousness may be so abnormally felt as to become painful. This increased sensitiveness to certain stimuli such as light, noise, or even music, a kind of a fatigue hyperæsthesia, is a frequent accompaniment of the neurasthenic state. How many neurasthenics exclaim, "How noises grate and jar on me!" When fatigue is carried to a point beyond the possibility of recovery by rest or nutrition it then becomes pathological. Exhaustion of the nervous system may take place either because abnormally high demands are made upon the nerve tissue, or because there is not sufficient compensation for the functioning of the tissue. Therefore, for the maintenance of an absolutely perfect function of the nervous system the relation of function to reparative and nutritive processes must be accurately balanced. If there is an excess of function, the nervous system, in the intervals of rest, may not be able to repair the loss sustained by its activity. As a result, either a progressive degeneration or a functional disintegration of the entire neuron follows, leading to many forms of organic or functional disorders of the nervous system. These functional disintegrations may lead to definite changes in the personality and thus cause such conditions as the neurasthenic, hysterical, and psychasthenic states. Chemical analyses and the microscope have revealed nothing in neurasthenia. In spite of the old dictum that there can be no thought or nerve activity without the presence of phosphorus, yet analyses of the brain in neurasthenia have shown no diminution or changes in its highly phosphorized constituents. Chemical investigations of the excreta have likewise been barren of results and there has not been the slightest evidence, experimental or otherwise, for the validity of the hazy auto-intoxication theory.

While it is true that fatigue may cause a neurasthenic state, it seems also true that neurasthenia is not a pure fatigue neurosis. This can be made clear, if attention be briefly directed to fatigue phenomena in the nervous system. As the result of careful experiments, it has been shown that the peripheral nerves, spinal cord, and brain are extremely resistant to fatigue, and that it is in the muscles that we must look for most fatigue phenomena. It is pointed out by Sherrington, that the reflex arcs in the spinal cord, which are composed of chains of nerve cells, "seem from experimental evidence to be relatively indefatigable." When the muscle is fatigued, its contractions are not so rapid as in normal muscles. That is why we work more slowly and with a sense of effort when we are tired. Now the sensations from these fatigued muscles enter consciousness and instead of "brain fag" or "nervous exhaustion," there is merely a consciousness of this muscular fatigue. The fatigue of neurasthenia is probably of this nature, because many cases of neurasthenia exist in which fatigue as a causative factor has been entirely absent. While at the beginning of the disease, there may be a genuine muscular fatigue, this fatigue ought to disappear after rest, because the muscles have had a chance to recuperate. This disappearance of fatigue phenomena in muscles, after rest, is in harmony with all the facts of experimental physiology. But in most cases of neurasthenia, even after a prolonged rest cure, the sense of fatigue continues. It may be indefinitely prolonged and even further rest will not serve to dissipate it. Now if the real muscular fatigue must have disappeared through rest, what, then, remains? Obviously, only the consciousness of the past muscular fatigue. The sense of fatigue has left its impression on the brain, in the same manner that a person feels a missing limb, long after it has been amputated. The limb left its impression on the brain, in what is vaguely termed the organic sensation. When the limb was amputated, this sensation remained as a memory, because of its long period of constant impression. So it is with the fatigue of neurasthenia. The real muscular fatigue has disappeared, only its memory, a false image of the fatigue, remains. Of course, by this we do not mean that the nervous system never becomes fatigued. This fatigue takes place only under special conditions, however, such as severe overwork without adequate repair by rest or nutrition. It is in this real fatigue of the nervous system, particularly after certain experiments in animals, that changes have been found in the nerve cells. These fatigue changes in the nerve cells are entirely absent in neurasthenic subjects. We do insist, however, that in most cases of neurasthenia we are not dealing with an exhaustion of the nervous system, but merely with a memory of past muscular fatigue.

There may be all grades of neurasthenia, from the slightest phenomena to the most severe types. It may be that the subject complains of only slight depression or fatigue symptoms, sometimes there are definite changes in the personality, on other occasions the neurasthenic state may be the outward expression of another functional disorder, particularly hysteria. In fact, neurasthenic symptoms occur so frequently in hysteria that they constitute one of the most important so-called stigmata of the disease. For instance, one neurasthenic showed peculiar changes in the organic sensations, in which she was unable to appreciate the taste of bitter, or tell the difference between heat and cold, neither had she any sensations of fatigue or hunger. Another one felt as if her head and body were apart, as if the "two hemispheres of my brain were separated," and at other times she experienced sensations "as if I were shrinking, shrinking away to nothing." In still another case, there existed a complete sense of change of personality, the patient stating, "It was as though I had possessed a dual personality." Miss Beauchamp, a case in which it was shown that the neurasthenic state was merely one of four personalities, presented many similar phenomena. Here, in addition to her normal self, there was a hypnotic personality known as B. I., and three other personalities known as B. II., B. III., and B. IV. Each of these personalities had a different degree of health. One personality was decidedly neurasthenic, demonstrating that neurasthenic symptoms are often an evidence of a functional disintegration.

Neurasthenia is very widely distributed in all countries. It occurs about as frequently in males as in females. Even children may have it, and it is fairly common at about the period of puberty. Heredity predisposes to the disease, and fatigue, worry, emotional factors, and certain sexual disorders are frequent causes. Slight or grave emotional shocks in railroad or other accidents, particularly where the accident is unexpected, may lead to the so-called traumatic neuroses, which are either hysterical or more frequently of the neurasthenic type. Mental overwork may cause neurasthenia, in that it more easily facilitates the dissociation of the personality, and the fatigue induced by this overwork tends to automatically keep up this dissociation. Certain types of what is called congenital neurasthenia, in which the subject from childhood up complains of physical weakness and mental insufficiencies, really belong to the psychasthenia group. The mental and physical make-up of such subjects is what may be termed a psychasthenic constitution.

Abnormal psychology interprets neurasthenia as a functional disorder, and like hysteria, multiple personality, and the psychasthenic states, it is one of the forms of dissociation of consciousness. This explains the frequent inefficiency of the purely physical treatment of the disease.

The disease, however, frequently has purely physical complications, such as gastric disorders, intestinal fermentation and a poor blood state, which, of course, need appropriate treatment. That these complications are the cause of the disease is very doubtful in the light of modern investigations, although certain purely physical diseases may lead to a condition strongly resembling neurasthenia, but probably not identical with it.

The sense of healthy personality depends upon the general feeling of comfort in our organic sensations, as they are conveyed to consciousness. A healthy personality is a unity, a synthesis of various organic and mental sensations. Anxiety, depression, fatigue, worry, if they do occur in the healthy individual, are usually transitory episodes. Any disturbance of the organic sensations can carry this anxiety, depression, or fatigue to an abnormal degree, and there arises a sense of discord between one's self and the outer world. In particular, abnormal fatigue or abnormal emotions tend to disturb the balance of organic sensations and a state of functional disintegration is produced with all its physical, intellectual, and emotional phenomena. The unity has fallen apart, and there results a state of weakened synthesis, disintegration, dissociation, call it what you will.

Fundamentally a change in the personality is produced, a dissociation of consciousness, and this dissociation may lead, according to its intensity, to either hysteria, multiple personality, or neurasthenia. Therefore neurasthenia, like hysteria, is a state of abnormal, functional disintegration. This disintegration or dissociation is an abnormal psychological phenomenon, and like all other phenomena of its particular type, it tends to take on an automatic activity and becomes a habit. Hence the stubborn persistence of all neurasthenic symptoms to treatment. The weakened synthesis in neurasthenia tends to the development of unstable psychic elements and the personality becomes disordered. The fatigue in particular, as was previously pointed out, is not real but is due to the persistence of certain abnormal organic sensations in consciousness. The real fatigue which first caused the neurasthenic dissociation has vanished, and in the abnormal mental state thus produced there is a tendency to repeat automatically the previous sensations of fatigue.

Neurasthenic symptoms, although mental, are not imaginary. The neurasthenic is a real sufferer. The catalogue of his ills is large and formidable, yet how different is the living neurasthenic from his inanimate counterpart of the text-books. The most striking point about the neurasthenic is his introspection, his continual morbid self-analysis. Only under the stress of intense emotions does the neurasthenic forget himself. The personality has become changed. Interest in things about him is lost, he feels broken up, depressed, anxious, cannot control his thoughts or feelings. The mental state of neurasthenia and its effect on the personality can perhaps best be conveyed by the following extracts from the letter of a highly intelligent patient:

"I found an excessive self-consciousness, extreme sensitiveness, that showed itself in a way I could neither understand nor overcome. It seemed to me the fear and apprehension with which I had lived and suffered so long had persisted. The way in which this fear was manifested was exceedingly trying, humiliating, and perplexing to me. Most unexpectedly a fear of some one with whom I was associated would seize me, not necessarily a person whom I disliked, but most often it would be some one for whom I felt the greatest respect, and even affection. This fear would become a veritable panic and would seem to take possession of me, enchaining my mind, body, and soul, making me helpless. I could not act out my real self, and found it impossible to express myself naturally, either by word or act, and internally I suffered intensely. Often the nervous agitation would be so great that I would be weak and even sore from its effects. As a rule I resisted this strange intangible influence, with all the energy of my being, but it was very seldom I was able to overcome it. As a rule it baffled me, and when I felt I had done all I could and failed, I would simply leave the place and person, feeling myself conquered by an unseen, unreal, evil force, outside, apparently, of myself. Under this malign influence I lost my sense of the proportion of things; this awful, diseased imagination assumed such a mountainous size in my thoughts and life, at times all else was secondary to it."

After a recovery through educational methods, the condition is described as follows:

"It would almost seem as though I were describing another person. My old self seems so far away and the old periods of depression and agony are like a bad dream from which I have awakened. The old sense of unreality and the feeling that I was alone, an exception to the rest of humanity, is a thing of the past. Now I found the old, morbid, dismal thoughts and habits which had become automatic and thoughtless, had been replaced by exactly the opposite thoughts and habits, and these are becoming more and more automatic and thoughtless."

Another patient described the neurasthenic state as follows:

"I am torn to pieces, I almost can feel every blood cell. I was much fatigued when I woke up this morning. I am just dead tired and trembling and shaking all over."

One of the most striking facts about the neurasthenic state is the automatic character of the symptoms. The continual self-analysis and the diminution of lack of outside interests tend to keep up these symptoms. The patient becomes obsessed by the idea of fatigue, that he must not overdo. In this state of weakened synthesis, the most unstable psychical elements develop. All the principal neurasthenic symptoms, such as fatigue, the fleeting pains, the headache, sleeplessness, sense of muscular weakness, can be explained on a psychological basis. In neurasthenia, as in hysteria, there is a narrowing of the field of personal consciousness.

The symptoms of neurasthenia are manifold. Since a minute description is beyond the scope of this discussion, we will mention very briefly the principal symptoms of neurasthenia. One of the most prominent complaints is a sense of fatigue, which is very slightly or not at all modified by rest, as most neurasthenics are decidedly more fatigued in the morning, even if they have slept well during the night. The fatigue is probably not a real fatigue, but a false one. Neurasthenics, when under stress of a painful emotion, either lose their sense of fatigue or cease to pay any further attention to it. A sense of fatigue which extends over a number of years, as we see it in many neurasthenics, which is not improved by rest, and which fails to cause collapse or a physical breakdown, cannot be identical with normal, physiological fatigue. According to Hartenberg[1] the fatigue of neurasthenia is merely the consciousness of the muscular weakness of this disease. This diminution of muscular energy and its rapid exhaustion in neurasthenia may be measured with the ergograph. By means of this instrument it can be demonstrated that muscular fatigue sets in very quickly, although the amount of energy may at first be equal to that of normal individuals. The diminution and the inhibition of muscular activity in neurasthenic states can be gradually overcome through continued work, a kind of process known in psychology as "warming up." This is one of the reasons for the therapeutic benefit derived from mild exercise in neurasthenia.

Depression, dull headaches, and sleeplessness are quite common in neurasthenia, the insomnia being due, in part at least, to a fixed idea. The neurasthenic frequently misinterprets his physical distress and pains and thus becomes decidedly hypochondriacal, imagining that he is

[1] P. Hartenberg: "Psychologie des Neurasthéniques," Paris, 1908.

suffering from all kinds of incurable diseases. The weakness of attention means to them a loss of memory; headache spells an incurable brain disease, etc. Most so-called "nervous dyspepsias" are merely symptoms of neurasthenia. Recent work on the effect of various emotions on the gastric-intestinal tract has led us to believe that many of these "nervous dyspepsias" are purely mental in origin. The mechanism of these false cases of "nervous indigestion" has already been elaborated upon, in the chapter on the emotions, so that it is unnecessary to repeat the discussion here.

Abnormal organic sensations frequently arise in neurasthenia, such as a feeling of depersonalization, numbness in the limbs, a subjective sense of muscular twitching, palpitation of the heart, a sense of emptiness in the head, or attacks of great anxiety, seemingly localized around the heart. Sometimes physical complications referable to a poor circulation of blood are present, such as a rapid pulse, flushing of the face, dizziness, tremor of the tongue and hands. As a rule, the reflexes are increased.

States of mental anxiety, termed an anxiety neurosis, frequently occur in neurasthenia and may be traced to abnormal manifestations of reactions to the sexual life. These states of anxiety strongly resemble the phobias of the psychasthenic neurosis; in fact, the phobia is often merely a protector from an outbreak of anxiety. These anxiety neuroses arise on a sexual basis and result from suppressed sexual excitement which becomes deflected and is manifested mentally as morbid anxiety and physically as the bodily accompaniment of this. In the compulsion neuroses too, attacks of anxiety may result from sexual reproaches in childhood which have been conserved in the unconscious.

The recent application of psycho-analytic methods to the treatment of stammering, has demonstrated that this speech disturbance is one of the protean forms of an anxiety neurosis and not merely a tic or spastic neurosis of co-ordination originating in childhood on a strong hereditary basis. All who have observed and treated cases of stammering have been impressed by one significant fact, namely, that in the large majority of instances the child did not begin to stammer until it had been talking freely and normally for several years. It is a significant fact too, that all stammerers show a dread of speaking with a feeling of inhibition only in certain situations, in fact, a genuine attack of anxiety, and these psychic accompaniments of stammering can frequently be overcome by some form of suggestive therapy. In stammering we are dealing, therefore, with a form of morbid anxiety due to unconscious emotional complexes, probably early childhood memories. Many cases of stammering show excessive timidity and embarrassment in childhood, which on analysis will sometimes be found to arise out of erotic fantasies. In fact, in a case of stammering in an adult, which I had occasion to treat, certain elements of infantile speech were actually preserved. In another case of stammering which I had occasion to submit to the psycho-analytic treatment, it could be demonstrated that the speech disturbance was a reaction of defence, in order to keep from consciousness painful memories and undesirable thoughts by repressing these into the unconscious. This manifested itself particularly upon certain words and letters, proving that pathogenic memory complexes from early childhood caused the stammering and that the speech neurosis was not due to a mere phonetic difficulty. Since stammering is due to unconscious influences, the proper treatment is psychological, directed to remove the deeply-rooted dread or anxiety from the unconscious. This is best accomplished through psycho-analysis, which removes the baneful influence of the unconscious complexes upon speech.

It must not be supposed, because neurasthenia is one form of a mental dissociation, that psychotherapy must be used in the treatment of the disease to the exclusion of everything else. While a certain amount of emphasis should be placed on psychotherapy, yet physical treatment must not be neglected. This physical treatment helps to remedy the abnormal organic sensations which make the mind of the neurasthenic so miserable, and thus, in its way, it has a beneficial psychotherapeutic effect. This explains the efficacy of electricity, massage, modified rest, hydrotherapy, certain drugs, in the treatment of neurasthenia. There is no one panacea for the treatment of the neurasthenic state, no universal remedy which will overcome the fatigue, depression, or anxiety, or which will make the dissociated consciousness whole again. The treatment of the neurasthenic is a delicate problem, the individual must be studied as well as the disease, and success can be achieved only by a judicious combination of mental and physical methods. Above all, the neurasthenic needs re-education, but whether this re-education should be simple or complex is dependent on many factors.

CHAPTER VIII

PSYCHO-EPILEPTIC ATTACKS

Recently it has been recognized there occasionally occur conditions which stimulate attacks of real epilepsy. On close analysis, however, it is found that these attacks have only a superficial resemblance to epilepsy, and that they are purely functional in nature. In all probability such conditions represent certain types of dissociations of consciousness. These attacks are known as psycho-epilepsy, a name which indicates the purely psychical and functional nature of the attacks and their differentiation from true, organic epilepsy. Whether the condition should be classed under hysteria, or as an episode in the course of a psychasthenic neurosis, is still an open question. The subject is an important one, however, because accounts are frequently published by the medico-religious cults and others, of the cure of epilepsy through purely psychotherapeutic methods. These so-called epileptic attacks are undoubtedly of a psycho-epileptic character, as genuine epilepsy is an organic disease which only simulates a functional disorder and which does not yield to any form of psychotherapy.

These psycho-epileptic attacks seem to be of several varieties. They may take the form of genuine convulsions, so far as the outward appearance is concerned, these convulsions being either general or more rarely limited to a special part of the body. In one of my cases, the right arm alone was involved in the psycho-epileptic attack and the purely functional nature of the disorder was proven through a searching analysis of the condition and its final cure through psychotherapeutic methods. In other conditions the attack may consist of a momentary confusion, intense anxiety, or even a feeling of depersonalization. This type may or may not be associated with a sense of unreality. One patient described his condition "as if my personality was gone. I see, hear, walk, converse, my mentality goes on, but the thing I call I, is changed." There is still a third form which these attacks seem to assume, a form which can be clearly differentiated from the other two. Here the attacks consist of peculiar momentary feelings of depression or numbness, without any loss or diminution of consciousness, and passing in a wave-like manner from one portion of the body to the other. Here the associated mental state is either anxiety, depression, or fear.

Now the important question arises—how can we distinguish these conditions from genuine epilepsy? When we come to consider the convulsions, we find that there is usually no history of epilepsy or fainting attacks in early youth. The attacks may be induced by emotional stress or mental or physical exertion. The seizures are of the nature of states of mental dissociation, which recur automatically and have an independent activity. The genesis of the individual attacks is usually some emotional experience. Furthermore, the memory for the attacks is only apparently lost and may be recovered through appropriate psychological methods, either in its entirety or as isolated fragments. So far as my experience with amnesia is concerned, it is almost impossible to restore the amnesic periods in genuine, organic epilepsy. Finally, most important of all, it is possible to reproduce an attack automatically. In one case in which the fit consisted of a spasm of the left arm, an attack was reproduced when the subject was placed in a state of abstraction. There is never an impairment of intellect or memory in these conditions, no matter how frequent the attacks may be, whereas one of the important signs of genuine epilepsy is a gradual deterioration of the intellect and memory.

When the attacks consist merely of periodic

anxiety and depression they can frequently be reproduced at will by allowing the mind to dwell upon the attacks and can even be prevented by directing the mind along other channels. The feeling of depersonalization, of unreality, the possibility of artificial reproduction of the attacks and of the artificial recovery of the amnesic period, shows that we are probably dealing with a process of mental dissociation, in the form of automatic upheavals or uprushings from the subconscious, entirely removed from the domain of the will.

So we see that these conditions may be differentiated from genuine epilepsy, although it must be admitted that this differentiation is difficult and only possible through close study and analysis. The purely psychic character of the attacks is shown in their origin in anxiety or other emotions, the complete or abortive persistence of the anxiety in the attacks, the cleavage of the personality, their automatic character, and the possibility of their artificial reproduction or the artificial synthesis of the lost memory for the attack. The condition may be cured by some form of psychotherapy, either suggestion or the synthesis of the dissociated state. In the disease called psychasthenia, there frequently occur attacks of intense dreaminess and unreality, beginning and ending suddenly, which are closely related to the condition of psycho-epilepsy, if indeed they are not identical with it. In fact, there are certain features in common between psycho-epilepsy and these psychasthenic attacks. These attacks are called psycholeptic crises and have been already discussed in the chapter devoted to psychasthenia. Likewise in hysteria, localized or general convulsions may occur, which strongly simulate a real epilepsy. Gowers[1] has described psycho-epileptic attacks, the symptoms consisting principally of periodic attacks of intense fear or of intense depression, usually beginning and ending suddenly, but of more or less protracted duration. After a discussion of the condition, he asks the rather pertinent question—whether this prolonged mental state represents a condition of the brain which, if compressed into a moment, would have involved a loss of consciousness? The answer to this important question can only be determined by further analysis of cases of psycho-epilepsy. Brief reports of a few cases which came under personal observation will serve to make this subject clearer.

The first case is that of a young woman, seventeen years of age, who for two years had suffered from peculiar "staring spells," which would come on and end suddenly, and were un-

[1] "The Borderland of Epilepsy," 1907.

associated with any definite warning or aura. There was no dizziness or loss of consciousness in the attacks. For several months before coming under observation she had been subject every morning to different attacks of the following description. On being awakened and after fully awake for a minute or two, she would suddenly have an attack consisting of an indistinct blubbering, followed immediately by a spasm of the left arm which would take an ill-directed reaching attitude as if grasping for something. The eyes would be wide open and staring and there was complete loss of consciousness. The attack would cease abruptly when the patient was sharply spoken to or when she was roughly shaken. There was complete amnesia for the attack and also for the short period after being awakened (retrograde amnesia). For several months these attacks had occurred every morning with a clock-like precision, always on awakening and always in an identical manner. There was no foaming at the mouth or biting of the tongue. Once, while the patient was placed in abstraction by listening to a monotonous sound stimulus, an attack developed which in every way corresponded to the description. There were no special dreams, while the association tests yielded nothing of value. Recovery took place under psychotherapeutic methods.

In another patient the attacks consisted of a wavelike, "deathly sensation," starting on the left side of the abdomen, thence ascending to the left side of the head and then descending down the left arm, ending usually in a numbness and tingling of the fingers of the left hand. The entire attack was short, lasting usually for one-half to one minute, and sometimes, but not always, followed by a feeling of drowsiness. In the attacks there was no feeling of unreality nor of depersonalization, consciousness was unaffected, the left arm and leg could be moved; in fact, an attack would occasionally come on while she was sewing, but without any interruption of the act. Most of the attacks occurred during the day, although occasionally an attack would take place at night and awaken her. There was never any loss of memory for the attacks and no feeling of anxiety or depression preceding them.

The effect of an emotional experience in causing psycho-epileptic attacks is well shown in the following case. A year previous to coming under observation, the patient witnessed a Jewish massacre in one of the Russian cities. She hid in a cellar for eight days in a state of great fear, and once, when the cellar door was slammed on an approaching mob, she immediately had a convulsive attack. Ever since, particularly when the eyes were closed, she would see horrible scenes of the massacre before her and a convulsion would follow. Once she dreamed of the massacre, at another time that her husband had been killed by the mob, and on both occasions she awoke in a convulsion. Again we have here the production of a psycho-epileptic attack through association of ideas.

CHAPTER IX

COLORED HEARING

COLORED hearing may be defined as a condition in which certain sounds (such as vowels or musical tones) produce a simultaneous sensation of a certain definite color. In other words, there is a deflection of sensation from one sensory organ to a different sensory centre in the brain, due either to an abnormal irradiation or spreading of the sensory impulse or to a strong emotional association dating from early childhood. The entire group of phenomena is termed a synæsthesia. There may be different types of synæsthesia corresponding to the different sensory end-organs stimulated, such as colored hearing, colored taste, or colored pain. The condition is a rare one, and therefore the number of carefully studied cases has been limited.

In one of Marinesco's cases[1] the subject was a woman, thirty-five years of age, with some neuropathic heredity, in whom the synæsthesia

[1] G. Marinesco: "Contribution à l'Étude des Synesthésies, Particulièrement de l'Audition Colorée."—*Journal de Psychologie Normal et Pathologique.*—Sept.-Oct., 1912.

first made its appearance at about the age of six. At this period her own name "Marie" was gray to her, while that of her sister, "Jeanne," always produced a sensation of blue. She would often compare the pretty color of her sister's name with the "ugly" color sensation caused by her own name. As with most subjects afflicted with colored hearing, up to the age of fourteen or fifteen she did not have the slightest doubt but that everyone experienced a sensation of color on hearing a spoken word. At this period she heard of colored hearing and began to realize for the first time that the phenomenon was not a common one.

In this case the colors associated with words and sounds were clear and in some instances quite intense, sometimes opaque and sometimes semi-transparent. Certain words were described "as transparent as water," for example the word "Ana" was a transparent bluish-green "like an opal." The color sensations were exteriorized, usually in the form of either a regular or irregular geometrical figure or resembling cloud-like masses of color. Certain vowels and words produced merely colored masses. Abstract terms were colored more intensely than concrete expressions. It is interesting to note that certain colors were more prominent in certain languages, for instance, rose in Roumanian, yellow in English, black in German, and yellowish-white in French. The noise of the wind was "gray," the music of Wagner "gray and yellow," while the music of Chopin was designated as "luminous." Poetry also produced certain colors which varied according to the different poets; for instance, the verses of Baudelaire were described as "less luminous" than those of Lamartine.

Many of the colors of words were due to predominance of the color of a certain letter or a mixture of the individual letters constituting the word. Colored thinking was likewise present. The synæsthesia also comprised the sense of smell, in that music gave the impression of perfume, for instance funeral marches produced a smell of chrysanthemums or tube-roses. It appears that there exists a mathematical or physiological relationship or association between the different sounds and their corresponding colors. In many instances the synæsthesia consisted of a mixture of two or more colors, rather than an elementary sensation corresponding to the primary colors of the spectrum. The color of the word may be due to a mixture of the individual colors of the several vowels and consonants which constitute the word. In some instances, on the contrary, a word will have the single color of the predominating hue of one of its vowels; for example, the word "Ion" in one case was designated as "yellow" because the elementary vowel "o" produced a sensation of "yellow."

There are two types of colored hearing; the first or most frequent in which a sensation of color is merely perceived, and the second, by far the less frequent, in which the colored images are intensely exteriorized in regular or irregular geometrical forms, a kind of hallucinatory colored hearing. Long words seem to produce larger colored images than short words.

According to Flournoy's classification, there are three divisions of visual synæsthesia (colored hearing), viz.:—

1. Photisms (luminous or colored).
2. Figures (symbols or diagrams).
3. Personifications (things or persons).

Concerning the intensity of the images, Flournoy distinguishes the following various degrees: simple ideas of color or of figures (first degree); clearer images, more "felt" (second degree); clear images, localized inside or outside of the head (inferior stage of the second degree); perceptions or actual hallucinations objectively localized (superior stage of the second-class, the chromatiseurs).

A matter of importance is concerned with the

question,—whether colored hearing is a normal physiological phenomenon arising from the peculiar psychological make-up of the afflicted individual, or a pathological condition? Only a few cases have been recorded in which the subjects of colored hearing were markedly free from nervous or mental symptoms during the greater part of their lives, and developed a mental disease before death. It seems, therefore, that the synæsthesias are neither pathological phenomena nor manifestations of a so-called degeneration. The condition is probably a psychological phenomenon, whose mechanism at present is not clearly understood, as shown by the various theories which have been put forth to explain the condition. Histological and physiological data have shown that the color sensations of the synæsthesias do not take place in the nerve elements of the retina, but rather in the visual centers of the brain. Four principal hypotheses have been put forth to explain the condition, as follows:—

(1) Incomplete anatomical differentiation of the sense of vision and audition or rather of their cortical centers. (Embryological hypothesis.)

(2) There may exist special anastomoses between the cortical centers of sight and hearing, in which, after auditory perception, the visual

center thereby becomes simultaneously stimulated.

(3) The theory of nerve irradiation, in which the stimulation of one center passes over the others, varying with the individual and with the intensity of the sensation provoked. (Fechner.)

(4) The psychological theory, based upon the emotional value of certain associations called forth by the word or sound heard or thought. (Flournoy.) Recent psycho-analytic investigations have also traced the genesis of colored hearing to certain unconscious sexual complexes arising in childhood. (H. V. Hug-Hellmuth and O. Pfister.)

In a case which came under personal observation [1] the various synæsthesias encountered (colored hearing and thinking, taste synæsthesia) while limited in their scope yet were quite intense. The subject was an intelligent woman forty-one years of age, of a decided visual type. The synæsthesia could be traced back to the earliest years of childhood. Physically the subject was in perfect condition. There was no psychopathic or neuropathic heredity and no similar synæsthetic disorder existing in any member of the family. She does not remember

[1] Isador H. Coriat: "A Case of Synesthesia."—*Journal Abnormal Psychology.*—Vol. VIII., No. 1, 1913.

the time when she did not have the colored hearing and thinking.

In this subject the synæsthesia was rather rudimentary and limited in its scope, in that only one color, blue in its various shades, was distinctly suggested by sounds. The shade of the color varied according to the sounds or thoughts. She remembered that once, when very young, she was given a doll dressed in blue. She immediately named her "Lucy Blue," while her sister's doll, which was dressed in red, she gave the name "Lucy Red." Her sister could not seem to comprehend this linking of a color with a name. Pieces of colored glass delighted her, while a kaleidoscope always produced a feeling of great satisfaction. Red sunsets were depressing; to use the subject's expression, "they were so beautiful that they hurt."

Certain sounds were blue and the principal words associated with the colored hearing were as follows:—

"Nellie"—pale blue, an unlimited sky blue (spatial sense).

"Lucy"—a clear sapphire.

"Bertha"—a deep Prussian blue.

Sometimes "Nellie" is described as "pale, soft blue, but very clear."

Further analysis demonstrated, that the predominating color of these three words was produced by the color of a combined vowel and consonant within the word. For instance, in "Lucy," the sound "loo" caused the color; in "Nellie," "el" produced the predominating color effect, while in "Bertha" the letters "er" colored the word. "L" alone without the vowel, or "R" alone, did not produce a blue sensation. It seemed, therefore, that the vowel sounds were the instigators of the synæsthesia, although why the letter "E" produced a pale blue color in one case and a Prussian blue in the other, could not be determined. Strangely enough the French words "Berthe," "allemand," and "berceau," although containing the same vowel combination, produced no color sensation, although "Berthe" appeared "higher" (to use the subject's description) than "Bertha." Unlike other reported cases, therefore, particularly the one studied by Marinesco, the synæsthesia was limited to the phonetic combinations of one language, in this case, English.

Conversely, showing the subject a blue or red disc, such as those used for taking the field of vision, produced no association with a word or sound. Tests with a tuning fork and watch demonstrated hearing to be normal. A (long) is not colored, but sounds "cool." The long vowels suggested position on a chromatic scale, rather than color, but these positions were not very clear to her. For instance:

ā = do
ē = re
ī = do (second octave)

The vowel sounds also produced other sensation, as follows:

ā = cool sound
ă = no sound
ē = high cool sound
ĕ = no sound
ī = very high sound
ĭ = no sound

Long and short u, produced no sensation.

Numbers never produced colors in her, but she always associated the cardinal numbers with a sort of visualized geometrical line arrangement, i.e., ascending up to twenty, dropping to ten, and then gradually ascending again. The days of the week and the names of the months produced no colors. " Sunday," however, appeared " taller " than other days. All the other days of the week were of uniform height except " Saturday," which is " half as tall " as " Sunday." The seasons of the year were always peculiarly symbolized by a spiral spring, oval in shape, the ends indicating spring and autumn, the sides the summer and winter. Music produced an intoxicating effect on her, but did not stimulate colors. Separate notes of the scale and the sounds of various musical instruments failed to produce colors.

Tests with the normal spectrum gave interesting results in emotional states produced by colors:

Color	*Emotional States*
Purple,	Repulsive and depressive.
Blue,	Not satisfied.
Green,	Not satisfied.
Yellow,	Flash of light.
Red,	Nothing.

The word " Bertha " was localized in the blue-purple end of the spectrum. No color was strong enough for " Lucy " or light enough for " Nellie."

Both hearing the words and vowels and the thinking of them produced the same sensation of color; therefore, colored thinking was present in addition to colored hearing. An interesting gustatory synæsthesia (colored taste) was also present, but not to the extent of a genuine sensation. A quotation from Ruskin has always appealed to her:—" We should love beautiful colors as a child loves good things to eat." Beautiful colors have always " tasted good " to her, while color discords were nauseating and produced the effect of a blow. She expressed the condition as follows: "If I like a color, it leaves a delightful taste in my mouth, like the sensation when one thinks of beautiful food," or "when I put my mind intently on the colors I taste them. I can taste blue." There was no olfactory synæsthesia. Direct tests of smell and taste proved the olfactory and gustatory sensations to be normal, but these tests did not stimulate any photisms. This taste synæsthesia was less intense than the colored hearing or thinking.

An analysis of the synæsthesia itself, particularly the colored hearing, gave some interesting results. The synæsthesia had not varied since it was first noticed during the earliest years of childhood. It was purely a waking process and not due to unconscious associations of sounds with colors dating from the earliest years of life. This was shown by two facts: first, that in the subject's dreams sounds have never been associated with colors, and second, because an analysis conducted in the abstraction through means of free association procedures gave negative results. That the phenomenon was a cortical one, possibly physiological, is shown by the facts that neither positive nor negative after-images could be produced with colors of the synæsthesia, and secondly, the colors were always seen in the left half of each visual field, but not exteriorized. The color was always definite, distinct, and invariable, and the same sound or word was always associated with the same color. The color and sound occurred simultaneously and instantly, the sound seemed to " melt " (to use the subject's expression) into the color. A reversion of the process, that is, by thinking of the specific color, never produced the word or sound associated with that particular color. The vowels in the words designated, and not the consonants, were the instigators of the photism. Closing of the eyes did not increase the intensity of the images produced. The color was very luminous, would persist for some time after she had ceased hearing the word or thinking it, and was not of definite shape or size, but rather like a "puddle," shading off a little at the edges.

To summarize briefly, we seem to be dealing with a limited but intense synæsthesia probably congenital in origin and remaining unchanged since childhood. There was no heredity or familial tendency. This is of interest, as in many recorded synæsthesias the hereditary tendency has been marked, for instance, in a case of Marinesco's and in one of familial colored hearing reported by Laiquel-Lavastine. Both colored hearing and thinking were present, in which variants of blue predominated. There was also a rudimentary gustatory synæsthesia.

What are the cause and origin of this interesting phenomenon, this linking of sound with color, apparently contradictory to the law of the specific energy of the senses? Under normal conditions, any form of stimulation of the retina or optic nerve would always produce a sensation of light or color, or the stimulation of a "cold point" in the skin by a needle or a hot wire always causes a sensation of cold. The quality of the reaction is a constant one, in spite of the variations of stimulus used. Whether this specific invariable character of a sensation resulting from different stimuli is of peripheral or central origin, whether localized in nervous end structures or central projection fields of the brain cortex is a point which has not been entirely cleared up. It is probable, however, that the specificity resides as much in the end organs as in the cortex itself. A synæsthesia seems to be an irradiation of the specific reactions, a phenomenon which is well known in experimental physiology.

In any case the synæsthesia appears to be a cortical phenomenon, partly because of the impossibility of producing negative or positive after-images, and partly because the synæsthesia was irreversible. This irreversibility of the phenomenon would also seem to prove that it was not an emotional state, but rather a physiological condition, due possibly to a physiological irradiation of impulses. The fact, too, that in my case there were no unconscious linkings of colors with sound, and also that the photisms were instantaneous, and had not varied since they were first experienced in early childhood, would argue against the emotional explanation of the condition. This invariability of the color sensations in the synæsthesia for years has also been noted by Dressler in a case which was observed over a long period of time.

It seems, therefore, that we are probably dealing with an incomplete, almost congenital, differentiation of the sense of hearing or rather of the cortical projection fields corresponding to the peripheral auditory and visual neurons. On account of this incomplete differentiation, a stimulus (a word or thought) irradiates or is derailed to a cortical center which does not correspond physiologically to the peripheral neuron stimulated. That such an irradiation of nervous impulses does occur, has been demonstrated experimentally by Sherrington and can be explained on the basis of different conduction resistances offered by different fibers, probably an over-facility of conduction at different synapses.[1] Thus it seems that the theory of nerve irradiation, arising from a congenital defect of the nervous system, in which the stimulation of one center passes over into another, varying with the individual and with the intensity of the provoked sensation, appears at present the most satisfactory explanation of the various synæsthesias.

Another case of synæsthesia which I had the opportunity to study was a rare type of the condition, and occurred in an intelligent woman of forty years of age.[2] For years she had suffered with an hysterical hemicrania combined with neurasthenic symptoms and in addition there had been attacks of somnambulism and, on one occasion, a transitory paralysis of the legs. A right hemihypoesthesia could be demonstrated, while the field of vision was normal for form and color.

The type of synæsthesia from which this subject suffered may be called "colored pain." As far back as she can remember, pain had produced in her a sensation of color. When a young girl, attacks of severe abdominal pain from which she suffered were referred to as "long blue-black." The colors produced by

[1] A synapse may be defined as the membrane of physiological connection between nerve cells.

[2] Isador H. Coriat: "An Unusual Type of Synesthesia."—*Journal Abnormal Psychology*, Vol. VIII, No. 2, 1913.

pain were distinct and clear and various kinds of pain always produced the same invariable color. The color sensations were distinctly visualized as a mass of color, of no particular shape. If the pain, however, involved a jagged, longitudinal or round area, the color stimulated by this particular type of pain had a corresponding geometrical figure. Colors were produced only when the pain was severe and persistent. Slight pain usually failed to produce colors. When, however, the pain was at first slight and gradually became more intense, this increase in intensity gradually produced a sensation of color which increased in vividness parallel with the increase in the intensity of the pain. This parallelism between color sensations and intense pain was probably a kind of summation of stimuli from the peripheral pain points.

Certain emotional associations were likewise present in these color phenomena, since the pains which produced color sensations were usually those which frightened her and were associated with fear. Conversely, certain colors like yellow and green produced a depressing effect in the subject, while other colors like red and blue were referred to as soothing. In the synæsthesia, the duration of the color sensation was the same as that of the pain which produced it, varying in its intensity and disappearing simultaneously with the disappearance of the pain.

Each type of pain produced its individual and invariable color, for instance: Hollow pain, blue color; sore pain, red color; deep headache, vivid scarlet; superficial headache, white color; shooting neuralgic pain, white color.

The hemicrania attacks always produced at first a feeling of "blueness" localized on the same side as the headache, and finally, as the intensity of the headache increased, a distinct blue color was produced.

Bearing in mind the physiological theory which I had formulated to explain these synæsthesic phenomena, namely, an irradiation of peripheral nervous impulses, some experiments were carried out by means of Von Frey's hair æsthesiometer.[1] Careful testing with this instrument could demonstrate a hemihypoesthesia, always corresponding to the side of the body on which the last attack of headache occurred. In the testing of both sides of the body with the æsthesiometer and attempting to stimulate the pain points, rather than the pressure points, there could be demonstrated an unusually prolonged persistence of the pain sensation after

[1] A delicate instrument to test sensation, by means of varying lengths of a hair.

the cessation of the stimulus. The duration of this persistence varied with the length of the testing hair in millimeters and was the same for both sides of the body. During this abnormal persistence of the sensation, there was a subjective feeling of fluctuation of the stimulus, that is, a periodic increase and decrease in the intensity of the pain perception which suddenly ceased, resembling somewhat the fluctuating fatigue of the field of vision in hysteria and neurasthenia. The condition was somewhat analogous to the prolonged persistence of a visual after-image.

The exact figures were as follows:—

Hair length of æsthesiometer	Persistence of sensation
40 mm.	17.2 secs.
30 mm.	43.8 secs.
20 mm.	66.6 secs.
10 mm.	84.8 secs.

The hair length could be easily measured on the scale of the instrument, while the time was accurately taken with a stop-watch.

Comparative tests in a normal individual, with the same varying hair lengths (40 mm. to 10 mm.), showed a persistence of sensation varying from 2.5 secs. to 3.8 secs. on the palms of the hands, and from 5.4 secs. to 7.2 secs. on the face. These figures were thus markedly smaller than in the synæsthesic subject and probably represented the normal persistence of an after-sensation on stimulating the pain points. Furthermore in the normal individual there was no fluctuation of the sensation, but it gradually decreased in intensity.

In the subject, too, it was possible to actually produce an artificial pain synæsthesia, with varying degrees of hair length of the æsthesiometer, a rather convincing proof that the condition was produced by a physiological irradiation of peripheral pain sensations. The figures and results were as follows:—

Hair length (mm.)	Right side (hypoesthetic)	Left side (normal)
40	no color sensation	no color sensation
30	" " "	" " "
20	" " "	" " "
10	" " "	slight redness
9	" " "	" "
8	" " "	more "
7	" " "	" "
6	" " "	distinct red sensation
5	slight redness	strong " "
4	" "	" " "
3	more "	" " "
2	" "	" " "

It will be noted that the beginning of the redness on the normal side was simultaneous with the time of greatest persistence of sensation

(10 mm. hair = 84.8 secs. persistence). Furthermore, the synæsthesia, on the normal side, could be artificially produced sooner and with a greater hair-length than on the hypoesthetic side.

In this case we seem to be dealing with a peculiar and unusual type of synæsthesia, in that an abnormal (or artificial) stimulation of the peripheral pain neurons of the skin stimulated at the same time, possibly through a physiological irradiation or a derailment of the pain-impulses, a sensation of color, a theory in harmony with the one I devised for the explanation of colored hearing. The fact that the synæsthesia could be artificially produced by peripheral stimuli does not militate against the condition being a central phenomenon.

In certain writers, for instance in the so-called French symbolist poets (Rimbaud particularly, in his famous sonnet in which he designates the color of the vowels, Marie, Baudelaire, Verlaine), colored hearing seems to have been present. The phenomenon was also found in Lafcadio Hearn and is described by him with his usual psychological insight. "For me words have color, form, character. . . . The readers do not feel as you do about words. They can't be supposed to know that you think the letter A is blush-crimson, and the letter E pale-sky-blue."[1]

Sometimes artists will also show a rudimentary unconscious linking of sound with color, probably due to the nature of their work. I had the opportunity to observe the condition in one artist, in whom the synæsthesia developed only after he had begun to study painting in his early youth. In this subject, harsh and loud music produced instantaneously a sensation of red and yellow while soft music caused a violet and blue sensation. A clash of cymbals produced a red-yellow sensation, a harp, a blue-violet sensation. The colors were intense and persisting during the entire duration of the music. The colors were designated as pure, "as if they came out of a tube." In the red-yellow synæsthesia, sometimes the red would predominate, sometimes the yellow. The violet-green synæsthesia resembled the color of waves on the water. As in my other cases, there was no reversibility of the synæsthesia, namely, none of the colors were able to produce musical sensations.

[1] "The Japanese Letters of Lafcadio Hearn."—Edited by Elizabeth Bisland, 1910.

CHAPTER X

THE PREVENTION OF THE NEUROSES

MODERN medicine concerns itself more with the prevention of disease than its cure. What then has abnormal psychology to teach us concerning the prevention of the psycho-neuroses, a group of diseases which more than any other incapacitates the individual and produces far-reaching effects upon our social organization? It seemed wise, before bringing this book to a close, to add a few words on the prevention of the psycho-neuroses, as far as this lies within our power. To begin with, in the normal individual, that is, the one who is free from a nervous taint, but who is liable to social frictions, curiosities of character and oddities, a psycho-analysis of his innermost tendencies would be of great benefit in giving him the clue for a better control of them and thus a better adjustment to surroundings and to the capabilities of life and action. In a way such an analysis might prevent any delusional interpretation of conflicts with the environment, so characteristic of the paranoiac mental make-up and thus give the clue to an intelligent and well-adapted adjustment.

It is in the child, however, that our efforts will be most productive, for, as was repeatedly shown in these pages, many of the adult psychoneuroses have their origin in the unconscious mental conflicts and repressions, usually of a sexual character, in early childhood. In fact so early may they appear, that the amnesia or forgetting of the events later in life tends to make one incriminate a more or less hypothetical hereditary disposition, rather than one's own unconscious and repressed thoughts. In children precocious sexual excitement should be avoided and children should not be exposed to an over-caressing, excessive parental affection. Otherwise this persistence of infantile fixation in the son or daughter might lead to various pathological reactions in adult life. (Œdipus-complex.) The only or "favorite" child is particularly liable to be spoiled by the development of these complexes. The baneful results of these unconscious complexes are well known, leading on the one hand to homo-sexuality with its misery and unhappiness and on the other to sexual anæsthesia, which latter is the basis of so many divorces on the ground of "conjugal incompatibility."

The uninitiated mother or father will tend to deny this important fact and interpret it as only a scientific fancy in the mind of the writer. But modern psycho-pathological investigations have shown that these unconscious conflicts lead a dynamic existence, conflicts repressed and hidden even from the parents and only brought out through psycho-analytic investigation.

Thus the prevention of the psycho-neuroses is to be found in the individual rather than in the minimizing of the injurious influences of the rush and progress of modern civilization. An individual breaks down, not so much from fatigue or overwork or from "brain fag" (whatever that may mean), but from his own mental conflicts, from sexual self-reproaches dating from childhood and from the injurious repression of the sexual instinct.

There are several ways of directing the sexual feelings and converting or transferring them to other emotional spheres. The best method of controlling suppressed sexual emotions is to change or attach these to higher artistic or intellectual interests and not allow free sexual expression or the running rampant in sexual vice.[1] This process, called sublimation, is a deflection of the sexual aim and the utilizing of

[1] See my paper "Psycho-Analysis and the Sexual Hygiene of Children."—*The Child,* January, 1912.

sexual energy for other purposes of cultural demands. The help derived from psychoanalysis is partly through this sublimating process.

Culture and social conventionalities are built upon a repression of instincts, a strangling of emotions, and the revenge of the nervous system upon this repression is the breaking out of a psycho-neurosis. Our inconsistencies in this regard are startling: one must not, for instance, act in a voluptuous manner in public, unless it be in some form of a social dance, and even our language is full of this repression and veiled sexual symbolism. Hysterical outbreaks of violence, such as characterize the so-called militant suffragettes in England, are probably the result of a repression to which certain classes of women think they have been subjected by the opposite sex, and so here again, as in the hysteria of an individual, the sexual conflict is the dynamic force at work. In a significant phrase of Adler's,[1] it is a reaction against the "masculine protest"—that is, an insistence on independence, a feeling that to give up would mean surrender and thus an over-compensation arises in the form of aggression. Freud well says, "Before everything else, however, there must be opened in the general thought a chance

[1] Alfred Adler: "Ueber den Nervosen Charakter."—1912.

for the discussion of the sexual problem; one must be able to speak of these things without being pronounced a disturber of the peace or a delver in the vulgar instinct, and there remains enough work here for a century in which our civilization must learn to live according to the demands of our sexuality." If we are to have a natural, healthy sexual education, it must be, not like what is now sweeping like a sexual epidemic all over the world, and teaching the child and the adult what they must *not* do, but rather what they must do, an avoidance of sexual errors and a transforming or sublimation of the various emotional repressions into intellectual work and athletic activity. This sexual enlightenment in the child, if properly done, can do much to prevent the mental conflicts and the erotic fantasies which are so productive of harm in later years. Thus the prevention of nervous diseases is our individual problem, no amount of propaganda or teaching can do any good, unless the individual oversight of the child is given its proper attention. By avoiding repression, mental conflicts, and emotional shocks we can in a large measure circumvent, if not entirely prevent, the psychoneuroses. Children should be impressed with the fact that sexuality is clean and the affairs of sexual life should not be made a secret any more than their food or their religious beliefs.

For this unwarrantable attitude blame must be placed upon the unconscious elements of society. As the social unconscious which is really a repository for childhood ideas and primitive beliefs is able to produce myths and folk-lore, in many instances these being merely disguises and symbolizations for repressed sexual emotions, so the unconscious of the modern social organization is constantly suppressing sexual truths in the struggle against facts of sex. Thus arise prudery and frigidity, the shutting of the eyes of society and the individual against the naked facts, so valuable for the welfare of the race. It is this unwarranted suppression for which society pays the price, in the form of the various psycho-neuroses.

Thus repression may lead to conversion into bodily symptoms as in hysteria, or when a compensating thought is substituted for the repression, to psychasthenia and the compulsion neuroses. The outward projection of a repressed but forbidden wish may manifest itself in diseases such as paranoia or in certain abnormal beliefs, as in the mediæval conceptions of the devil. In fact, in times less enlightened than ours, the yielding to a forbidden sexual wish was often attributed to demoniac possession or to the influence of witches. When the unconscious breaks through into consciousness, and the unconscious wish thus comes into conflict with reality, a psycho-neurosis develops. Thus psycho-analytic interpretations are of value, in not only enabling us to understand the mechanism of certain nervous diseases, but the mechanism of society as well.

In bringing this book to a conclusion, a brief recapitulation and survey may not be without service. The ground covered is a wide one, while the experimental and clinical researches on abnormal psychology, with its practical application to medicine, are becoming more extensive and assuming an increasing importance for thinking men and women. Yet the field is new and the principles, although fundamental, are only partially defined. Much remains to be done, particularly on the nature of consciousness and the unconscious in its normal and abnormal states and of the mysterious relations existing between the mind and the body. This latter problem in particular is now the subject of exact experimental research, whereas formerly it entered only into the field of philosophical dialectic. The present status of abnormal psychology may be summed up in the pertinent language of Professor James.

In speaking of the present situation in philosophy, referring particularly to Bergson, Professor James says: "What really exists is not things made, but things in the making. Once made they are dead."

The earlier portion of the book, dealing with the various theories of the subconscious, is especially open to new light. The theories given and most favored are those which exact experiment has shown to be of most value to psychopathology and psychotherapeutics. For obvious reasons, I have not included any philosophical conception of the subconscious such as that of Von Hartmann. My principal object has been threefold, first, to strip the subconscious of any supernormal ability or power—second, to limit it to the various mental functions established by brain physiology, thus making it synonymous with mental dissociation and with complex mental processes of which we are unaware—and third, to show how certain functional nervous disorders may be produced by perversions of unconscious mental processes. For this purpose, certain methods of exploring the subconscious mental life, according to the principles of experimental physiology and psychology, have been discussed rather fully, thus clearing the way for a correct view of the place occupied by automatism and the effect of repressed emotions in the domain of psychopathology. The broad field of Freud's theories of the unconscious, with their bearing upon dreams, the neuroses and psycho-analysis, upon society, literature, and folk-lore, is of incalculable value. Its investigations have already done much to prevent, as well as to cure, certain diseases, and the future of psycho-analysis thus becomes of paramount importance for the race as well as for the individual. Psycho-analysis thus becomes synthetic as well as analytical, it can reassociate the destructive forces at work in the unconscious of the individual and point the way for a natural outlet of his energies and inherent creative ability in the form of what is termed "sublimation."

The establishment of the fact that certain functional nervous disturbances, technically known as the psycho-neuroses, are caused by subconscious or dissociated activities, may perhaps be called one of the triumphs of modern research in abnormal psychology. The part played by these dissociated mental processes in the origin of certain functional disorders, is perhaps more extensive than many physicians are at present disposed to concede, but clinical evidence is fast accumulating to show that these disturbances can only be understood if this interpretation is placed upon them, thus clearing the way for an intelligent psycho-therapeutic treatment. We must remember that from the moment an action falls from the domain of the purposive into that of the habitual, it ceases to be under the direct control of consciousness and becomes allied to certain automatisms, either unconscious or subconscious. What is true of purposive actions also holds true as regards conscious thought. It is this mechanism which enters into the causation of certain psycho-neuroses. It is not improbable that states of mind may originate certain functional disorders, as in a reverse manner physical maladies may give rise to morbid states of mind. We refer particularly to the effect of the emotions upon the gastro-intestinal tract, as established by recent exact physiological research.

The subject of abnormal psychology is one that has but recently been critically examined, and therefore the vast territory covered by this important branch of medical science has been only partially explored. The object of these pages has been to discuss only so much as has been already ascertained from exact experiment and clinical research. It is impossible to state at present how far these researches may extend, but sufficient is already known to enable us to formulate certain fundamental principles, which are of great value in certain psychotherapeutic procedures. The literature on the subject is already vast, and for the general reader I have attempted to give a summary of only the most important researches. In presenting these facts and indicating their bearing upon psychotherapeutic methods, I feel that my task for the present is as complete as I can make it, and as such I am content to leave it to the patient study of the impartial reader.

THE END

INDEX